# The Child's Construction of Knowledge

*Piaget for Teaching Children*

# The Child's Construction of Knowledge

Piaget for Teaching Children

GEORGE E. FORMAN
UNIVERSITY OF MASSACHUSETTS

DAVID S. KUSCHNER
UNIVERSITY OF NORTH DAKOTA

National Association for the Education of Young Children
Washington, D.C.

**National Association for the Education of Young Children**
**1509 16th Street, NW**
**Washington, DC 20036–1426**
**202-232-8777 or 800-424-2460**
**Website: http://www.naeyc.org**

The National Association for the Education of Young Children (NAEYC) attempts through its publications program to provide a forum for discussion of major issues and ideas in our field. We hope to provoke thought and promote professional growth. The views expressed or implied are not necessarily those of the Association. NAEYC wishes to thank the authors, who donated much time and effort to develop this book as a contribution to our profession.

ISBN 0–912674–92–X
(This book was previously published by Wadsworth Publishing Company, Inc., under ISBN 0–8185–0231–2.)

NAEYC #116

Interior and Cover Design: *Jamie S. Brooks*
Illustrations: *Jean Fabian Wiley and Pamela Wilson*
Photographs: *Art Mann*

**Printed in the United States of America**

# Foreword

It is a great pleasure for me to introduce this book by George E. Forman and David S. Kuschner. My pleasure comes not only from the fact that the authors and I share a common orientation toward education but also from their recognition of the integral relationship between theory and practice. Goethe said that every fact is already a theory; in the same way, every classroom practice presupposes a particular conception of the child or theory of knowledge. In Chapter Three, Forman and Kuschner deal in detail with this relationship between conception and action.

When Piaget first came upon the scene in the late 1950s, this relationship was not always recognized. At that time (and, to a certain extent, today), there were many direct applications of Piaget's work to education, without a real understanding of his revolutionary conception of the child. Such applications, however well intentioned, failed and failed badly. The reason is that, if Piaget's procedures and findings are used without regard to his theory of knowledge, then these procedures and findings are eventually transformed in keeping with the educator's prior conception of the child. This is not unlike Piaget's own response to a new bike that was given to him for his 75th birthday. He was most pleased to have it but asked if he could put the seat from his old bicycle on the new one since it was so comfortable. Later he asked if he might change the handlebars, and still later he wanted his old pedals. He was not really committed, intellectually, to the new bike, and soon the new bike was translated into a version of the old one. The same thing happens to Piagetian procedures and practices when they are used without an understanding of Piagetian theory. When children are given M & M's for performing on a conservation task, one can be sure that there is no real commitment to the Piagetian position. In Chapter Five, Forman and Kuschner point out the disadvantages of shaping responses by external reinforcement. Their emphasis on cognitive conflict as an inducement to learning is clearly a commitment to the Piagetian position.

Please understand that I am not saying that everyone should adopt this position. Piaget is far from having all the answers; furthermore, the human psyche is too complex for any theory—at least at our present stage of knowledge—to encompass it all. And different perspectives and approaches are valuable in that they challenge and produce changes in competing systems.

It was quite a dramatic moment when, two years ago in Philadelphia, Piaget conceded that static comparisons might result in conservation. One wonders how

v

96753

this newly acknowledged role of static comparisons fits with Forman and Kuschner's concentration on the importance of transformations, the procedures by which states change. Considering the traditional concentration on static states, their emphasis on transformations seems well taken. When Piaget said that static states could facilitate conservation, he did not mean to gainsay the role of transformations but only to acknowledge the potential value of both.

So I am not saying that everyone should become a Piagetian—which would be sad—but only that it is important that those who say that they are working in the Piagetian tradition understand and commit themselves to the conception of the child that is the fountainhead of that position. And it is the fact that Forman and Kuschner have taken Piaget's theory, as well as his practice, seriously that so pleases me. Beginning with a theory of knowledge and progressing through a theory of development, learning, and then teaching, the authors have recognized how each level of theory influences the others. As Chapter Nine shows, they have tried in a deliberate manner to innovate practice founded on theoretical principles. This is not an easy task, because Piaget has not always been explicit about educational practice. Here educators must simply go it alone and introduce practice that seems most suited to the theory.

Inevitably there will be disagreements. The apostles are seldom in accord. But what unites them is a common conviction—a belief, if you will— that guides and directs their actions and that provides a conceptual unity despite practical diversity. Being something of an apostle myself, I am not always in agreement with what Forman and Kuschner have to say about classroom practice. But each leads according to his own light, and who is to say that one light is brighter than the other? What matters most is that Forman and Kuschner know what it is they are doing and have recognized how important a conceptual basis is for classroom practice. I believe that teachers can learn and profit from this book.

*David Elkind*

# Preface

This book is a personal work, a diary of thoughts and experiences. It is not a review of the research in early childhood education, nor is it an eclectic collection of ideas on how to teach young children. This book is the result of one rather bored research psychologist's being turned on by the delight of a 2-year-old named Bret when he accidentally stood a body-sized log on end. The joy on the child's face, in his entire posture, made me put away the tools of laboratory research and join Bret and many other children since him in the sandboxes and blocks corners from New Orleans to Nashville, Buffalo, and Amherst. It was in Amherst that I had the good fortune of meeting David Kuschner. Together we planned this text with a commitment to using developmental theory to design curricula for young children. This commitment was accompanied by two basic goals: to highlight the constructivism in Piaget's epistemology and to provide a useful pedagogical tool for teachers of 2-year-olds, as well as of older preschool children.

Piaget says that knowledge is active construction, not passive copying. Construction is the only way in which we can deal with the countless "missing" events in our day-to-day experience. A hidden object, an object no longer visible, still exists. We know this, and children, too, know, because they have constructed something called "space" in which objects exist even when they cannot see them. We believe that the root metaphor that underlies Piaget's theory of knowledge is profoundly different from the philosophies that underlie traditional preschool pedagogy. This metaphor is *change*. From beginning to end this text asks the teacher to think of the world as a process, not as a series of immutable categories. Knowledge is the understanding of the process by which objects and events change.* Only when children understand this process are they able to cope with the apparent discontinuities of their everyday world. Knowing is more than doing; knowing is also reflecting on how the doing was done. In this text we discuss both the theoretical importance of and the teaching techniques for inviting children to reflect on the form of actions—for example, driving tricycles through water puddles to make tracks, making imprints in rolled-out play dough, and drawing the spiraling fall of a feather.

*We would like to credit David Elkind's "Conservation and Concept Formation" (1969b) as the source of our taking the concept of change so seriously.

With regard to our second goal, this book emphasizes what the 2-year-old—as well as the 3- and the 4- and the 5-year-old—*can* do. Very young children may not have achieved the level of abstract thinking or learned how to thoroughly master their language, but they have an incredibly competent practical intelligence. It is to that intelligence that we direct teachers' attention so they can build on it. We do so by using developmental theory to emphasize the extreme value of practical activities and spontaneous play for very young children. It is crucial, we believe, that teachers fully appreciate this value, because it is through practical activities and spontaneous play that the 2- and 3-year-old acquire the necessary basis for understanding language, mathematics, and even social relationships.

This text can be effectively used in child development courses to add practice to theory, as well as in early childhood education courses to add theory to practice. We are now successfully using this book in our undergraduate course in early childhood curriculum at the University of Massachusetts at Amherst. Our course builds from theory to practice, with each student creating and field-testing learning encounters that use the format described in Chapter Nine. This text, because of the speculative nature of some sections, could well generate many exciting and researchable questions for students in child psychology courses. Nothing would please us more than knowing that practitioners and educational researchers are using this book as a heuristic device to define significant issues in early childhood education and child development. An accompanying activities book containing more than 100 learning encounters, by George Forman and Fleet Hill, is available from Addison-Wesley, Menlo Park, California. This activities book is titled *Constructive Play: Applying Piaget in the Preschool.*

Our acknowledgments begin with a tribute to several influential people. By far my greatest lessons regarding how children learn came from Irving E. Sigel during the two years I spent as Curriculum Director of the Early Childhood Education Project (ECEP) at SUNY/Buffalo. It was the combination of working with graduate students, talking late into the night, and watching videotapes for hundreds of hours that made me begin to fully appreciate the nature of the very young child at work during play. Willis Overton, also then at SUNY/Buffalo, was a delightful and accessible Piagetian scholar. The conversations, videotaping, and exchange of curriculum ideas continued at Amherst when David Kuschner and I began a two-year study of children's spontaneous block play, funded by the National Institute of Education.

The learning encounters presented in Chapter Nine have been field-tested in a demonstration program at the University of Massachusetts. We have named this program The School for Constructive Play, a name that reflects our commitment to Piaget's theory known as *constructivism*. The success of our program has been the result of our excellent staff—Fleet Hill and Peter Oldziey (Head Teachers), Lisa Pritcher, Clara Blum, Barbara Kay, George Fine, and Tom Healy. I would like to give particular thanks to Tom who spent the summer of 1976 reviewing curriculum theory and early childhood education models and who contributed several ingenious ideas to Chapter Nine. We extend similar thanks to David Fernie for creative suggestions on the design and use of the Plexiglas easel, which has become standard equipment in our classroom. And we thank Arthur Mann, who took the excellent photographs that appear in this book. The photographs were taken at The School for Constructive Play, and they capture, thanks to Art's sensitivity, critical moments in learning encounters.

This book was first released by Brooks/Cole, Monterey, California, but because of a shift in their product line the book was discontinued after its second printing. We are grateful to Brooks/Cole for their support of the book and its production, with special thanks to Fiorella Ljunggren. Now we are extremely pleased that NAEYC, under the direction of Jan Brown, has decided to release this book in soft-cover, making it again available and more affordable to the general public. This second release promises to give the book a second life and hopefully a new type of life to early childhood program staff who have not yet read the unique ideas presented in this book.

*George E. Forman*

Amherst, Massachusetts
September 1983

# Contents

Section 1: Introduction     1

*1   The Special Nature of This Book*     3

Purpose     4
Knowledge     4
Development     7
Learning     10
Teaching     12
Outline of the Book     19
Suggestions for Further Reading     21


Section 2: Purpose and Knowledge     23

*2   The Purpose of Early Childhood Education*     25

An Overall Purpose     25
Categories of Knowledge     34
Summary     45
Suggestions for Further Reading     46

*3   The Child Constructs Knowledge*     47

The Copy Theory of Knowledge: The Child Learns by
   Closely Attending     47
The Constructivist Theory of Knowledge: The Child Learns by
   Changing Objects     50
Piaget's Concept of Transformation     52
The Advantage of Thinking about How Objects Change     54
Transformational Thinking in Science, Mathematics, and the
   Everyday World     58
Using Transformations in Preschool Education     61
Summary     63
Suggestions for Further Reading     65

Section 3: Development and Learning   67

4   *Stages and Dimensions of Development*   69

Piaget's Theory of Developmental Stages   69
Dimensions of Development   79
Summary   91
Suggestions for Further Reading   93

5   *Behavior Modification and Conflict Inducement*   94

Behavior Modification Defined   95
False Assumptions regarding Behavior Modification   96
Controversy about the Level of Learning   99
Intrinsic Reinforcement   103
Conflict Inducement in Early Childhood Education   107
Behavior Modification Supports Conflict Inducement   114
Summary   117
Suggestions for Further Reading   118

Section 4: The Practice of Teaching   121

6   *Entering the Child's World*   123

The Problem of Entry   123
The Importance of a Theoretical Base   124
The Importance of Close Observation   128
Imitating the Child as a Means of Entry   131
Sensing the Critical Moment to Enter   135
An Exemplary Learning Encounter Using Sand Play   137
Summary   141
Suggestions for Further Reading   142

7   *Expanding and Generalizing the Learning Encounter*   143

Expanding the Learning Encounter in Progress   143
Generalizing Learning across Encounters   151
Summary   167
Suggestions for Further Reading   168

8   *Improving the Quality of Teaching*   169

Discovering Basic Assumptions   169
Openness to Change   174
Going beyond the Particular Behavior   177
Monitoring Teacher-Child Interaction   183
Preparing the Educational Environment   187
Summary   191
Suggestions for Further Reading   192

Section 5: Practical Suggestions    193

9    *Suggested Learning Encounters*    195

    Definition of Terms    195
Six Learning Encounters and Their Rationales    198
Additional Ideas for Learning Encounters    217


References    230

Index    237

# Section 1
# Introduction

# Chapter One

# The Special Nature of This Book

This book is about children—2 to 5 years old—playing, exploring, inventing, and learning with other children and with adults. Our purpose in writing this book is to present recent progress in the understanding of child development and the implications of this progress for early childhood education—in particular, Piaget's work. Jean Piaget, a Swiss scientist interested in how the child constructs knowledge, has caused a rethinking of what should be done in the classroom, especially in preschool education. The theory that underlies Piaget's work is not easy to understand (1) because we have been conditioned to emphasize the environmental determinants of behavior and (2) because we have oversimplified our answer to the question "What has the child learned?" This book, by keeping theory in close contact with practice, attempts to bring parents and teachers closer to an understanding of why certain experiences are beneficial to the child—for example, why hide-and-seek games are universal across cultures, why patty-cake games are an early form of mathematical thinking, and why the negativism of the 2-year-old is a necessary part of his or her self-development. This book is based on a theory that is comprehensive enough to help teachers and parents make decisions in many areas of child development. And it is to that end that we have directed our efforts.

Our attempt to relate theory and practice begins by stating what we believe to be the purpose of early childhood education—the construction of knowledge in order to improve the quality of life. For this overall purpose, outlined in Chapter Two, we need a set of educated guesses regarding what knowledge is, what stages define its development, how knowledge is learned, and how we can teach the learner. In other words, we need theory to guide our practice and practice to improve our theory. When we speak of theory here, we are using the term in a broad sense, because we are, in fact, speaking of four interrelated theories: a theory of knowledge, a theory of development, a theory of learning, and a theory of teaching. If theory and practice are to influence *each other,* these four theories must be interrelated. A theory of teaching that does not derive from a theory of development represents a split between theory and practice. Ideally, a theory of knowledge leads to a theory of development, which in turn leads to a theory of learning, which in turn leads to a theory of teaching. Later in the book we will discuss at length each of these theories. For the time being, we limit our discussion to a few introductory comments that are intended as mere signposts, as warning signs that tell you where to break with the traditional way of thinking about young children. Each of the following topics is covered at length in the chapters to come, in the same order in which we are discussing them here: purpose, knowledge, development, learning, and teaching.

## Purpose

Perhaps the purpose of early childhood education as we have stated it—the construction of knowledge in order to improve the quality of life—is not that new. But the emphasis here is on the word *construction.* A good education provides the student with means to construct and use knowledge, with skills to construct coherence from scattered facts. Knowledge, and the capacity to apply it, should not be limited to impersonal "data" but should extend to very personal matters as well. We have taken a comprehensive view of the good life; so we must look at many forms of knowledge and how each contributes to the attainment of that good life. In Chapter Two we discuss in depth what we see as the purpose of early childhood education, focusing on adaptation (which we define as the ability to use knowledge), and then we proceed to examine four categories of knowledge.

## Knowledge

A theory of knowledge explains how it is that we know *anything,* not just how we know something specific, such as the fact that glass is made from sand. What are the sources of knowledge? Does all knowledge come from our five senses? Is knowledge no more than the organization of sights, sounds, smells, tastes, and sensations of touch, heat, cold, and pain? Is there a source of knowledge that exists independent of these sensory inputs? Piaget says yes, there is. Somehow our mind knows how to organize sensory input in ways that automatically improve our interaction with the world around us. Through biological evolution our brain has developed definite schemes—what might be called universal structures—that interpret sensory information.

What difference does a theory of knowledge make for early childhood educators? If a teacher believes that knowledge develops by learning what-goes-with-what as something occurs in the environment, that teacher will see the environment as a stimulus and the child as a respondent to that stimulus. If a teacher believes that knowledge develops by transforming the environment and matching it to mental schemes that already exist, that teacher will see the environment as a hint and the child as an active constructor of useful hypotheses about what is. Piaget takes the latter view and over and over makes the point that knowledge of what is is always an inference and that we have no direct sensory contact with the "truth." The world as we sense it is either a continuously changing flux, and we must infer where to make the freeze-frames, or a multiplicity of separate pieces, and we must infer what to combine with what and what wholes to create from these pieces. Piaget tells us that the way we choose to cut and paste is not given in the objective world. We must add something to what we see and hear. We add inferences. We add inferences even to understand the simple "fact" that the toy hidden under the blanket still exists.

A theory of knowledge that assumes that reality is constructed, rather than learned by looking closer, will most certainly value spontaneous play, problem solving, and self-regulated learning in early education. Piaget's theory of knowledge instructs us, indirectly, to examine the child's task as one of dealing with the continuities and discontinuities in the world about him.[1] Through self-regulation the child can put to use his biologically given competence to construct a meaningful interpretation of reality. Piaget respects the beauty of biological adaptation and asks us to see the child's attempts to solve problems as no less than expressions of beauty.

Knowledge comes from our culture as well as from our biological inheritance. Knowledge from culture is given to us in full-blown form. We are taught Boyle's law, for example, without repeating Boyle's original process of discovery. We learn

Knowledge is constructed by self-regulated play.

[1]Frequent use of the generic masculine pronoun doesn't in any way reflect a sexist approach to human beings, be they small children or adults, students or teachers. When we use the generic masculine, we do so exclusively out of concern for the smooth flow of reading and exposition of ideas.

the names of objects that our culture has, by convention, decided to use. The relation between biology and knowledge is different from the relation between culture and knowledge. Biology gives us the competence to make inferences—any inference —while culture gives us guides regarding what inferences have been useful to those who have come before us. Self-regulated construction of knowledge does not mean that the child must reinvent the wheel and begin where early man began. It does mean that the child mentally constructs the basic relation between structure and function (round-means-roll), even though the wisdom of his culture places him in situations that make that invention highly probable. Piaget's theory of knowledge shouts to us that ignoring our biological heritage is as absurd as ignoring our cultural heritage. Intelligent behavior results from an interaction between the natural operations of the mind and the accumulated knowledge of the culture.

In Chapter Three we focus on change: in order to know something, the child must deal with how things change. Knowledge is more than observing and remembering the shape, position, and color of objects. For reasons that lie deep within our basic assumptions about child development, preschool curricula heretofore have not emphasized change. Colors, shapes, textures, and tones are discriminated, but the child is less than often given the means to produce similarities and differences. He may be asked to identify similarities and differences, but how often is he asked to change one state until it is similar to another or different by a set degree? It is through the process of transforming one state into another that the child learns two things at once: (1) how the two states are different and (2) how they are the same. A circle transformed into a square is different in curvature but similar in closure. These two properties of geometric form become coordinated (literally co-ordinated, in that both properties are ordered at the same time). In Chapter Three and elsewhere in the book, when we say that the child learns by doing, we mean that the child learns by transforming states of objects, situations, himself, fantasy, and any other possible knowledge state. We cannot say this too often. Knowledge is constructed by the child in his attempts to understand what is different and what remains the same across changing states. We have the biological competence to actively construct reality, and the natural processes by which we assimilate and construct knowledge should be understood in order to improve early education.

Often we educators fail to study these natural processes. We assume that teaching a 4-year-old how to pronounce individual letters is a good way to begin reading instruction. Why can't we learn from observing the infant? Does an infant learn to recognize her mother's face by looking at the nose, then at the mouth, ear, chin, and so forth? If she does learn the mother's face this way, fine; that is not the point. The point is that we don't look to infant learning for guidance in creating curricula in early education. Classroom learning is made dissimilar from the strategies the child has been using, and using well, all his preceding life. Piaget laments the separation between the natural and the institutional, between early learning and later instruction, between a theory of knowledge and a theory of teaching. Piaget describes in detail the continuity between the biological reflexes of the first months of life and the intelligent behavior of the subsequent stages through adolescence. We have used Piaget's understanding of development to guide us in designing curricula for children aged 2 to 5.

## Development

Developmental theory increases our awareness of where the child has been and where the child will probably go. The walking 2-year-old was the crawling 1-year-old and will be the running and jumping 3-year-old. We early childhood educators have for many decades been using, and using well, our knowledge of motor development to improve the preschool experience. We have done an equally fine job in applying our understanding of social-emotional development. But somehow we have fallen behind in our use of cognitive developmental theory. One of our most unfortunate choices was to treat cognitive development as separate from motor development and social-emotional development. Thinking integrates it all. Motor development requires judgments of weight, balance, trajectory, and even strategy. Social-emotional development requires judgments of another person's intentions and of one's own feelings, constructive use of anger, and, most certainly, strategies. We have, as Kamii (1974) has so aptly phrased it, "one intelligence indivisible." We solicit the reader to use the term *cognitive development* in this broad sense—the operation of the mind as it deals with movement, feelings, and academic subjects.[2]

A comprehensive theory of development helps us do two things. As we said earlier, it helps us integrate social-emotional, motor, and cognitive aspects of the curriculum. It also helps us understand how infant development influences early childhood development and how early childhood development influences later development. The first of these two things pertains to the whole child at a given age; the second, to the whole child across age stages. Piaget's theory is most helpful on both counts. For the moment let's look at development across age stages.

Piaget (1970) is quite serious when he looks at an infant's search for a lost toy as an early form of logical thinking. He is equally serious when he studies the 3-year-old's explorations of a flexible spring as an early form of education in mathematics. To Piaget, and to an increasing number of modern thinkers, the roots of science are found in the free play of young children. The reason why the tools of science (math, logic, and the experimental method) are so efficient is that they began, thousands of years ago, with the reflex of the infant and the intuitions of the 3-year-old and continued to grow in complexity gradually, generation by generation, to their present level. There is obviously no need for educators to duplicate this process, with all its false starts and false hypotheses. But there is a need for us to understand this continuity, to see the infant's groping as a foundation for the preschooler's reasoning and the adolescent's formal logic.

We can look at a child's development in two different—and, in our opinion, both wrong—ways: (1) as a continuous change without qualitative differences between age stages and (2) as a set of qualitatively different stages without continuity between themselves. If we take the first approach, we see the child as a little adult, who learns more and more but does not basically change his approach to the world as he grows older. He just knows less and can physically do less. If we take the sec-

---

[2]At the risk of sounding flippant, but as a help in remembering the message, we can describe cognition as the mind's attempts to deal with motion, emotion, and promotion.

ond approach, we see the child as indeed different from the adult. We see him progressing toward adulthood through stages, but each stage is quite unrelated to the preceding and to the succeeding ones. All that matters is the fact that the child must pass through all the stages, one after the other one. He outgrows each stage, which is not the same thing as saying that he uses an earlier stage in some essential manner to complete his progress through the subsequent stage. Piaget, as we shall see, holds neither view. He sees each stage not as a springboard for the next one but as an integral part of it. The stages are both continuous, in that the child knows an increasing amount, and discontinuous, in that the child's basic approach to the world undergoes qualitative changes. The whole process is an integrated one, because the gains of one stage are used in subsequent stages, not outgrown. We have represented these three different views of development in a schematic form in Figure 1-1.

The implications of Piaget's view for preschool education are profound. Instead of sitting back, satisfied that a 3-year-old has passed through infancy suc-

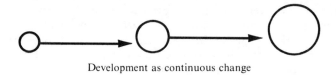

Development as continuous change

Development as discontinuous change

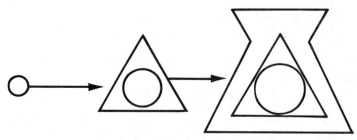

Development as the integration of
continuous and discontinuous change

*Figure 1-1*. Three views of development.

cessfully, and then forgetting it, we look closely at infancy for curriculum ideas. Infancy is no longer perceived as a rite of passage, a stage to be forgotten in form and content once completed. Infancy is over, but it is not outgrown. The discoveries that we make in infancy are implicitly used in all our subsequent discoveries. This means that the preschool teacher looks at curriculum as analogous to infant development. Where is the analogy?

Piaget (1970) relates the bodily movements of the infant to the mental manipulations of the older child. As we will explain in Chapter Four, when the infant learns how to detour around obstacles, he is preparing himself to understand that a span of string doesn't change in length when it changes in shape. The detour problem in infancy is a precursor of the conservation-of-length problem in early childhood. (A *precursor* is a more elementary form of a problem that the child will encounter when older.)

So, how is the detour problem an elementary form of conservation of length? How is learning to negotiate detours in infancy going to help the 7-year-old who is trying to solve a problem of conservation of length? A detour problem properly solved indicates that the infant understands that there are two routes that pass between the same two points. Both the usual route and the detour begin at the same point and end at the same point. The child solving the conservation-of-length problem must also know that the straight string and the curved string are still one and the same string. The string was curved, but the starting and end points are the same. The string was not stretched, only repositioned. The infant has learned that he can crawl from one place to another by different routes that begin and end at the same points. This early experience helps him understand later that a string can be positioned in different ways without necessarily being stretched. Note that his conclusion that the string was not stretched is not tantamount to his success at conserving the total length of the string. He may still think that the curved string is shorter. Eventually, the fact that the string was not stretched takes on greater implication, and the child makes the correct conclusion regarding conservation of length. The point labored here is that the detour problem is an elementary form of length conservation. The former is contained in the latter; yet, in order to solve the latter, the child must know more than the fact that two routes can span the same two points.

Our preceding discussion supports Piaget's view of development as a continuous process. But, as we said earlier, Piaget also says that development is discontinuous. How, then, are later stages discontinuous with regard to earlier stages? The answer to this question lies in the change that the child's consciousness of action undergoes as he grows older. Action involves personal effort and energy, but it also involves form. The form of action can itself be an object of reflection, independent of personal effort. In fact, if the child thinks about the personal effort needed to walk the curves of a bent piece of string, he might erroneously conclude that a bent string is "longer" than a straight string. Length in this case is confused with amount of effort. However, as the child grows older, he reflects more on the form of his own motions (for example, detours) and becomes less susceptible to making errors of personification. This depersonification of action defines the child's development and takes some years to accomplish. When it occurs, the cognitive ability of the child takes on a new power, which we choose to view as qualitatively different from that of earlier stages—qualitatively different, but continuous and inclusive of the cognitive abilities of earlier stages. Later stages are, in effect, a reanalysis of previous accomplishments, an increased awareness of form independent of time and effort, and a consciousness that was not there before. One of the goals of this book is to demonstrate that development is a continuing process of becoming more and more conscious of form, be it physical action or mental operation.

Chapter Four offers the reader a useful scheme to organize preschool curricula in terms of three dimensions of development—social-emotional, cognitive, and language. These dimensions accentuate child growth and should help the teacher make decisions on how to simplify a task for a young child or make a task more challenging for an older child. According to these three dimensions of development, the child grows from reactive to active thinker; he begins to use logical sources of knowledge instead of empirical ones and to assume a relative perspective instead of an absolute one. We are not suggesting that early education be a push to accelerate development along these dimensions. What we are suggesting is that these dimensions be more appropriately used to help the teacher understand where a child is currently. As we hope will be clear in this text, the aim of early education is not to accelerate development but to expand the range of application of a child's current stage, so that the child himself will climb to the higher levels of development.

## Learning

In Chapter Five we present two different views of how children learn. Both views are correct, but they ask different questions. The first view asks "What are the external events that control the frequency of behavior?" and "What stimulus signals to the child that a particular response at a particular moment will lead to a happy consequence?" The second view asks "What mental events explain how the child understands a complex problem?" and "What conflicting ideas must the child deal with in order to solve problems correctly?" The first view—call it behavior modification—is concerned mainly with the frequency of behavior; the second—call it cognitive conflict—is concerned mainly with the form of behavior (as an indication of the form of thinking).

We turn to different views to give us practical help in different situations. Although this "division of labor" is never exclusive, you might wonder which of the two views we have just discussed would be more useful if you tried to answer the following questions: Why are children so noisy the first half hour of the day? Why does Clara have so much trouble building a three-block bridge? Why is Herbie afraid of the water table? Why does Alphonse get upset whenever his cookie snack is broken in half? Sometimes we teachers want to know why a child is not doing something that we have reason to believe he could do if he were appropriately motivated. Here the principles of behavior modification can be helpful, because we are dealing with response rate, or what might be called performance. At other times we teachers want to know why a child can't do something that we have reason to believe he couldn't do even when appropriately motivated. Here the principles of cognitive conflict can be helpful, because we are dealing with response form as an indication of thinking, or what might be called competence.

We hasten to add that at no point in development should one think that the child is "incompetent." Competence, as we use the term in this text, is no more than a description of the thought patterns a child is probably using at a particular stage of development. We lay heavy the claim that the early stages should not be treated as stages of "incompetence." These stages are, in their own right, a period of great competence (Stone, Murphy, & Smith, 1973), like all subsequent stages, and they are just as necessary, as we explained when we discussed the concept of precursors. Similarly, the early stages of learning a particular concept, filled as they are with errors, are necessary. In Chapter Five we give our reasons for stating that errors are indicators not of incompetence but of an active and useful thinking process.

In our coverage of learning principles we distinguish active and useful thinking from rote learning, comment on those instances in which rote learning is the only alternative, and differentiate the process of discovery from the process of invention.

We would go against the stated purpose of this book if we were to discuss theory without keeping in close contact with practice. The principles of learning are related to the practice of teaching. A teacher may use behavior modification to foster a positive learning atmosphere (reducing distracting noise, for example) and to support the child's explorations of materials (protecting one child's space by redi-

Conflict can cause children to rethink their habitual approaches to objects and events.

recting another child, for example). A teacher may also use cognitive conflict, such as handing a child large objects that are extremely light and small objects that are extremely heavy. Cognitive conflict can cause children to rethink their habitual approaches to objects and events. The use of learning theory in the classroom brings us to the sections in the book that deal with teaching.

## Teaching

Educators have known for a long time that subject matter presents different degrees of difficulty and, consequently, that easier subjects should be taught before the more difficult ones—reading before writing, arithmetic before algebra, and so on. More recently educators have also come to understand that children at different ages have different styles of learning, no matter what the content of the lesson. For example, the learning styles of 2-year-olds and 5-year-olds—the objects of our special interest in this book—are quite different. This means that the general approach to teaching 2-year-olds will necessarily be different from the general approach to teaching 5-year-olds. Chapter Four discusses developmental differences in detail; but, as an introduction to this very important topic, we present some of these differences in Table 1-1. Then we discuss the implications that these developmental differences carry for teaching 2- and 5-year-olds.

Take developmental differences in language skills. The advanced language skills of the 5-year-old allow many types of classroom activities that are not possible with the 2-year-old. The following example, taken from the records of the Early Childhood Education Project, an experimental preschool for 2-year-olds (Sigel, Secrist, & Forman, 1973), vividly portrays the limits of verbal instructions. Actually, the children in this example were 3 years old, but even with children of that age staging problems could not be done easily by using language to set task constraints (instructions that require the child to inhibit a natural tendency).

The children were brought into a small playroom containing a table covered with green felt. On the felt the teacher had placed four or five toy houses. The children were asked to drive a toy car from one house to the next; but in order to do so they had to arrange cardboard strips into the necessary system of roadways. The object of the lesson was to teach the children concepts in distance, order, and spatial relations, such as parallel and perpendicular (at a practical level, of course). The lesson was a failure, because the children didn't understand why they couldn't drive their toy cars across the felt from one house to another. Even the (excessive) repetition of the rule "You can't drive on the grass" combined with pretend squeals from the teacher because a child was "stuck in the grass" didn't inhibit the child's natural tendency to drive the car anywhere.

These task constraints are among the most difficult for the child under 5 to follow. When the child is 5 years old, he is usually somewhat test-sophisticated and follows these arbitrary rules even though he doesn't understand the reasons for them. Most 5-year-olds are socialized to the idea that during a "lesson" there are a certain number of constraints that are arbitrarily given. This test sophistication increases with classroom experience and could be the reason why 7-year-olds

*Table 1-1.* Developmental Differences between Ages 2 and 5.

| *The 2-year-old* | *The 5-year-old* |
|---|---|
| *Social-emotional characteristics* | |
| Is engrossed in his own manipulations of objects. | Includes others in his explorations of the physical world. |
| Imitates the actions of objects and others as he sees them. | Goes beyond what he sees; invents sociodramatic themes in play. |
| Spends a lot of his time watching as well as acting. | Is able to pick up a lot of information from a momentary glance. |
| Self-directive, varies abruptly in his amenability to be influenced by an adult. | Socially tractable, waits for instructions and responds appropriately. |
| Strong in self-set goals, has difficulty inhibiting an action once initiated. | Can change an intended action in mid-flight at the verbal suggestion of an adult. |
| His emotional mood changes abruptly, but intensity is often short-lived. | His emotional mood can pervade several situations and is manifested in themes of social play and in approach to materials. |
| *General cognitive characteristics* | |
| His goals exceed his means; preparing materials sometimes frustrates him as he attempts to reach his intended goal; is sidetracked on means. | Has mastered the simple means of preparing and wielding materials; anticipates definite products. |
| Has no clear sense of the continuity of past, present, and future but can anticipate physical consequences of his actions. | Is beginning to see the continuity of his own past, present, and future but has difficulty generalizing this to other persons. |
| Treats pictures as static shots of things rather than as momentary freezes of ongoing actions. | Can infer the course of action from a sequence of pictures. |
| His preferred mode of exploration is manual manipulation combined with observation. | Can visually explore the physical world in advance of manipulation in order to pick up information needed to guide goal-directed behavior. |
| Has difficulty coordinating his actions with those of other children in group games. | Has no difficulty coordinating his actions with those of others and is beginning to anticipate the meaning of game rules. |
| *Language characteristics* | |
| His sentences omit adjectives and adverbs necessary for explicit communication. | Has more effective ability to express desires and ask questions. |
| Uses language primarily to express personal desires and immediate needs. | Uses language to gather information about things in general—for example, origins and reasons. |
| His language is episodic and refers to single events and objects. | His language develops an idea or question, and his sentences build upon each other around a core theme. |
| His language is quite bound to the spatial and temporal present or to familiar contingencies. | Can use language metaphorically and to invent novel contingencies he doesn't actually see. |
| Adult's language can be used to activate him if the physical setting is right. | Adult's language can be used to set task constraints and to have him modify the physical setting. |

appear qualitatively superior to 5-year-olds on test performance (White, 1968). The "readiness" to learn is in part determined by the child's acceptance and ability to decipher the scores of implicit social rules required for a good performance. Rules like "Don't touch the material until I tell you how" and "Listen carefully now, because you'll have to remember this later" are all rules of the game that the 5-year-old has internalized but that the 2-year-old has not.

Given these developmental differences, our whole approach to teaching children aged 2 to 3 years should be different from our approach to teaching children aged 4 to 5 years. The 2-year-olds' preference for manipulating real objects, their limited language competence, their difficulty in integrating the overall theme of events separated in time, their insistence on following through their self-set goals, and the interaction between their emotional and cognitive worlds—all combine to suggest that educational programs for 2-year-olds need to be more individual- than group-oriented. Very young children learn language by hearing words that describe their current ongoing actions (Bloom, Lightbown, & Hood, 1975). They then imitate and expand these words and phrases as they repeat the action context in which they first heard the words. This match between personal action and new words is difficult to implement when the teacher is working with groups of children. Nor can the teacher working in groups anticipate the intention of a single child enough to know when to put the child's actions into words. Children "overgeneralize" new words and phrases (Clark, 1973). Therefore, through their own actions and observations of those actions and how they affect others, children limit the field of application of the new words. These overgeneralizations can be quite inventive, as the following example illustrates.

> A two-year-old girl was taking a bath and making her doll "dive" into the water and "dive out" of it, commenting: "There, she drowns-in; now she drowns-out!" [Chukovsky, 1974, p. 7].

Would a teacher or parent surrounded by three or four simultaneous monologues be able to decipher the implied difference between "drowns" and this child's more temporary "drowns-in" and "drowns-out"? Would the same teacher have the time to formulate a game that capitalizes on this opportunity to distinguish between the permanent effects of drowning and the temporary effects of diving? If he did, would the other children profit, in a vicarious manner, from watching the game with that one child? Given that the *inventive* use of words in relation to one's *own* actions is important for language development and given that teachers and parents need sufficient time to observe the child's language-action context before they can move effectively into the idiosyncratic world of the 2-year-old, programs for very young children need to emphasize one-to-one learning encounters. This emphasis is maintained throughout this book, with suggestions for more group involvement as the children grow older.

Very young children's difficulty with continuity and transitions between activities and events presents special requirements for their education. The 2-year-old is likely to remember what she did with a particular object as she picks it up again. Handling an object on Tuesday brings to mind what was done with that object on Monday. Setting stimuli—like telling the child "Let's shovel the sand"—may cause the child to grasp the shovel, but her pausing look and general hefting of the shovel suggest that she doesn't quite remember the game until the weight, leverage, and sight of the object in her hand recall yesterday's fun. Of course, this pausing time is gradually reduced with increased experience, but the meaning of objects is contained in lifting, rotating, and, more generally, moving the objects in the initial stages of experience. A child thwarted in these early attempts to internalize the motor schemes as part of the object's meaning may have difficulty generalizing the use of that object across a wide variety of situations (Piaget, 1973). The action on the object aids to establish a continuity between encounters with that object on different days.

We have seen 2-year-olds engage in sort of abbreviated motor rituals upon first approaching a familiar object. After this abbreviated motor ritual has been played through, the child elaborates the ritual or shifts to more inventive uses of the object. It is apparent that the initial motor ritual helps the child make his past knowledge of the object more continuous with his present discoveries about the object. A case in point comes from a series of videotapes made at the Early Childhood Education Project (Sigel, Secrist, & Forman, 1973).

Spencer, age 2½, was sitting at a table playing with an assortment of wooden rings, circles, square frames, and solid squares. His teacher was sitting next to

The handling of an object determines its meaning.

him engaged in parallel play, as was the style of this program. The teacher saw Spencer poke his finger inside the ring and drag the ring across the table surface. The teacher did the same but added to this movement a back-and-forth alternation, making the ring spin in a rotary fashion. Spencer then modified his finger movement in kind, making his ring spin around his finger.

It was noticed that in subsequent videotapes on sessions separated by several days, Spencer, upon seeing the ring, would engage in this motor ritual before using the ring in any new manner. This motor ritual could have been Spencer's way of making sure that this object was indeed the familiar ring. Once this assurance was obtained, Spencer could learn more about the object without losing what he already knew of it. The motor ritual improved the continuity between new knowledge and old knowledge.

What would happen if the teacher said on each new session "Let's try this" and then demonstrated something new? The continuity with the past could be broken. Young children have difficulty coordinating successive experiences into a general theme. Programs for the very young should allow the children themselves to make the first move; then the teacher might embellish the action, as the teacher in the example above did.

The importance of letting the child free-play with materials is not as great with

"Distancing" acts cause the child to consider the nonpresent.

the 4- and 5-year-olds, but the need to reinforce the continuity between yesterday and today is just as great. The ways of providing this continuity are, of course, different from those one would use with very young children. With the 4- and 5-year-old it is language that represents the mediator from one day to the next. Saying to a 4-year-old "Let's do what we did here yesterday" can cause the child to immediately search for the necessary props. Language serves as a representation of the nonpresent. "What we did here yesterday" is not in the immediate present but is some "distance" in time from the present. The fact that 4- and 5-year-olds can use language to span temporal distances does not mean that their competence comes without practice. The transition from the 2-year-old's use of the language to refer to the immediately present to the 5-year-old's use of the language to represent the nonpresent is facilitated by teachers and parents. Questions like "What will happen if . . . ?" and "What do we need to finish this . . . ?" asked by adults require the child to think about relatively distant times. Sigel (1972) refers to these teaching techniques as "distancing" acts—that is, acts the teacher performs in order to facilitate the child's ability to coordinate the past and future with the present through the use of language. The transition from the use of language to signify present events to the use of language to signify past and future events as well becomes an objective of preschool education. This and other objectives will be discussed at length in Chapter Two.

A 2-year-old lives on the edge of her emotions; her joy, anger, surprise, and disappointment blend inextricably with her cognition, use of memory, attention, anticipation, and problem solving. This has profound implications for preschool programs. For the 2-year-old child the emotional payoff for exploring new material must be direct and come almost immediately. If a task is not exciting, if it doesn't arouse emotion, the child will move on to another task. Encouraging the child to persist at the task "to make Daddy proud" or "so that you can go outside and play" delays emotional gratification, besides involving concepts that the child may not understand. It is important for very young children to find emotional gratification in the materials themselves. Since the child at this age is very sensitive to sources of emotional gratification, sources external to the materials have a way of distracting the child from the task at hand (Miller & Estes, 1961). Materials are explored for sources of satisfaction, for the fun, surprise, and variation (Fiske & Maddi, 1961). Exploring materials objectively and systematically for sources of information is not a frequent activity of the 2-year-old. When we see a child of this age systematically varying the use of some item, more often than not the child is doing so to discover new ways of creating the same exciting effect (Piaget, 1973). The 5-year-old can engage in a more detached exploration in search of physical features that may or may not have an exciting effect; he will permute all possible combinations of square and circular blocks with the seriousness of an accountant. The 2-year-old, instead, dives into the materials, stacking and crashing down her constructions as her delight directs her. The materials are almost a direct extension of the child. If it is standing that she has just mastered herself, it may be stacking that she is intrigued with when she plays with the blocks. The projection of her self and the concomitant emotions help her understand the materials (Werner, 1948). The overtness of her emotions provides the continuity between what she knows about herself and what she is trying to know about physical materials.

How often we hear young children describe inanimate objects in terms of living things—"The cup fell because it was tired." Very young children, too, engage in animistic thinking. A 2-year-old bends the manikin doll at the torso and then clutches his own stomach in mock pain. The projection of his own emotions into the physical world about him is essential to the child's understanding of the physical world. The initial blending of emotions and cognition improves the chances that the child's world view will not be fragmented and made up of unrelated pieces of information.

It is important not to begin the socialization process too quickly. In most Western cultures socialization is a process of weaning the child from his emotional and intuitive world. Children are continually told to calm down, to pay attention to the material, and to listen to others. They are not told to get excited, to let attention wander, and to listen to themselves. Programs for 2- and 3-year-olds should do just this. Children's excitement is a good indication of what tasks have sufficient continuity with their current knowledge base. If children didn't see some continuity themselves, if they had no expectation about the situations before them, they would not get excited—an idea that will be developed more fully in Chapter Six.

It is not enough to justify a classroom activity with the glib reason that "the children enjoy it." We must have some insight regarding why children enjoy an activity. Even if we establish the children's natural preferences as the number-one criterion for including an activity in the day's schedule, if we don't know why the children enjoy that activity, we are unable to make any further contributions to their development. If we look closely and are able to determine exactly when a child laughs or when he seems surprised or when he gets frustrated, we are closer to understanding what knowledge the child is constructing. The emotions of young children are the window to their thoughts. A 2-year-old girl laughs when she sees a wadded ball of paper begin to uncurl. Is she on the brink of understanding the contradiction inherent in an inert object in spontaneous motion? The observant teacher could move in at this point, gently expanding the girl's awareness.

Becoming objective about one's own emotions has its advantages, of course. The intensity of emotions can prevent the exploration of alternatives. The delight of an act that leads to a loud "pop" could reduce the chances that the child will vary his approach to the object. The intensity of a fear reaction could also create a rigidity in solving the problem of how to escape the source of that fear. Disappointment and frustration have similar constraining effects on cognition (Barker, Dembo, & Lewin, 1941). Nonemotional objectivity is essential for adaptive behavior in many situations. Yet, if we oversocialize the child in this direction, we find that the child gets better and better at solving problems that are increasingly irrelevant to his emotional life or we find that the child gets better and better at solving only a certain type of problem. Problems that require creative leaps and intuitive synthesis of experiences become difficult. The most adaptive child is one who can draw on both a detached intellect and a passionate intuition (Bruner, 1967). To recite an old saw: Genius is the power to be childlike at will.

What implications for preschool programs can we derive from the fact that 2-year-olds have less language competence than 5-year-olds? As we stated earlier, very young children have difficulty internalizing verbal instructions that constrain their natural responses to materials. The example of the children at the Early Childhood Education Project, who keep driving the toy cars over the felt, is a case in point. This example suggests that the teacher, rather than spending an excessive amount of energy "shaping" the child's behavior, might spend that energy more profitably in another way. For very young children the educational objective is often formulated on the spot. The teacher prepares the environment with materials known to have excited the children in the past. The children arrive and begin to play. The teacher observes for some minutes, long enough to get a feeling of the children's intentions. Then the teacher begins to imitate the children, modifying their actions slightly in a direction that she thinks will expand the children's thinking. The children, who have already developed an affinity for this person imitating them, observe these modifications and then imitate the teacher. At that point the imitated becomes the imitator, and the teacher has made an entry into the child's world.

This process of parallel play with very young children is quite different from what is usually done with 4- and 5-year-olds. With older children teachers often use verbal instructions to set both goals and means: "Let's make puppets. Lisa, get me the scissors, and we will cut out shapes for the eyes, nose, and mouth." Other children are encouraged to participate in the group activity. In activities like this the attention is concentrated on table-top materials and directed toward a preconceived product. Children who are 4 and 5 years old have developed the classroom skills necessary to internalize the instructions, sit around the table spending much of their time waiting for their turns for teacher's assistance, work toward the preconceived goal, and be less territorial about the space to their right and left. Although 2-year-olds can sit around a table and roll play dough, with this younger group more complex activities begin to break down unless the materials themselves provide exciting consequences. Since 2-year-olds are oriented more toward the actual properties of objects than toward their potential properties, we may assume that the potential puppet in an ordinary paper bag is not part of the 2-year-olds' world. If we say to a 2-year-old "Come, let's make this bag into a puppet," she might hear it as "Come here because it will please me if you do." She does not sense any greater purpose.

This means that the teacher will have to go to the younger child rather than ask the child to come to him. The teacher will be found next to the child—kneeling near the water table, standing by the slide, sitting next to the toy bus, and steadying the basin while the child washes the doll. If the teacher wants to work with the children at table-top activities, he should begin playing with the materials by himself. Interested children will come to him without his asking. We feel that the element of choice is extremely important for the very young child. Since his world is full of so many novel and unrelated events, we don't need to impose any greater fragmentation by diverting him from self-set objectives. Asking a child to stop his current task and to work on one that an adult has structured destroys the organic construction of the child's reality.

## Outline of the Book

The organization of this book is based on layers of theory. Section 2, "Purpose and Knowledge," comprises two chapters. Chapter Two opens with a statement of the general purpose of early childhood education. We take seriously the charge that knowledge can improve the quality of life and emphasize, as have Dewey and Piaget, that knowing how to use knowledge is the overarching purpose of education. This brings us to a discussion, in Chapter Three, of the nature of knowledge itself. What constitutes an act of knowing? What are the sources of knowledge, and what are its limits?

Section 3, "Development and Learning," contains two chapters: Chapter Four on development and Chapter Five on learning. In Chapter Four we present Piaget's theory of development, which derives from his broader theory of knowledge. The learning principles discussed in Chapter Five also derive from the theoretical position we have taken on the nature of development. Knowledge is an act of constructing relations. Development is defined by reference to important stages of this constructive process. Learning involves the specific conflicts that provoke the learner to reconstruct old ideas. The progression from knowledge to development to learning is a progression from the general to the specific.

Section 4, "The Practice of Teaching," contains three chapters. All of them examine the practice of teaching in light of the theories of knowledge, development, and learning. These three chapters are based on a sequence of questions. Chapter Six asks "How does the teacher enter the child's world?" Chapter Seven asks "Once the teacher has made a successful entry into the child's world, how does he or she expand that particular encounter?" and "How can the teacher generalize learning from one encounter to another encounter later in the day or in the week?" Chapter Eight asks "How can teachers improve their skills through review and staff meetings?"

Section 5, "Practical Suggestions," consists of one chapter (Chapter Nine), which deals with learning encounters that can be applied in the classroom or at home. These practical suggestions are the closest we come to "packaging" the curriculum presented in this book. We hope the packaging is loose enough to encourage the reader to tie things together in different ways to meet the needs of individual children.

Figure 1-2 summarizes the layers of theory, each deriving from the preceding one, that govern the organization of the chapters in this book. We state the purpose of education as the acquisition of the capacity to use knowledge, we define knowledge, we discuss the development of knowledge through different age-related

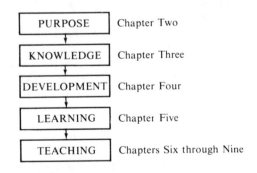

*Figure 1-2.* The five layers of theory used to organize this book.

stages, and we examine the process of learning, which assures development, and the practice of teaching, which facilitates learning. We sincerely believe that the continuity from a theory of knowledge to the practice of teaching can reduce the unnatural separation between theory and practice.

## Suggestions for Further Reading

Evans, E. D. *Contemporary influences in early childhood education* (2nd ed.). New York: Holt, Rinehart & Winston, 1975. An excellent and thorough review of different models of early childhood education programs, including programs based on Piaget's theory.

Inhelder, B., & Chipman, H. H. (Eds.). *Piaget and his school: A reader in developmental psychology.* New York: Springer-Verlag, 1976. A comprehensive collection of articles dealing with theory and research and a valuable source of information on many aspects of Piaget's work.

Schwebel, M., & Raph, J. (Eds.). *Piaget in the classroom.* New York: Basic Books, 1973. A fine collection of articles investigating the educational implications of Piaget's theory.

# Section 2
# Purpose and Knowledge

# Chapter Two

# The Purpose of Early Childhood Education

## An Overall Purpose

The general purpose of education, in any setting, is to provide the individual with means to improve his or her quality of life. These means vary from gaining an intellectual perspective of the status quo to mastering a vocational skill, from learning how to view change to learning how to change views, from learning how to do to learning what to do. The overall objective of education might be summarized, as Whitehead (1967, p. 4) does, as "the acquisition of the art of the utilization of knowledge" for the purpose of improving the quality of life.

These general comments imply two essential points. First, education is more than the acquisition of knowledge; it is learning how knowledge can be used—that is, learning the function of knowledge. Second, education is relevant to the quality of life. Through education we can become happier, more interested, more aware, and, most of all, more adaptable.

*Adaptability*

In our context, adaptability can be defined in alternative ways, depending on one's view of the environment from which children draw their nourishment. If one sees that environment as filled with choices, then adaptability is defined as the ability to cope with new information and make reasoned decisions. If one sees that environment as fixed and with few options, then adaptability is defined as the ability to perform well in one of the given options.

The specificity of instruction increases when teachers anticipate a fixed future for their students. This attitude, known in future studies as a closed view, leads a teacher to give students direct instruction on those skills that are currently marketable. By "marketable skills" we mean those academic skills that the preschooler must sell to the elementary school teacher. When a teacher's view of the future is more open, classroom activities tend to focus less on marketable skills and more on the child's total cognitive framework. This open view, which admits of the possibility that an environment can undergo profound changes in the course of 20 years, equates adaptability with general problem solving.

Given the rate of change that has characterized all areas of our culture—from technology to social consciousness—in the last one hundred years, the open view seems more appropriate for the general objective of education. The role of the family, the role of women, the role of government, the influence of mass communication, and the demand of the public for full disclosure on everything from food ingredients to government files are just a few, random areas in which these changes have taken place most dramatically. Not only are there more alternatives available, but people feel that they have a right to these alternatives. Choice is being returned to the consumer rather than being left to the producer. This means that the many rather than the few will have to be equipped to make judicious decisions.

Even the teacher wary of changing patterns cannot afford to drill students to the point of rote acceptance of tradition. In the years to come, these students, particularly women, will be challenged—if not in adolescence (Erikson, 1963), then later in life. Teachers need to search for the source of tradition and to understand its value, but then they must teach the students the process of searching, not the product of the search. Only through the ability to handle discrepant information and to search for implicit assumptions that may or may not be warranted, can the future citizen justify tradition in the face of opposing views. Teaching reasoning skills may increase the commitment to existing traditions, but it also improves the student's ability to make choices—and it takes courageous teachers to foster this ability. Such teachers—and there are many—believe that through practiced objectivity students can conserve the value of tradition and, at the same time, modify these traditions to fit the demands of the future.

As defined by Piaget, adaptation (the result of adaptability) is always a process of partial change—partial because some things remain the same. As we shall see throughout this text, development, and therefore adaptation, implies a continuity of experience and the conservation of the past. The infant grasps the newly presented sharp object in a way that is different from the way he used to grasp the familiar round object; yet, in both cases he opens his fingers wide before making contact with the object. The 2-year-old laughs at her father wearing a clown's hat, because she knows that the person is the same, even though he temporarily looks different. The high school history student understands that taxation without representation is not to be replaced by no taxation at all. Adaptive change always involves a double understanding: understanding of the value of the past and understanding of the requirements of the present. The capacity to coordinate past and present assures adaptation to the future.

The skills required to do more than just accept the new, the skills required to coordinate old ideas with new demands, are high-level skills. Often the person must do more than remember facts; he or she must invent procedures for discovering the facts and create an organizational system for interpreting those facts. Perhaps the 2-year-old does not laugh when she first sees her father donning a pointed hat. She is leery, but she knows how to acquire information that will reduce her anxiety. She pulls the clown's hat away from her father's head, sees the usual profile, and then laughs. She can adjust to this new situation because she knows how to acquire relevant information. The adaptable person can invent procedures that relate the past to the present. A 7-year-old is initially confused by the fact that this set of ten objects looks bigger than that set of ten objects which is spread apart. He is uncertain but knows the information that is relevant to reducing that uncertainty. He pushes the ten objects together again to reestablish the one-to-one correspondence, thereby verifying the equivalence of the two sets. He knows a procedure that relates the past to the present. Adaptation, as the term is used in this book, is the ability to invent procedures for establishing the continuity across experiences. The importance of the concept of continuity will be made explicit in Chapter Three.

*The Process of Teaching*

If, as we maintain, the aim of education is to improve the general adaptation of the individual and if adaptation is the ability to invent procedures for establishing the continuity across experiences, it follows that our teaching process must be one that assures that continuity across experiences is maintained. A good method for destroying continuity is to ask children questions out of the blue; a good method for facilitating continuity is to teach children how to ask their own questions—in other words, to give the child the time and support he or she needs to construct the knowledge relevant to an area of interest.

> Lauri had recently learned to hammer large nails into wooden boards. She would hold the nail head up vertically over the board and strike the nail head with her hammer. One day she found a bolt mixed in with her nails. She held the bolt vertically and struck it on its head. Of course, the bolt did not penetrate the wood. After watching the child try over and over again to drive the bolt through the wood, Lauri's teacher asked her "Why doesn't the bolt stick in the wood?"
> After Lauri indicated that she hadn't the slightest idea why, the teacher showed her the tip of a bolt and the tip of a nail side by side. "Look at the ends here. What is the difference?"
> Lauri had no trouble with this. "This one [the nail] is pointy." That answer satisfied the teacher tremendously. But had Lauri related the pointedness of the nail to the original problem—the bolt's failure to penetrate? Later in the day the teacher saw Lauri getting frustrated again in her attempts to hammer the bolt through the wood.

In spite of appearances to the contrary, the teacher's question in the above example was indeed out of the blue, because it was not directly related to the problem. The child did not see the connection between the shape of the point and its function. The child knew two things: nails are pointy, and bolts don't stick in wood. These are two isolated facts. The continuity between pointed-and-penetrating and blunt-and-nonpenetrating was completely missed by Lauri.

Possibly a better questioning procedure by the teacher could have assured greater continuity between known facts and Lauri's particular problem. Questioning procedures will be discussed in detail in Chapters Three and Five. The general point we are making here is that teaching procedures should be judged by the degree to which they facilitate continuity. Our assumption is that relating facts is more difficult for the child than the initial learning of isolated facts. The child doesn't necessarily learn how to use a fact at the same time that he or she learns the fact. Teaching is a process of helping children learn how to use facts.

One form of continuity, known as *transfer of learning,* has been identified by educators for some time. Transfer of learning involves generalizing the application of one successful problem-solving procedure to similar problems. Transfer of learning is usually assured by presenting the child with a range of similar problems. As the child succeeds on the first one, the time it takes him to master subsequent problems is reduced. The child literally learns how to learn (see Harlow, 1959). This means that the teacher, in preparing the preschool environment, needs to think about what makes one problem similar to another. Similarity of this type cannot be determined by superficial features such as the actual material the child uses or the commercial label on the material. In this text we have tried to provide the reader with a theoretical perspective that makes possible accurate analyses of task similarity. This theoretical perspective, further discussed in Chapter Six, is essential.

In sum, the process of teaching needs to assure two types of continuity: (1) continuity across the potentially interrelated facts that are needed to explain a problem, and (2) continuity across various problems that can be solved by a general procedure. These objectives can be met by providing the child with the time and context she needs to construct her own questions in order to relate facts and to construct her own analogies in order to relate problems.

*Knowing the Knower*

What shall the child learn? What knowledge is useful toward the goal of greater adaptation as we have defined it? Having identified the aim of education as learning and inventing procedures for relating facts and problems, what specifically can we say about these procedures? This section attempts to answer these questions by discussing the proposition that adaptation improves with consciousness of the means by which the knower constructs the known (see Piaget, 1976). The young child, oblivious to his own spatial perspective or subjective state, cannot understand that facts are relative to the process of observing. Knowing the role of the observer will improve the utilization of knowledge.

As Piaget (1970) repeatedly states, the knower plays an active role in learning the known. The knower adds something that is not *in* the external world—links, comparisons, contrasts, and other organizational operations. When we read Piaget carefully, we begin to realize that there is no physical fact that can stand independent of some system of relations that gives it meaning. The color red, surely thought by many to be a raw, uninterpreted sensation, is not understood as red until it is implicitly compared by the observer to colors that are not red (Kamii, 1974). Our eyes may be stimulated by the red band of light, but that wavelength does not become *known* to us as red until we *think* (albeit automatically) about it, compare red to not-red, or, in more general terms, compare $A$ to not-$A$. At some other time we can look at the same stimulus $A$ and compare it to something else—for example, to a darker object. The stimulus can be either a red object or a light object, depending on what relations we construct to react to the stimulus. There are an infinite number of not-$A$ comparisons that are possible, and it is the observer who makes the choice, not the environment. As Piaget would say, the object can be *assimilated* to an infinite number of schemata (or mental frameworks). It is important for children, adults, everyone to become conscious of this assimilatory process.

Just as the assimilatory process attributes meaning to physical objects, it also attributes meaning to social objects. What social rules I choose to obey depends on what social group I identify as my own. When I talk to others, I perceive what I say as polite or rude depending on the concept I have of myself in the presence of others and on the concept I presume others have of me. Whether I perceive a comment of mine as an insult or a compliment depends on my values and my current mood. Education gives us the means to see ourselves in context and to understand that our personality traits and our habitual ways of reacting combine with current situations to determine our behavior. Education keeps us wary of simplistic explanations, such as the view that behavior is determined exclusively by either temperament or environment. Education continually relates the known to the knower—a process that begins during the first five years of life.

Knowledge of the knower describes a general basis for education. But there is a major obstacle to the knower-known relation, and that obstacle is discontinuity. We have difficulty reconstructing the relation between the knower and the known because we must use inference to bridge discontinuous events. There are always "gaps in empiricism" (Piaget & Inhelder, 1969a), as the following example illustrates. A child says "I'm angry." He treats as a fact that his emotion is anger. But the child's parent questions him. As it turns out, the child's anger is only a surface emotion that masks a deeper fear of punishment. The parent suspected as much, because on a previous occasion the child had been punished in the same situation in which he now expresses anger. His anger is, in fact, a defense against the punishment that he fears may be forthcoming. But the child had failed to relate these two discontinuous events, and, as long as these two events remain discontinuous in the child's mind, he is deprived of an insight into the biased methods he uses to assess his emotions. Self-knowledge proceeds from the process of understanding the relation between the knower and the known, and this process occurs by relating discontinuous events to one another and to the self.

Discontinuity thwarts our awareness of the knower-known relation in the physical world also. A steel ball bearing rolls down a groove and collides with three resting ball bearings. The last ball bearing, at the opposite end, separates from the row and rolls forward. How does the young child account for this action and reaction? The problem is the apparent discontinuity between the movement of the first ball bearing and the movement of the last ball bearing, never touched by the first one. The child under 4 explains this "magical" action at a distance by saying "The first ball sneaks around and hits the one at the end" or "They all bump each other around" (see Piaget & Garcia, 1974). These comments derive from the child's intuitions about cause and effect, intuitions based on the child's personal relations to objects; that is, a pushed object rolls. His self-to-object perspective is interfering with his object-to-object perspective. He fills in the gap (the discontinuity) between action and reaction with an intuition that is a projection of himself into the object-to-object relation (Karplus, 1972). It is the discontinuity of physical events that causes us the greatest difficulty, and it is when we must deal with discontinuity that we are most likely to blur the knower-known relation (see Forman, 1975).

Awareness of the knower-known relation is a fundamental aim of education. What facilitates this awareness? Representation. The human mind has developed

One teacher or two?—discontinuities with which the child must deal.

ways to transcend the discontinuities that fall about capriciously and that thwart awareness. Mental imagery and language are important means of representation. Representation is the human mind's method of making the discontinuous more continuous. What happened yesterday can be represented in mental imagery or words and then related to what is happening today. The construction of these relations and a reflection on these relations make what we call an awareness of the knower-known relation. The child becomes aware that the situation that is making him angry now is similar to the situation that led to punishment yesterday. Through his ability to represent the previous situation, he is at least in the position to consider the knower-known relation and entertain the possibility that his perception is biased. Without representational competence the child would continue to react to each situation de novo, without contrast to not-$A$, without consciousness of the role of self in the perception of self. Through representation the child can span discontinuous events—two emotionally laden situations, two actions of ball bearings, two different objects at different times ($A$ then not-$A$), and the same object at different times ($A$ then $A$).

These considerations should form the matrix of a general design for a curriculum whose aim is an increased awareness of the knower-known relation. As we said earlier, the main difficulty in understanding this relation is the relative discontinuity between events. The major vehicle for reducing discontinuity is representation. We propose that curriculum for young children be organized according to categories based on the concepts of discontinuity and representation rather than be broken down along the conventional lines presented in Table 2-1. Discontinuity and representation are the key dimensions we used to organize the learning encounters presented in Chapter Nine. The first section of that chapter relates the definitions of these terms to the actual classroom practices. We feel that, by emphasizing the knower-known relation, education can become more integrated and more true to the child's developmental level. Development is a process of becoming more and more aware of the arbitrariness of "facts" and of the usefulness of this arbitrariness for human discourse. The teacher who understands this important point is likely to become more protective of children's need to invent their "facts," so that they can study the process of invention, and not just know the known.

With these considerations in mind, let's now rethink Table 2-1. There is no harm in keeping the same subject-area headings. We are asking that you rethink fundamental processes, not arbitrary subject-matter categories. Consider these old categories from this new perspective: development is an increase in the understanding of the *knower-known relation* through a process of *representation* that allows the person to bring *discontinuities* together.

We have taken the asterisked examples from the various categories in Table 2-1 and rewritten them in Table 2-2 according to this general statement regarding development.

What are the discontinuities with which the child must cope through representation in order to effectively deal with the knower-known relation? In removing his coat, the 2-year-old must move the coat sleeve from on-the-arm to off-the-arm. He cannot do this in one continuous tug on the sleeve by pulling it directly away from the wrist. The sleeve must go up and over and around the wrist and hand. It must make a detour. The discontinuity—that is, the detour—is forced on the child by the body itself. The discontinuity is managed by getting a firm view of the self as an object in space. The child doesn't try to take the sleeve off by pulling it "through" his wrist. He constructs the relation between himself (the knower) and the sleeve (the known).

Here is one more example, this one from premathematical thinking. When the child takes one block in each hand and places the two blocks side by side in a row on the table, does she think that that one row contains two blocks? Or, better put, how does she know that the whole is composed of two parts? She looks at the row, recalls that she had put the two blocks together, and reasons that she could indeed pull them apart if she chose. Twoness is conserved in oneness by virtue of the child's awareness of the relation between the knower (her actions) and the known (the construction of a row). The discontinuity between the instrumental actions and the final construction is bridged by the child's recollection—her representation—of these actions as she looks at the construction. Once again we see that representation bridges a discontinuity, improves the child's awareness of the knower-known relation, and, in the process, helps her conserve the parts within the whole.

Although the other examples in Table 2-2 are probably not truly self-explanatory, we hope that they are at least hints of what we have in mind. The last chapter of this book discusses curriculum units as basic ways of dealing with discontinuity and elaborates them in detail. We trust that you will remember the hints contained in Table 2-2 when you read Chapter Nine.

*Table 2-1.* Traditional Subject Areas for Early Education.

|  | 2- and 3-year-olds | 4- and 5-year-olds |
|---|---|---|
| *Self-help skills* | *Help child don clothes. Facilitate toileting. Set limits on running. | *Instruct child to watch for traffic. Teach use of materials. Teach child how to ask for directions. |
| *Social development* | *Teach child to share. Help child improve impulse control. Define classroom rules. | *Teach child a sense of fairness. Teach group cooperation. Show child how to negotiate with others. |
| *Language development* | Teach vocabulary. Use words that relate to pictures at hand. *Give child verbal instructions. | *Encourage communication between children. Play word games that contain puns and metaphors. |
| *Perceptual development* | Present shapes and ask for their names. *Ask child to pair matching hues, tones, and textures. Have child search for embedded figures. | *Ask child to interpret line drawings. Ask child to interpret the signs of seasons and other natural phenomena. Ask child to find the missing part of a whole figure. |
| *Motor development* | *Provide child with ladders for climbing. Let child play on a seesaw. Give child crayons and paper. | *Teach child a dance. Play kickball with a group of children. Give children figures to copy with crayon. |
| *Science* | *Ask child to predict an effect. Let child change flour into paste. Have child dilute a red liquid into a pink hue. | *Teach child to use a lever. Teach child the relation between heat and expansion of metal. Teach child how to read a clock. |
| *Mathematics* | Have child copy a repeated rhythm. *Comment on the symmetry of a child's block construction. Identify parts versus wholes. | Put objects in sets with one-to-one correspondence. Teach child to count a set of objects. *Teach child relative concepts such as bigger and longer. |
| *Art* | *Teach child expressive movement. Have child experiment with paints and collages. Foster basic sense of musical rhythm and melody. | *Teach child mime and dance. Encourage child to produce deliberate designs and scenes with paint. Teach children to produce rhythms and melodies in concert with one another. |

*These examples have been rewritten in Table 2-2 to highlight the knower-known relation.

*Table 2-2.* Subject Areas Defined as an Increased Understanding of the Knower-Known Relation.

| | 2- and 3-year-olds | 4- and 5-year-olds |
|---|---|---|
| *Self-help skills* | Help child account for body position in donning clothes. | Help child understand that perspective of auto drivers is different from that of pedestrians. |
| *Social development* | Relate sharing to both snatching and receiving. | Compare actions and intentions and discuss the differences. |
| *Language development* | Respond to the child's requests literally, so that he understands his own language. | Place children in dyads— one as listener and the other as speaker—to improve language as a means of transforming the unknown into the known. |
| *Perceptual development* | Compare a red object with a white object seen through a red filter. | Have two children interpret a drawing to the group. Ask others what cues the two children used in their interpretations. |
| *Motor development* | Compare walking the rungs of a horizontal ladder with climbing a vertical ladder. | Teach children a dance using videotapes. Edit tapes to show contrast between model and child. |
| *Science* | Have child explore the limits of himself as an agent of change to relate movement of self with movement of objects. | Have child predict the outcome of a lever in action. Vary the task in the hope that the child's self-contradictions will become apparent. |
| *Mathematics* | Watch and encourage child to advance from symmetrical actions (such as clapping) to symmetrical constructions. | Compare the lengths of two sticks, sometimes parallel and sometimes nonparallel, in the hope that contradictory judgments will improve the knower-known relation. |
| *Art* | Imitate child's rhythmical actions and lead child to exaggerate and prolong spontaneous rhythms. | Ask child to "become the sluggish liquid." Relate child's actions to liquid. Knowing the liquid is contained in the doing of the knower. |

## Categories of Knowledge

In Table 2-2 we have begun to challenge the traditional way of categorizing preschool curricula. Let's carry this challenge further by working with categories of knowledge rather than with the specific objectives alone. From a Piagetian perspective, what are the major categories of knowledge?

Piaget distinguishes three categories of knowledge on the basis of their primary source. Physical knowledge comes from physical objects, social knowledge comes from people, and logico-mathematical knowledge comes from the way we move ourselves and other objects. Piaget's distinction between physical knowledge and logico-mathematical knowledge causes most readers some difficulty. The difficulty arises, in part, because logico-mathematical knowledge plays an important role in all other forms of knowledge. In fact, there is an interaction among all three sources of knowledge. Logico-mathematical knowledge develops as the child becomes more conscious of the form of his own actions and of his own thought processes. This knowledge, in turn, increases the power of his understanding of information from physical objects and social beings.

Do not confuse the logico-mathematical category with either formal logic or mathematics per se. Piaget chooses this term only to draw our attention to the structure of action and thought—for example, the mathematical elegance of an infant finding a hidden toy. It is a category that in the preschool years should never be taught in a pure and abstract form (Kamii & DeVries, 1977; Piaget & Garcia, 1974). Even though logic and mathematics can be taught as pure, formal systems in high school and college, in the early years logico-mathematical relations are used in action and thought but are not explicitly known as such. As we said in the previous section, the education of the child involves a developing consciousness of thought itself, but it does not presuppose this consciousness.

We have added a fourth category to the three defined by Piaget. This fourth category does not, properly speaking, relate to a source of knowledge but, rather, to the result of using the other three sources. This category, *self-knowledge,* results from coordinating information from others, from physical objects, and from an awareness of movement and thought. We have chosen to highlight self-knowledge because so many readers assume that Piaget's theory is irrelevant to social-emotional development. Such is not the case. The child's knowledge about himself, his role, potential, and bias can best be studied as a subvariety of general cognitive development.[1]

### Physical Knowledge

The source of physical knowledge is the object in the physical environment. Physical knowledge results whenever the child makes an association between a particular action and a particular object: this round object continues to move when I push it across the table; this square object does not. The basic cognitive process involved in the development of physical knowledge is *discrimination.* The child

---

[1]For an excellent review of this relatively new area of research see C. Shantz, The Development of Social Cognition, in E. M. Hetherington (Ed.), *Review of Child Development Research* (Vol. 5, Chap. 5). Chicago: University of Chicago Press, 1976.

makes a discrimination between this object and other objects. He knows what this object will do under the effect of his own actions. In fact the child's ability to anticipate the physical results of his actions on a particular object is the only index we have that the child has discriminated that object from similar objects.

Children can learn about objects by means other than physically acting on them. The inquisitive Hawaiian child approaches a sea urchin washed to the shore. "No!" his mother warns. "That will hurt you" she says pointing to the prickly spines. The child heeds his mother and does not venture to touch the object, nor does he in the future. He gingerly touches many other objects on the beach but avoids the sea urchins. This means that he has learned a discrimination, but it is a discrimination that he did not learn through his own actions on the object. Piaget would say that this child's knowledge, having been given to him by another person, is an instance of social knowledge. Social knowledge comes from people. Social knowledge can be about anything.

By associating action with object, the child acquires a wide range of physical knowledge. A 4-year-old girl may fully understand that she must pour water more slowly into a skinny glass than into a wide glass. She has learned, by observing the consequences of her own actions, that the water level rises faster in the skinny glass than in the wide glass. She probably doesn't know *why* this is so, but she does know that a difference exists between the two situations. Nor is she necessarily aware of the implication of being able to pour the same water in these two different vessels—namely, that, although one vessel seems to contain more than the other, the two vessels actually contain the same amount. The cognitive act of relating one action (changing the vessel) to another action (transferring the same water) and making a conclusion (water is conserved in quantity) requires a conscious use of logico-mathematical thought.

It is difficult to say much more about the development of physical knowledge without discussing logico-mathematical knowledge, because the latter is necessary for the child to develop an understanding of physical events. At the cost of oversimplifying things, we will risk here a distinction between physical and logico-mathematical knowledge. Physical knowledge comes from relating different actions on the same object to the same action on different objects. Logico-mathematical knowledge comes from relating one action that changes objects to another action that changes objects. The form of one action is related to the form and consequence of another action. For example, if a puppet is placed on top of a pillow and that pillow is then raised from the floor to the table top, the puppet is still *on top* of the pillow. Changing the relation between the pillow and the floor does not change the relation between the puppet and the pillow. However, inverting the pillow would: the puppet would be *underneath* the pillow. This knowledge does not come from a simple observation of the effect of one action on one object. This knowledge—knowing the difference between *on top* and *underneath*—comes from a mental comparison of the form and effect of one action-object relation with the form and effect of another action-object relation. The child does not learn the concepts *on top* and *underneath* from the physical objects in the way he learns that the puppet will break if dropped but the pillow will not. These concepts of spatial relations (a form of logico-mathematical knowledge) come from reflection on the actions themselves.

Do we really need to go into such detail about types of knowledge? Our answer is an emphatic "Yes!" because it is the failure to distinguish types of knowledge that makes preschool curricula inadequate. The preschool curriculum should help children reflect on the organization of their actions and not simply lead them to discover the effects of their actions on an object. To understand just how the child constructs knowledge, we must understand the difference between physical knowledge and logico-mathematical knowledge.

*Logico-Mathematical Knowledge*

As we just said, this category of knowledge comes from reflecting on the coordination of actions. It derives from learning how to coordinate physical actions, and yet it is more than simple know-how. In his most recent book, *The Grasp of Consciousness,* Piaget describes through an experiment this difference between doing and understanding the coordination of actions. A 4-year-old child is asked to swing around a ball on a string and release the string so that the ball will fly into a box tacked to a wall directly in front of the child. After several minutes of practice the child develops sufficient skill to hit the target almost every time. Then the child is asked at what point in the circular movement of the ball he released the string. Most of the children who participated in the experiment answered that they had released the string when the ball was directly opposite the box. Their answers were, of course, wrong because, had they waited until the ball was there, the release would have caused the ball to fly in a tangent, missing the target altogether. Knowing how to do something is not the same as understanding how actions relate to one another.

Where is the "logic" in the more advanced ability to understand the coordination of actions required by this task? Or, to put it in other words, in what way does the child exhibit logical thought when he is able to tell the experimenter where he actually released the string? Piaget explains that the older child, around age 11, reflects on the rotary action of the sling (action $A$) and on the linear path of the released ball (action $B$). This child knows that the path of the released ball is a continuation of the path of the spinning ball. Therefore, the path of the released ball cannot be perpendicular to the path of the spinning ball; that is, the release point cannot be directly opposite the box. The rotation of the ball on the string is at the same time the beginning of a linear path whenever the ball is released; the rotary action and the linear action are not two separate actions. Reflecting on the coordination of these two actions leads the child to make an *inference;* to wit, the ball is not released directly opposite the box. He is not told, nor is he shown. His understanding is the result of making an inference based on his knowledge of action-to-action relations. Therein lies the logic in logico-mathematical knowledge.

We have jumped from the practical knowledge of the 4-year-old to the logical inferences of the 11-year-old. By this we don't mean to imply that logico-mathematical knowledge is relevant only to high school curricula. Logico-mathematical knowledge develops slowly, beginning with the first coordinations of movements in infancy. In the next chapter we will be more specific about the relationship between the sensorimotor coordinations of the first two years of life and the conceptual coordinations of later years. Here we are concerned with distinguishing the four categories of knowledge—physical, social, self-, and logico-mathematical —as clearly as possible, without dealing extensively with their courses of development. We admit that trying to define these terms without simultaneously tracing the development of the knowledge we are discussing is not an easy task. But it is a necessary task, because an understanding of how these categories differ and how they relate to one another is essential to an understanding of our approach to childhood education. We ask you to reread these sections after you have read Chapter Three. Right now we offer a few more examples in order to make definitions and distinctions as clear as possible.

What type of knowledge is reflected in the child's awareness that both cornflakes and watermelons are food? The answer rests in the source of this awareness. If the child has heard adults call both cornflakes and watermelons "food," his knowledge is socially derived. If the child infers that both watermelons and cornflakes are food because he reasons that all edible substances are called "food," watermelons and cornflakes are edible substances, and therefore both watermelons and cornflakes are food, his knowledge falls in the logico-mathematical category. If the child makes the additional inference that all the cornflakes in the world can never equal all the food (since the one is a subset of the other), that inference, too, is a form of logico-mathematical thinking. Logico-mathematical knowledge pertains to the use of factual information to generate new knowledge. Certainly, helping the child use knowledge creatively is an important objective of education.

What role does language play in logico-mathematical knowledge? Language is necessary but not sufficient, as the following example illustrates. A 3-year-old says "This doll is missing something. Where is the doll's arm?" The teacher helps the child find the missing part and then asks the child "Which is bigger, the whole doll or the doll's arm?" The child answers "This one," pointing to the torso exclusive of the arm. This answer does not address the teacher's question, nor could a child of this age begin to understand the part-whole relation implicit in the question (Inhelder & Piaget, 1964). The child has tried to answer the teacher's question by looking at the doll. The older child would have known that a whole is always, by necessity, larger than any of its parts. Concepts like this cannot be taught by teaching the child to name objects. The child was asked to do more than to identify the arm as part of the body. He was asked to think about the meaning of the part-whole relation and about the implications that such relation has for size comparisons. Language alone does not assure that the mental manipulations will be carried out (see Furth, 1966).

One final point about logico-mathematical knowledge remains to be made. This form of knowledge depends on continuity. Logico-mathematical thinking can be applied only when two actions relate to the same object, or two classes are both subclasses of a common class, or two objects are initially established empirically as equivalent. Changing the shape of one ball of clay from round to flat carries no implication with regard to the amount of substance contained in another ball of clay. The 7-year-old knows that flattening a ball of clay does not change the amount of substance contained in that piece of clay—whatever its shape. A child of 7 understands that he is thinking about two states of the same object, an object transformed by an action that is irrelevant to quantity. If the flattened ball had been seen as a different object altogether, the child would feel compelled to empirically measure the quantity of the flattened piece. The fact that he knows that the flat piece is a transformed version of the round piece makes the empirical measurement unnecessary. He knows by inference—an inference based on the assumed continuity between these two states—that the identity remains the same. As we briefly mentioned in the section on adaptation, preschool curricula should facilitate the young child's awareness of the continuity between experiences. This in turn maximizes the child's use of logico-mathematical thinking, even though in the early years this form of thinking is primarily intuitive. As you will read in Chapter Three, a great deal of power comes with the discovery that two events are continuous despite outward appearances. If we give children the means to discover whether two events are continuous or discontinuous, we give them the power to construct logico-mathematical relations.

*Social Knowledge*

There is a large body of knowledge whose function is to improve conversation and other forms of interaction with other people. Most of this knowledge is arbitrary in the sense that the "facts" are merely social conventions. For example, it doesn't matter what you call an alligator. You could just as easily call it "pffypu." However, your warning "Beware of the pffypu" might not alert your listener to ripples in still water if he didn't share your convention. Knowledge that comes from the

Social knowledge is directly transmitted to the child by the culture.

culture alone is called by Piaget *social knowledge.* Vocabulary, rules of conduct, game rules, moral codes, and a thousand more pieces of information are given to the child as "facts." These "facts" cannot be discovered by the child alone. The child cannot discover an animal's name—or a social expectation—through a combination of logico-mathematical and physical knowledge alone. Social knowledge, by definition, must be directly transmitted in some form to the child by his culture.

While it is true that all social knowledge is transmitted by the culture, is it also true that all knowledge is acquired through the culture's social knowledge? The answer is no, and a brief digression into the distinction between rote knowledge and meaningful knowledge will make the point clear. A sixth grader is told that the earth is round. The teacher proceeds to relate the rising and setting sun to the rotation of the earth, brings out a miniature model of our planetary system, and helps the child understand the evidence that led early astronomers to conclude that the earth is round. The child listens carefully, reconstructs these pieces of information in the manner described by the teacher, and comes away with a new understanding of the earth.

Another sixth grader is also told that the earth is round. But her teacher then adds that this is why, if we continued to sail westward, we would eventually return to our starting point. The child asks "How do you know that the world is round?" and the teacher answers "Because early sailors sailed in one direction and eventually returned to their starting point." For this teacher the fact that the earth is round rests solely on the social truth that early sailors circumnavigated the globe. The child is given no recourse beyond this statement of history. In spite of the fact that the child may go on and use this premise constructively and creatively, the premise itself is a piece of socially given rote knowledge.

Rote knowledge is knowledge that could be learned meaningfully but is not— like the premise in our second example. Meaningful knowledge is knowledge that is gradually constructed from previous knowledge—like the new understanding of the earth gained by the child in our first example. And social knowledge is knowledge that can never be constructed, since it is no more than arbitrary social convention. Social knowledge can be learned but cannot be constructed. Rote knowledge can be learned, can be constructed, but is not constructed. Meaningful knowledge can be constructed and is constructed. All three forms of knowledge can be useful.

Social knowledge can help the child remember, attend to, compare, and otherwise process information. A child who is given the term "baseball game" has less to keep in memory when comparing different games than another child left with his own mental images of the unnamed activity. Rote knowledge, too, can be useful, especially in the early stages of learning a concept. Were children to reconstruct the origin of every first premise, their education would surely be retarded. In fact, it is the reconstruction of first premises that becomes the main concern of our most sophisticated levels of science and philosophy. Inevitably, meaningful knowledge derives from premises that are themselves discontinuous with regard to the child's personal discoveries and intuitions. While we recommend throughout this text that discontinuity between personal discovery and first premises be minimized, we acknowledge that some discontinuity must exist until the mental capabilities of the child are fully developed. We said "some" because allowing for much discontinuity would create a Catch-22 situation. If we do nothing to bridge discontinuity, the child's mental capabilities will not fully develop. Therefore, the perpetual "problem of the match" (Hunt, 1969) between the child and the curriculum must be solved by the art of knowing which premises the child is ready to reconstruct. Rote knowledge and social knowledge are useful, but only if they are eventually placed in a logico-mathematical system that helps the child "go beyond the information given" (Bruner, 1973).

The arbitrary conventions of social knowledge are not always conventions of convenience. They can also be conventions of value. These conventions—for example, the value assigned to being "self-sufficient"—are arbitrary in the fact that they are not necessarily the same across cultures; but within a given culture the agreed-upon value has a functional (nontrivial) relation to the maintenance of the culture. The relation between a word and an object is more trivial, since changing the word would have little effect on the cultural system at large as long as all participants agreed to the change. Changing values is not so trivial but no less arbitrary than changing word-object relations.

To what degree is social knowledge an aim of early childhood education? Undeniably, social knowledge is a fact of early childhood education. "When you go to the big school where your brother is, you'll have to sit quietly, listen, and do what the teacher says" one concerned teacher tells a 4-year-old. Another teacher explains "You can't just believe everything you hear. You have to keep asking until you really know what's true." In the science corner we hear the teacher say "Let's call this part [pointing to a balance beam] the pivot." And in the language-arts corner we hear "Pooh loves honey, as all bears do." A preschool program that doesn't offer the child a great deal of information resists our imagination. Social knowledge is there the moment children enter the classroom. They see it in the dress of their teacher, in the way the room is furnished, in the presence of certain materials, and in the very structure of the language they hear. Therefore, instead of asking *if* social knowledge is relevant to early childhood education, we should ask *what* social knowledge is relevant to early childhood education.

The answer to this question rests in large measure on the cultural heritage of teachers and parents. One program may teach that fighting is always wrong, and another may teach that fighting must follow certain rules of fairness. One program may teach that little boys don't dress up in women's clothes, and another may teach there are no rights or wrongs in the world of fantasy. The socialization process continues, either explicitly or implicitly, every minute of the child's day. The teaching staff should spend many hours clarifying their own values to themselves and realizing that these values are always superimposed on the child. There is no value-free curriculum; if there were, its very neutrality would represent its "value."

*Self-Knowledge*

As we mentioned earlier, self-knowledge is not itself a source of knowledge; rather, it is the result of the application of physical, logico-mathematical, and social knowledge. Through the coordination of all sources of knowledge the child gradually differentiates the self as a unique object and later as a unique personality. We have chosen to discuss the formation of self-knowledge as a separate category so that the reader will not erroneously conclude that Piaget's theory fails to relate to social-emotional development.

The infant is not born with the ability to differentiate between his own body and the external world. He may act as if he could affect objects at a distance, mainly because he is not aware of the difference between "body in contact with object" and "body not in contact with object." Better put, he has not yet constructed the object. Gradually he constructs the object concept and understands that he can cause the object to move only if his body, which is separate from the object, makes contact with the object. Knowing the cause-and-effect limits of the body is an early form of self-awareness.

The me/not-me distinction is also learned through a comparison of various sensations. When the infant touches his lips with his fingers, he receives two sensations, one in the lips and one in the fingers. When he touches his lips with an object, he feels only one sensation, the sensation in the lips. The difference between the double and the single sensory experience is used by the child to distinguish self (hand) from objects (rattle, teething ring, and so on). These sensory experiences are universal; they transcend culture and are fundamental to the child's construction of the me/not-me distinction (Gordon, 1975b, p. 86). The coordination of these two different sensory experiences occurs automatically; that is, the coordination is part of our biological competence.

Locomotion is another process by which the me/not-me distinction is made. As the infant crawls and later walks, objects pass across his visual field. At times, as objects pass across his visual field, he feels his own muscles at work—the muscles in his legs and the muscles in his neck as he turns his head. But at other times objects pass across his visual field when his muscles are not working. This contrast gives the child the means to distinguish the real movement of the objects themselves from their apparent movement, an illusion created by the child's crawling and walking. This differentiation between self-movement and object movement is another step in self-knowledge (Miller, 1962).

After the child has become aware of the boundaries of his own body and of the difference between self-induced and object-induced movement, he begins to construct the permanence of himself in the face of a fluctuating environment. This continuity of self is initially anchored to the child's primary caretaker. The mother leaves the infant, the infant cries, and she returns. The initial state of mother present is changed to that of mother absent, but it can be *reversed* to mother present again. The child becomes aware, at least at the practical level of action, that he does not cease to have an identity when his mother leaves. After all, he can reverse her absence. His awareness of his power affirms not only the continued existence of himself but also the continued existence of his caretaker, even across those times when the caretaker is not in sight.

Awareness of the caretaker's permanence seems to occur earlier than awareness of object permanence (Bell, 1970). By object permanence we mean the child's knowledge of how to make a hidden object reappear. The child knows that he can reverse the state of object absence by removing the shield that hides the object or by moving his head to peer around the shield. The object has a permanence that is independent of visual contact; that is, the object is part of the permanent not-me. The child's own body, the outside objects, and significant others are the anchor points essential to the construction of self-awareness (Gordon, 1975b).

The process of constructing self-knowledge is in fact no different from the process of constructing any of the conservations mentioned by Piaget—that is, conservation of number, length, substance, and so forth. Self-knowledge, as is true of all conservation concepts, involves the coordination of what remains the same with what does not remain the same. Take, for example, the child who is just learning that her mirror image is not another child. How does that child construct a system of relations that allows her to differentiate between another child seen through a plate glass and her own mirror image?

Look at what Emily does. She stands opposite the other child, Susan. Susan moves her arm from low to high. Emily is motionless. Sometimes this situation is reversed, and it is Emily who stands opposite the mirror. Now, when Emily moves her hand, the "child in the mirror" moves her hand, too, and everything else Emily does is perfectly mimicked by the mirror image. These visual experiences are combined with Emily's kinesthetic awareness of the movements of her own limbs in the following general system of relations.

Call the sense of movement (the kinesthetic sense) $B$. Call the visual sense $A$. Emily sees an arm in the mirror move; the image changes position from $A$ to $A'$. How does she come to understand that this change of position from $A$ to $A'$ is a reflection of herself? Throughout the entire movement from $A$ to $A'$, Emily is also aware that her muscles are tense and that they are moving; that is, that $B$ is constant. When the visual event stops, so does the child's kinesthetic feedback. Susan's arm changes position, too, but this visual change is not synchronized with Emily's kinesthetic feedback. Emily is old enough—say, 1 year old—to understand that her arm in two different places at two different times is still her arm. She takes this knowledge and relates it to the mirror image. The kinesthetic experience tells her that it is her arm that is now low, then high. Herein lies the continuity that makes it possible for the child to make an inference (albeit not at a conscious level) about the visual experience of $A$ changing to $A'$. Since the transformation of $A$ to $A'$ is continuous with the continuous experience of $B$, the visual experience must be an extension of the kinesthetic experience; that is, that sight is my reflection. Without the presence of $B$ throughout the $A$-to-$A'$ transformation, the child would have no basis for making the inference that what she saw was herself. Figure 2-1 diagrams the sight of

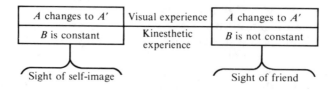

*Figure 2-1.* Differentiating self from other.

Emily's own image in motion and the sight of her friend Susan in motion. Since there is no invariant relation between $B$ and $A$ in the second case, $A$ is not constructed as an extension of self. The "conservation of self-identity" in the first case depends on the constancy of the kinesthetic sense. All conservation problems require an invariant dimension—some continuity that makes the conservation inference possible.

This process of discovering what belongs to the self and what does not belong to the self does not stop after the first year of life, nor does it stop after adulthood. The basic process involved in the construction of these distinctions remains the same. What does change is the range of application of self-awareness. Whereas in infancy the range of awareness pertains to the body and not-body, in adulthood the range pertains to my-culture and not-my-culture. The process still consists of contrasting a change in one dimension ($A$ to $A'$) with the constancy of another dimension ($B$ remains $B$). My culture kills cattle for food; their culture kills cute little seals for food ($A$ versus $A'$), but both cultures take advantage of harmless animals ($B$ is the same across both $A$ and $A'$). It is this coordination of the similarities and differences between our culture and another that gives us a greater appreciation of what we are ourselves (Metz-Hatch, 1975).

Two processes are basic to a construction of the self: *correspondence* and *transformation* (Metz-Hatch, 1975). These are Piagetian concepts and are part of logico-mathematical relations. Remember, we are emphasizing that the construction of a strong sense of self is no less a logico-mathematical process than the construction of an understanding of the lever. Correspondence refers to an awareness that two things are the same, that $B$ remains $B$. Transformation refers to both the awareness that two things are different and the awareness of the method by which one thing is made different from the other: $A$ changes to $A'$ by action $X$. When correspondences are coordinated with transformations, the child can make better adaptations to the environment, both social and physical. Transforming a row of counters by spreading them apart is not confused by a 6-year-old with transforming the row by adding new counters. He verifies that these two transformations make a numerical difference by realizing that one row still corresponds to another of an equal number of counters and that the action of adding new counters destroys this correspondence.

Let's now consider an example of how the coordination of transformations and correspondences can improve social adaptation. Mona has just learned to understand Herbie's feelings, even though the way he manifests them is different from the way she expresses those same emotions. Mona now understands that Herbie works slowly (call this $A$) when he is interested (call this $B$). Mona works quickly ($A'$) when she is interested $(B)$. Slowness is to Herbie what quickness is to Mona—that is, $AB = A'B$. The girl must not confuse Herbie's slowness with a lack of interest $(B')$; that is, $AB$ does not equal $A'B'$. By coordinating their differences in pace with their similarities in interest, Mona learns not to interrupt Herbie when he is working slowly. She has developed an empathy for him.

It is because of empathy that we see in others emotions that we ourselves have, even though their manifestations are different from ours. It is possible that empathy develops through the process of mentally transforming one's own outward behavior $(A')$ into the outward behavior of the other person $(A)$, while at the same time maintaining a constant emotional state $(B)$. Mona reflects on the fact that she can vary her own work pace without an appreciable change in her interest level. The continuity of her own emotions across these variations creates a sense of self from which Mona can generalize a sense of continuity with others. Awareness of constancy across variations within self may be gradually transferred to variations between self and others. This perceived constancy between self and others could be the dawn of empathy.

Perceiving similarity between self and others is the dawn of empathy.

In summary, the construction of self involves both a differentiation of the self and sense of continuity with others. A person who does not reintegrate the differentiated self into a social world of others remains aloof, insensitive, and alone. Social-emotional development requires both the protection of the child's autonomy and the establishment of linkages with other children. One theme of this text is that social-emotional development results from an increasing awareness that other people's actions are variations of one's own actions. This awareness is muted in both the oversocialized child, who has no sense of self, and the nonsocialized child, who has no sense of other. Social adaptation results from the ability to coordinate correspondence and transformation—that is, the ability to reconcile our essential sameness with the transformations that we undergo all the time. Gaining a sense of self and an understanding of others is no less a case of logico-mathematical thinking than is trying to balance a beam with equal weights. Self-knowledge, which includes by necessity an understanding of others, is certainly another important aim of early childhood education.

## Summary

Increasing children's adaptability should be the basic purpose of early childhood programs. However, the definitions and operationalization of the term *adaptability* varies from teacher to teacher. Piaget views adaptation as virtually synonymous with intellectual development and conceives it as the process by which individuals change and understand change within their environments. Through the process of assimilation, individuals apply general schemes to different objects and events in the environment. This minimizes environmental changes and differences, thus permitting the organism to retain a sense of continuity. At times, however, the environmental input and the organism are so discrepant that the organism itself is forced to change, which accounts for the process of accommodation. In this case the schemes themselves are modified or elaborated in order to adapt to the input. In a very real sense, the environment is changed during the process of assimilation, and the organism is changed during the process of accommodation.

What implications does the concept of adaptability as viewed by Piaget hold for early childhood education? The primary function of the teacher in terms of this question is that of assuring that children have the opportunity to deal with all types of change—for instance, applying the same actions to different objects, expressing emotions under different circumstances, and viewing an object or situation from different perspectives. In each case the aim is for the child to begin to deal with the concepts of continuity and discontinuity. Adaptation can be defined as the ability to establish continuity across experiences. The process of teaching, then, is one that strives to maintain continuity across experiences. The best way to achieve this goal is to structure a curriculum that allows a maximum amount of freedom for children to ask their own questions, to set their own problems, and to generate their own confusion. When children answer their own questions, solve their own problems, and bring order to their own confusion, we can be reasonably sure that continuity across experience has been maintained.

We have stated that development is an increase in the understanding of the knower-known relation through a process of representation. Representation allows the thinker to bring discontinuities together in order to discern the form of movement and thought. The movement of one steel ball striking three steel balls in a row is perceived initially as discontinuous with regard to the movement of the third steel ball separating from the others. The knower, in this initial stage, is unaware that he is using the self-starting ability of his own body to describe the last ball's movement. As the child becomes more aware of the difference between himself and the objects of his knowledge (the knower-known relation), he ceases to make these errors of personification. The movement of the last ball is seen as a continuation of the movement of the striking ball. The apparent discontinuity is bridged by an inference that there is only one force involved. The inference itself depends on the child's ability to represent past actions and past combinations of actions.

Maintaining continuity across experiences is a process. Although process and content are often spoken of separately, one cannot exist without the other. What are the proper contents of an early childhood program? Expressed slightly differently, what knowledges should be of concern to teachers of young children? Piaget has answered this question by dividing the types of knowledge children deal with into three categories: physical knowledge, logico-mathematical knowledge, and social knowledge. One way of understanding these categories is to consider the source from which children gain an understanding of the specific knowledge. Physical knowledge is a product of a child's actions on the physical world. Color is discovered by looking; the fact that an object breaks is discovered by dropping; and the taste of an object is discovered by tasting. In each case feedback comes directly from the object as a result of an action on the part of the child. Logico-mathematical knowledge is provided by feedback from actions. The child relates one action to another; for example, the action of placing checkers into a one-to-one correspondence is related to the action of spreading one row of checkers out. By relating these two actions the child gains the understanding of conservation of number and discontinuous quantity.

Social knowledge comes from the information provided by other people. It is a knowledge that cannot be learned simply by acting on objects. For example, no matter how hard one studies or manipulates a shiny, sharp object, one cannot discover the fact that it is called a thumbtack. That type of information can come only from other people, either directly (by being told) or indirectly (for example, through books). Customs, morals, and values are other examples of social knowledge.

Another area of knowledge important to the young child, but which is not stressed in Piaget's studies, is self-knowledge. A child constructs an understanding of self in the same way he or she constructs an understanding of space, number, and reality. The first major step is the differentiation of self from not-self. Here, too, the concept of continuity and discontinuity applies. For example, constant kinesthetic feedback across variations in position and action provides the child with information about his own body with relation to the environment.

The purpose of early childhood education, then, is to provide an environment in which children will have ample opportunity to experience changes (discontinuity) in all four areas of knowledge and the freedom to construct an understanding that bridges the differences (continuity).

## Suggestions for Further Reading

Isaacs, S. *Intellectual growth in young children.* New York: Schocken Books, 1964. This book by a pioneering British nursery educator provides a good discussion and some very nice supporting examples of the importance for children to pursue their own interests and ask their own questions.

Kohlberg, L., & Mayer, R. Development as the aim of education. *Harvard Educational Review,* 1972, *42*(4), 449–496. In this excellent article the authors discuss different ideologies underlying educational practices. They conclude that the ideas of Piaget and those of John Dewey provide the most viable theories for constructing educational curricula.

Piaget, J. Genetic epistemology. In R. I. Evans (Ed.), *Jean Piaget: The man and his ideas.* New York: Dutton, 1973. A very readable discussion of Piaget, which includes an explanation of the concepts of physical and logico-mathematical knowledge.

# Chapter Three

# The Child Constructs Knowledge

Every time a teacher works with a pupil, the teacher is expressing his assumptions about how children learn and what knowledge is. If he says to the child "This is a telephone" as the child looks at the object, he is probably assuming that (1) knowledge is an association between a word and an object and (2) this association is learned by looking at the object and listening to the word. Of course, the teacher may work with children in many other ways, but this particular approach does carry specific assumptions about learning and knowledge.

These assumptions can also be found in the current practices of preschool education at large, because the very existence of today's favorite methods of early childhood education implies the existence of today's prevalent assumptions about the learning process and the definition of knowledge. Judging from curriculum guides and programmatic descriptions (Evans, 1975) preschool teachers across the nation do favor one category of methods. This category of methods centers around the teacher's attempts to improve the child's perceptual discriminations—the child's ability to see and hear and feel small differences and general similarities among objects and to identify the physical features that make things the same or different. These methods presuppose that knowledge is mainly an accurate copy of what exists in an absolute, external reality. This theory is called *the copy theory of knowledge.* In the next section we shall define the theory, discuss its underlying assumptions, and then compare it with an alternative theory, known as the *constructivist theory of knowledge.*

## The Copy Theory of Knowledge: The Child Learns by Closely Attending

According to the copy theory of knowledge, the act of knowing can be likened to a photographic process. Wisdom, useful knowledge, and adaptation result from getting clear focus on the object. Ignorance, mistakes, and self-defeating behavior result from a blurred and poorly defined copy of what is out there in the world. Improvement takes place when the lenses are adjusted—that is, when the viewer makes some change in the way he looks at the world. The observer trains himself to minimize prejudice, correct for bias, maximize contrast, and employ many other means to guarantee that he gets an accurate impression of what is really there. At no point does the observer question the existence and form of his object. He questions only the fidelity of his print. He spends centuries improving the precision of his measuring instruments, his means of recording, his statistics; but he holds as absolute that the object to be measured exists independent of his attempts to measure it. Of course, the copy theorist realizes that a naturalist trying to photograph a colony of baboons will affect the behavior of the "objects" she is trying to measure; but the naturalist is advised only to "improve her lens" by improving her camouflage. The natural behavior of a baboon family is there to be photographed if the naturalist can improve her method of observing. At no point does the empirical scientist or the copy theorist—or, for that matter, most of us in the world—question the fundamental units of time and space that tell us when an image of reality has been improved. An inch is an inch, a second is a second, even though there are yardsticks and clocks that are less than precise. Precision can be achieved.

The copy theorist's views seem very reasonable to most of us. If we regard these views as self-evident truths, we teach young children in ways that are consistent with these views. If gaining knowledge is a matter of getting an increasingly precise copy of what is out there in external reality, then it is reasonable to teach young children how to look with greater care, how to listen with greater acuity, and how to touch and taste with greater discrimination. Preschool programs everywhere emphasize the early years as the time to "educate the senses," a phrase made famous by Maria Montessori (1967).

Discrimination training is the hallmark of the Montessori approach to early childhood education. The Montessori methods are designed to train the senses to make more and more refined distinctions among shapes, sounds, textures, and colors. For example, the child learns to make refined discriminations of size by placing small wooden cylinders into holes that are perfect size matches. The material itself informs the child of an error, since a small cylinder in a large hole will be loose and a large cylinder will not fit into a small hole. The objective is to educate the senses to "see" more precisely.

The preschool teacher of today also uses language to improve perceptual discriminations. She consistently uses one word to refer to a specific object and is careful not to use that word to refer to similar but essentially different objects. She doesn't call a glass a cup, a stool a chair, or a can a bucket. She encourages the child to do the same. If he calls a fuzzy object "nerf" and a prickly object "nerd," the teacher is pleased that the child has (1) noticed the difference and (2) associated the correct word with each object. If the child, at some initial stage of learning, calls the nerd a nerf, the teacher begins to focus the child's attention on the features (fuzzy versus prickly) that distinguish these two objects. She says to the child things such as "This is a nerd. This is a nerf," and that is enough. The object of the lesson—and a thousand more like it, repeated throughout the children's days—is to teach the child to look carefully and to see more than he saw before.

Teaching children to notice similarities among objects is as much a part of copy theory as teaching them to look for differences. In order to identify two objects as similar, the observer must be able to distinguish features in one object that are also in the other object. The ostrich is similar to the swan in that they both have feathers, long necks, and bills. On an outing to the zoo, the teacher encourages the child to look closely at these features and to isolate them as items that two different birds can each "have." A more refined copy of the external object improves our ability to see differences as well as similarities among elements in the external environment. Looking for similarity and difference, comparing and contrasting, and matching shapes, colors, and textures are prevalent themes in most commercially packaged preschool curricula. Almost every preschool has an abundant supply of lotto sets, form boards, and texture tiles for training the senses.

Teachers using these materials and methods make the implicit assumption that young children don't notice detail and that they don't spend enough time looking or listening before they act—in other words, that they respond to the global properties of their environment. Given these assumptions, the teacher's role is to teach the child how to look, how to note details, how to differentiate parts from the whole. A child repeatedly jabbing a jigsaw-puzzle piece in a space too small for it is asked to look more closely at the piece and to trace the contour of the piece with her finger. If a child misnames a triangle a square, the teacher calls his attention to the shape of the angles. If, when asked to sort pictures, the child places the horse with the dogs rather than with the other horses, the teacher assumes that the child has failed to notice some distinguishing feature of horses. The teacher tries, either by physically pointing or by drawing or by highlighting in color, to make each child aware of those features that function as criteria for sorting the pictures correctly. The curriculum-material designer and the teacher are implicitly assuming that a major objective of early childhood education is to guide attention to critical features of the environment *as it exists*. A corollary objective is to improve the systems that support precise observation, such as impulse control and task persistence.

Should we feel comfortable with this approach and these methods in our preschools today? How much does knowledge of something depend on precise observation of the environment as it exists static and frozen in time? As we will stress in the next section and as we have already mentioned in our discussion of logico-mathematical knowledge, precise observation is not enough. The child has to take his observations, no matter how accurate, and think about them. The fact that he has observed long necks on two different birds doesn't automatically lead the child to conclude that he has seen two different birds with a common feature. He could have seen the same bird twice. These fundamental distinctions of time and space—in this case the difference between seeing one object twice and two identical objects once—are taken for granted in the copy theory of knowledge. The copy theory exaggerates the importance of improving the precision of observation. Even extremely precise observation does not provide sufficient information to discriminate between the one-object-twice and the two-objects-once. We must have additional information, information regarding how objects change.

We now turn to Piaget, who repeatedly tells us that knowledge is not a copy of some absolute external reality but is, instead, a construct of the mind. His theory of knowledge has profound implications for the practice of preschool education, which are significantly different from those of a copy theory of knowledge. As you read the following discussion on the constructivist theory of knowledge, remember: for Piaget, *change makes the difference*.

## The Constructivist Theory of Knowledge:
## The Child Learns by Changing Objects

How does Piaget's theory of knowledge differ from the copy theory of knowledge? Instead of being the result of increasingly refined perceptual discriminations, knowledge is for Piaget the result of an active mind constructing relationships among objects (Furth, 1969). Of course, Piaget does not deny that the child must learn to take notice of the details of the physical objects; what he denies is that this is sufficient. There are many cases in which the child can misunderstand a situation even when he has seen all the physical properties clearly, as the following illustrates.

Suppose that Valerie, a 3-year-old, can perceptually distinguish a small wooden pyramid from a small wooden cube. We know she can distinguish the shapes of these two wooden blocks because she can name them correctly. However, when we watch her play with the blocks, we see that she tries to stack the cube on the apex of the pyramid. Naturally, when she releases her grip, the cube immediately falls to the table top. Valerie picks up the cube and tries it again on the apex of the

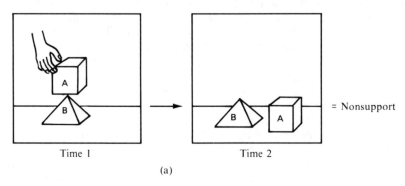

Time 1                    Time 2              = Nonsupport

(a)

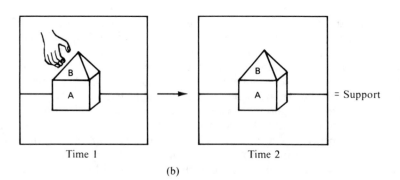

Time 1                    Time 2              = Support

(b)

*Figure 3-1.*

pyramid. She is likely to keep doing this again and again, as indeed we have seen children do when they are 2½ to 3 years of age (Forman, Kuschner, & Dempsey, 1975a). From the total context of Valerie's play we can determine that hers is an attempt to have the cube come to rest on the apex of the pyramid and not a deliberate attempt to make the cube fall.

What is the child's difficulty? It is not that she fails to *see* the apex of the pyramid. What she lacks is an understanding of the relationship among the cube, the vertical pull of gravity, and the apex of the pyramid. She sees the apex, but she does not get the point (sic). Telling her to look closely at the shape of the apex will not help her, unless she relates this information to the vertical pull of gravity and the flat surface of the cube. She may, of course, begin to construct these relationships in successive approximations. After failing to stack the cube, she may try to place the cube on the inclined but flat surface of one side of the pyramid. Although this placement is a little better, because it reduces the teetering that accompanied her attempts to place the cube on the apex, it does not offer stable support. When released, the cube will slide down the inclined face of the pyramid. Eventually Valerie will learn that, if she wants to stack cube and pyramid, she must put the pyramid on top of the cube and not the other way around. This adaptation to the material indicates that the child understands the relationship between nonhorizontal surfaces and support against gravity. Does this new understanding result from looking more closely at the objects?

What could it be that the child looks at more closely? We have already decided that she can see the apex and can discriminate the pyramid from the cube. It could not be gravity, because gravity cannot be seen, as a cube or pyramid can be seen. Gravity is no less than pure motion, the natural motion of unsupported objects. Gravity cannot be touched, heard, seen, smelled, or tasted. Gravity, or what is in actuality downward motion, is constructed by establishing relations among observable changes, changes in the position of the blocks. Similarly, support is a concept that is constructed by establishing relations among observable changes. So it is not physical features that the stacking novice fails to see when she continues to place the cube on the apex.

Somewhere in her explorations with these objects, Valerie begins to construct relations. Block *A* over block *B* at time 1 will invariably result at time 2 in *A* next to *B*. Call this set of events *nonsupport* (Figure 3-1a). Block *B* over block *A* at time 1 will quite often result at time 2 in *B* remaining on top of *A*. Call this set of events *support* (Figure 3-1b). To construct the relations necessary to distinguish support from nonsupport Valerie must go beyond recognizing shapes. Support can not be perceptually discriminated from nonsupport, because neither is *in* the external world of physical, touchable objects. Support is the result of the child actively changing spatial order (*A* over *B* being changed to *B* over *A*) and actively noticing in what temporal order subsequent spatial changes occur (*A* next to *B* or *B* still on *A*). Any mix-up in the coordination of these temporal and spatial states will lead the child into error.[1] The child actively constructs the correct coordination between temporal

[1]Please understand that errors are essential to learning. They function to ensure that new knowledge is coordinated with old knowledge (see Chapter Five).

order and spatial order. According to Piaget and Inhelder (1969b), the child actively transforms the world of objects to understand the relation between himself and objects and the relation between objects and objects. In order to understand this statement, we must investigate one of Piaget's most important concepts—transformation—which has profound implications for early childhood education.

## Piaget's Concept of Transformation

According to Piaget, knowledge develops through learning how objects move, how they change position and shape, and how they change in their relation to themselves and other objects. For example, the infant learns that when an object changes position, the identity of that object does not change. A favorite toy, rotated and now seen from the rear, is still the same toy that was seen a few moments earlier from the front. The child lets us know that he recognizes the toy from the new perspective by grasping the toy and immediately rotating it back into a more familiar state (position). The object has changed position but is not a different toy. At the initial stage of development the infant has no notion that these rotations are variations of the same object (Piaget, 1954). In this earlier stage the child will gaze at the old object from a new perspective as if it were a new toy altogether. Looking closely at the toy from this new perspective is not enough for the child to realize that the second state of the toy is related to the first. The child gradually constructs these relations with experience. But, in order to construct these relations, he needs to *transform* the object—that is, move it through space while observing the shifts in state from different perspectives and reversing those shifts back to the object's original state (Poincaré, 1946).

If we want to understand what precisely the child is doing, we must make a distinction between the resting, static states of an object and the movement of the object between these static states. Let's adopt the convention of designating the initial state of an object as state $A$—the favorite toy seen in its usual perspective—and the following state of the object as state $A'$—the toy seen from the rear. We call *transformation* the rotation (movement) from $A$ to $A'$. The child in our example didn't actually observe this transformation. He saw the object in state $A$, then he saw it in state $A'$ (from the rear); but he didn't observe the transformation of $A$ into $A'$. However, when the child saw state $A'$, not only did he remember state $A$ but he also knew what sort of transformation of $A'$ would reinstate $A$. Piaget emphasizes that knowledge is more than remembering some past situation (state $A$); it is also knowing how to get there (rotation). Knowing how to get from $A'$ to $A$ is the same thing as knowing that $A'$ and $A$ are variations of the same object. Not knowing how to get from $A'$ to $A$ is the same thing as thinking that $A$ and $A'$ are two different objects.

A few other examples of transformations may be helpful. A bag of jelly beans is poured into a shallow dish. Call the initial static state of the jelly beans in the bag state $A$ and their following state in the shallow dish state $A'$. Most 5- and 6-year-olds know that the number of jelly beans in the bag is the same as the number of jelly beans in the dish. The reason they know is because they know *how A became A'*—

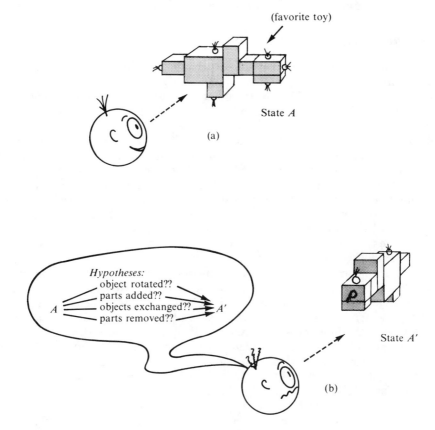

*Figure 3-2.* The child must know how states change. The type of change (the transformation) determines what state $A'$ really is.

that is, how $A$ was transformed into $A'$. No jelly beans were added or subtracted; the beans simply changed their position.

The child who has seen the transformation—that is, the jelly beans being poured from the bag into the dish—can reason that all those jelly delights in the dish can be put back into the bag and fill the bag to the same degree as before; therefore the beans in the dish equal the beans in the bag. To express these relations with our notation, we say that the change from $A$ to $A'$ can be reversed, so that $A'$ is changed back to $A$. This awareness that $A'$ can be reversed to $A$ has special importance in many problem-solving situations (Piaget, 1970). When the child can think about how objects change from one state to another, he can also think about how these objects may change again to their initial state. This ability to think of change in two directions—$A$ to $A'$ and $A'$ to $A$—is an essential mental ability.

### The Advantage of Thinking about How Objects Change

*The Apparent versus the Real*

Being able to think about how objects change permits the child to distinguish the apparent from the real. The infant may behave as if the hidden object didn't exist at all. But by relating the displacement of the rattle toward the pillow to the reappearance of the rattle from behind the pillow, the infant gradually constructs this relation to mean that the nonexistence of the object is not real. The object still exists in reality behind the pillow that temporarily blocks the infant's view of the object. The 4-year-old may insist that the jelly beans spread out in the plate are more numerous than those packed tightly in the bag. But with further experience she constructs all the relations from $A$ to $A'$ and back to $A$, understands the transformations, and in so doing knows that the greater number of jelly beans in the dish is only apparent. A golf ball dropped on a carpet crowded with marbles looks bigger than the same golf ball dropped on a carpet crowded with baseballs. But the child who can relate the two instances of dropping the golf ball knows that it is the same ball and that the change in size is only an apparent change.

Here are instead two examples of how an unobserved transformation can cause difficulty to the child. Tim, a preschooler busily working in the sandbox, lifts his head just at the point when the noise level in the room has increased because of some excitement in the gerbil corner and says "Where did those kids come from?" The increase in the number of children is only apparent, since the same children have been around—albeit more quietly—the whole morning. But Tim has not observed the other children for a while and assumes that the increase in noise is due to an increase in the number of children in the room. Adrian presses a finger against Toby's side and says "What's that?" referring to Toby's bulge around the middle. The last time Adrian saw Toby, he was ten pounds lighter. Since Adrian has not seen the gradual onset of Toby's extra weight, she assumes that the bulge is not really part of her friend's girth. In both these examples the apparent can be distinguished from the real by knowing how one state changes into another.

*Placing Static States along a Continuum of Change*

When transformations are considered, any given state of an object is automatically placed somewhere along a continuum of change. This is another advantage of thinking about how objects change. When the child sees a given static state $A$, he also thinks of $A'$ and of many of the states between $A$ and $A'$. He understands that $A$ is a potential $A'$ and that $A'$ is a potential $A$. The child's ability to do this rests on a mental reconstruction of the path along which the real object moves. This ability to reconstruct the continuum of movement is often an essential component of problem solving. Piaget (1954) gives the example of a child who had to reconstruct the trajectory of a real object—more specifically, the swing of a door. The child approached the door as she was carrying an armful of toys. She laid the toys down by the door in order to open the door, which was hinged to swing inward. However, when she had just turned the knob, she realized that, if she continued to open the door, its trajectory would carry it crashing into the toys. The child then momentarily released her grasp on the knob, moved the toys to the side, and then continued to open the door without obstruction (see also Woodcock, 1941, p. 157).

Although these early encounters that demand an anticipation of trajectories of real objects are necessary precursors (antecedents) of the use of more symbolic representations of movement, they do not appear to be sufficient for such representations. A child may be able to predict that, if a mop leaning against a wall falls down, it will knock a certain picture off the wall in the course of its fall; and, yet, that child will not necessarily be able to order a set of pictures representing the falling mop in its various stages of falling. Even after observing the trajectory of the mop pivoting through an arc from a vertical to a horizontal position, the 4-year-old will have difficulty placing the set of pictures in the correct order (Piaget & Inhelder, 1971). The child may know that each picture represents the same object, albeit at different times, but has difficulty reproducing the progression without inversions. How often do our books for young children presuppose this ability to "see" movement in a series of pictures? Our culture so often asks the child to look at the picture of an object in state $A$ and at the same time think of the continuation of that state toward some later state $A'$. A picture of a girl under a ball in midair could be interpreted as the girl throwing the ball up or as the girl about to catch the falling ball. If the child looking at this picture cannot construct the implicit movement in the correct direction, that child may miss the significance of the picture altogether.

Thinking about how objects move in a continuum—considering their intermediate positions—has definite advantages for constructing the meaning of pictures. It also has other, more sophisticated advantages. Although these advantages may apply only to older students, a discussion of these more complicated uses of transformation is appropriate because it describes the ultimate use of preschool experiences. Our discussion deals with how transformations are used to solve problems of logic, problems that older students could not solve were it not for their prior experience, when they were much younger, with such things as opening doors, finding hidden objects, and retracing their steps through their house. Our view of the role of preschool experiences in problem solving is shared by many researchers of cognitive development (see, for example, Mischel, 1971).

The advantage of thinking in terms of a continuum of movement was made extremely clear to us when we gave a group of college students the following problem of geometry. We showed them the open end of a rectangular cardboard sleeve that slipped over a box of ordinary kitchen matches and asked them to consider the surface area created by the open end of this cardboard sleeve (area $A$). We stated clearly that we were not referring to the perimeter but, rather, to the area (see Figure 3-3a). Then we pressed the top of the cardboard sleeve, bending it over slightly, to make the parallelogram seen in Figure 3-3b. Call this transformed area $A'$. At this point we asked the question "Is area $A'$ the same as area $A$, or is area $A'$ larger than or smaller than area $A$?"

About three fourths of the students answered that area $A'$ was the same as area $A$. When questioned further, individual students gave some interesting reasons for their answers. One said that the amount of area that was lost on the left was gained on the right. This student was using a type of thinking called *compensation;* that is, one change is compensated for another that is its reciprocal. Another student applied what he thought to be the formula for computing area. If the formula

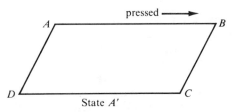

*Figure 3-3a*. Rectangle *ABCD* is a cardboard sleeve in upright position. State *A* is the area of the interior of the rectangle.

*Figure 3-3b*. Rectangle *ABCD* has now been pressed down slightly. As a result, the shape of the end of the cardboard sleeve has changed from a rectangle to parallelogram *ABCD* seen in this figure. Is the area of the cardboard sleeve in state *A* the same as that in state *A'*?

for computing area is length times width, and since the length of side *AD* does not change at any point, area *A'* is equal to area *A*. Of course, area *A'* is smaller than area *A;* but these students, and many more since we first administered this test, believed that the two areas were equal. One can correct the error by learning the right formula for computing the area of a parallelogram,[2] but this is not the route we are suggesting here. There is a more direct, more intuitive way of reasoning that area *A'* is smaller than area *A*. This more direct route involves thinking of the continuation of the transformation from *A* to *A'*. What if *A'* is pressed further, so that the cardboard sleeve is completely collapsed? Call this area *A"*.

When they thought about area *A"*, most of the students who had said that area *A'* was equal to area *A* gasped at the absurdity of their answer. They realized immediately that if *A"* was smaller than *A*, then *A'* must also be smaller than *A*. They realized this because they placed *A'* along the continuum of *A*-*A"*: if *A"* is smaller than *A*, *A'* is by logic necessarily smaller than *A*. This type of reasoning has far deeper implications than one might think at first. The person who realizes that *A* can become *A"* also realizes that the process of transformation from *A* to *A"* begins with a very small change—in this case *A'*—therefore, no matter how small the change, *A'* must be smaller than *A*, because *A'* is a potential *A"*.

### Coordinating Similarities with Differences

Thinking in terms of how objects change has a third important advantage. As the child thinks about changes from *A* to *A'*, she learns not only how objects differ but also how they are the same. This coordination of similarity with difference— knowing how two objects are simultaneously similar and different—is central to cognitive development. If a 4-year-old is given a moldable copper circle, she may

---

[2]The formula for computing the area of a parallelogram is width times altitude, not width times length of the slanted side. The altitude is the vertical distance between the base and the ceiling of the parallelogram. The altitude lessens as *A* is transformed to *A'*, and therefore the area of *A'* is smaller than that of *A*.

change it into a variety of shapes, including a square. If she changes the circular loop into a square, she is, by her very actions, doing two things at once: she is maintaining the closure of the wire as she transforms the circle into a square, and she is changing the curves in the circle to straight lines in the square. In other words, she is actually coordinating, in action, the similarity and differences between circle and square. If she were simply shown a circle and a square, as done with lotto games and form boards, she might readily identify the differences between the two shapes; but would she be as quick to note their similarities? Seeing a ready-made circle and square side by side doesn't give the child any clue regarding how the circle can be transformed into a square and vice versa. Having the child think about transformation is important because it encourages thinking about what remains invariant across change, not just what changes.

As we said earlier, conservation of sameness in difference, of what remains invariant across change, is another very useful mental operation. But, in order to conserve the invariant properties, the child must think about change in both directions—$A$ to $A'$ and $A'$ back to $A$. Recall our earlier discussion about the conservation of number. Spreading five jelly beans that were in a compact row only appears to change their number; in fact their number is conserved—that is, remains the same —in spite of the change in the positioning of the beans. For, after all, the spread-out beans can be retransformed into a compacted row of beans, just as they were before. The coordination of similarity and differences is fundamental to the child's understanding of conservation concepts; weight remains the same across changes in shape, number remains the same across changes in spatial distribution, and so forth.

Sometimes the preschool teacher assumes that the child coordinates similarity and difference, when in practice the child does not. The following is an actual case observed by one of us. A teacher showed Marion the picture of a doll and the picture of a dog and then shot that question heard round the world "How are these two pictures the same, and how are they different?" Marion looked, thought, and said "This one [pointing to the doll] has eyes, and this one [pointing to the dog] has eyes." Teacher pushed onward "And, yes, how are they different?" Marion: "Well, this one [doll] has shoes, and this one [dog] has a tail."

The comparison of shoes with tail will probably come as a surprise to the listener (see McCarthy & Kirk, 1961). We are likely to accept a comparison between shoes and paws or sash and tail, but not a comparison between shoes and tail. Why? Because the conventional use of a comparison of difference implies variation on a common dimension—shoeness, tailness, or some common attribute that remains invariant. "The doll has shoes, but the dog has bare feet" is a more conventional response to a question concerning difference. This more conventional response, unlike Marion's answer, expresses a coordination of difference within similarity. In a sense it expresses a classification (the formation of hierarchies) of a superordinate similarity and subordinate differences. The superordinate similarity is the property common to both objects—doll and dog—and the subordinate differences are the two properties that distinguish the two objects. Reasoning in this manner about two objects is a step toward the hierarchical classification system we use to categorize a whole host of objects. For example, tents and houses are both classes of dwellings, one class portable and the other class permanent. Thinking about how objects change is a probable source of the ability to coordinate superordinate and subordinate properties (Inhelder & Piaget, 1964). Both doll and dog are animals with eyes. But the doll has shoes, and the dog does not; the dog has not had shoes added to its feet. Rather than looking more closely at each static picture, the child would do well to think about how the subject of one picture is a variation (a transformation) of the subject in the other picture. How can *A* be made to look like *A'*? As we headlined at the beginning of the discussion of Piaget's theory of knowledge, *change makes the difference*. We can further appreciate the importance of this principle by looking at its role in the development of modern science.

One changes randomly; the other is determined.

## Transformational Thinking in Science, Mathematics, and the Everyday World

At a level much more advanced than preschool education, knowledge has been the result of the discovery of continuities (see Kuhn, 1970). In physics the continuity between heat and movement, between flame and friction, opened the world of thermodynamics. In psychology the continuity between normal shifts in mood and neurosis led to new discoveries regarding treatment of the mentally disturbed. Freud stopped looking for demons that suddenly overcome a person and began looking at those childhood experiences that can gradually transform a normal person into an individual ridden by phobias. Freud's development of a therapeutic procedure for reversing the change from normal $A$ to neurotic $A'$ back to normal $A$ is a classic example of transformational thinking. His therapeutic approach, which consists essentially of talking about past experiences, would be absurd without the assumption that neurosis is a reversible transformation of normality, an exaggerated continuation of normal fears. Darwin also made a scientific breakthrough by thinking about how objects change. The greater apes were no longer seen as a species that had always had its present form but, rather, as a species that had undergone profound changes and whose early stages had represented the origin of both homo sapiens and the greater apes. Einstein brought science significantly forward by mathematically describing the continuity of matter and energy. The notion that something as apparently inert as a mineral can be transformed into a chain reaction of incredible force must be the most miraculous transformational idea of the century.

The concept of transformation also influenced mathematics, particularly geometry. Until the second half of the 19th century, Euclid's geometry of straight lines that were forever parallel when extended and of triangles whose angles always totaled 180 degrees held the day as truth. Then Riemann proposed that the sum of the angles of a triangle drawn on the surface of a sphere is more than 180 degrees and that parallel lines will eventually meet. As a result of Riemann's elliptical geometry, Euclidean space was seen as only one type of space, a flat space, and mathematicians accepted the idea that many types of geometry can be developed by transforming the type of space in which objects exist (Weyl, 1963). Klein went so far as to deduce several types of geometry, each defined by the properties that remain invariant under transformation. For example, topology is a type of geometry defined by the properties of geometric figures that do not change when space is stretched. Topology is sometimes called "rubber sheet geometry" because, if you draw on a rubber sheet two triangles that are near but not touching each other, stretching that rubber sheet will not change the fact that the two figures are both closed figures and that they are nonoverlapping. These invariant relations—closure and overlap—are topological relations, while relations such as curved versus straight and long versus short are Euclidean relations. Euclidean relations do change when space is stretched. Thus Klein demonstrated that Euclidean geometry is a system of relations that assumes that certain transformations will not be made—that is, that space is rigid and flat.

Students in our Western culture are constantly confronted with problems that involve the concept of transformation—how something came to be and what transformation produced a given state. The concept of transformation also requires the coordination of continuity within discontinuity. The number sequence itself is perhaps the most obvious example of coordinating the discontinuity of countable elements with the continuity of an ordered relation (see Chapter Two). The discovery of how one element is a transformation of another element is a theme that begins in infancy and carries the human mind to its most sophisticated limits.

In the everyday world the child attuned to process, the child sensitive to change, is simply more likely to be adaptive and therefore more likely to think intelligently. Such a child will resist the temptation to associate every thing with every other thing, an endeavor bound to overwhelm the mind and make the mind go random. Yet the copy theory of knowledge suggests that humans are equally responsive to all possible pairings of stimuli. The mind is described as a blank tablet, etched by the come-what-may of exposure. And, mind you, these theories are not obsolete; they are quite modern (Hilgard & Bower, 1966). Even the more cognitive versions of copy theory assume, perhaps by their silence on the matter, that any two things can be linked by a verbal mediator; for example, both watermelon and cornflakes can be called food. While this is true, associations of this kind are the product of what Piaget calls social knowledge, a matter of convention learned by rote. Copy theory has decidedly little to offer to someone interested in what the child spontaneously learns at an early age and in how that early learning affects all subsequent learning processes. Piaget's emphasis on transformations comes closer to providing a clue to an understanding of these processes.

In the world of natural events certain changes do occur, and others do not occur. For example, objects do not change position without a change in time; that is, one object cannot be in two places at the same time. Another example is the fact that a ripening fruit will change in color without changing significantly in shape or texture. The change from green to yellow without a change in shape indicates that the banana is ready to eat. Now, it could well be that on some distant planet where the objects float in a thick atmosphere, the banana rises from the fruit bowl as it becomes more and more mature. It could well be that on this distant planet nothing changes in color, even though all colors of the rainbow can be found there. Then, on that planet, changes in the floating height would have an ecological importance, but diversity in color would not.[3]

If one reads Piaget's theory carefully, one understands that not all associative pairings are of equal value or of equal possibility. Intelligence, to Piaget (1970), increases when we become sensitized to changes. The teacher should help the child associate states that are transformations on each other, not just random associations. If the teacher approaches preschool experiences in this fashion, it is unlikely that the child will be learning rote, linguistic conventions. The child will depend less on what something is named and more on what something can become. When the child learns that $A$ can become $A'$, he also learns a method of checking his own conclusions (see Chomsky, 1972). If he is not sure that $A$ and $A'$ are related, he attempts to transform one into the other. If his attempt is successful and, starting with $A$, he ends up with $A'$, he is more confident in his use of words to classify these objects. Transformations also provide a means to make discoveries, to generate new relations, to see that $A$ and $A'$ and $A''$ may all be related, since the $A$-to-$A'$ transformation can be expanded further to include $A''$ (see page 56). The extrapolation of the transformation helps the child reason. This brings us to a discussion of practical applications of the concept of transformation in preschool education.

---

[3]We should also note that our biological equipment sets constraints on what specific transformations we process. For example, a change from horizontal to vertical may be much more noticeable than a change from one diagonal to another, because of the presence of special receptors called *statocysts,* which continuously register the vertical pull of gravity (Gibson, 1966).

## Using Transformations in Preschool Education

The abundance of static printed curriculum materials in preschool classrooms is difficult to reconcile with an emphasis on thinking about change. Pictures, puzzles, and number cards with dots fixed in one pattern do little to help the child coordinate differences within similarity, place properties on a continuum, or distinguish the real from the apparent. The emphasis on transformation suggests certain other procedures in preschool teaching.

### Questioning

Asking the child "What will this [pointing to a soda straw] look like if you bend it here?" is more in line with transformational teaching than asking the child to identify some static property by questions like "What do we call this?" Asking "How can you get the lid back on?" is more transformational than asking "Where does the lid belong?" because the latter requires only that the child make a straight associa-

Ask children how events change.

tion between lid and jar. "What can we do to make this one the same as that one?" is a great improvement over "Tell me how these two objects are different." In addition to drawing the children's thoughts toward movement, the transformational approach also gives them an opportunity to express their instrumentality in affecting their environment. Children are more than passive recipients of verbal labels passed down from an adult culture; they are active agents of change.

To use the transformational approach correctly, the teacher should look for opportunities to engage the child in thinking about opposition. If the child makes a general comment, the teacher might challenge him to think about the opposite of what he means. At times a question regarding the opposite is the only way to clear an ambiguity. The child says "I want to play the drum with Spencer!" The teacher responds "Does that mean you don't want to play the tambourine with Spencer?" Child: "What? Just let me play something with Spencer!" The child's original sentence was unclear. Was it the instrument or the partner that he preferred? It turned out to be the partner. The teacher took the child's original sentence and transformed a portion of it as a means to clarify its intent. By changing the word *drum* to *tambourine,* the teacher was in essence seeking to find if this change made a difference to the child. It did not. A consistent use of these techniques should help the children think about how well their sentences express their intended meaning. The objective of using oppositional transformation is to teach children to think of key words in their sentences as variables, not as static absolutes automatically known by the listener. In order to clearly understand the meaning of a sentence, it is at times necessary to ask the counterquestion "As opposed to what?" This oppositional transformation tells the listener which of several possible variables is being emphasized—in the case at hand, instrument or partner.

*Presenting Discontinuous Material*

As we have mentioned, learning to identify the process of continuous transformation when given only discrete, static states is essential to knowledge. Consider the following situation, which we actually witnessed and which involved a teacher and a 4-year-old boy. The teacher held a caterpillar in her left hand and an anesthetized butterfly in her right hand. She was explaining to the boy that the butterfly *(A')* had been in its previous stage a caterpillar *(A).* "This butterfly [holding up *A'*] used to be a caterpillar [holding up *A*]" she said. The boy was utterly confused. How could that dead butterfly have been the caterpillar, when the caterpillar was still a caterpillar? Of course, the teacher was not implying that the butterfly had literally been that particular caterpillar but, rather, that the caterpillar was a representative of the class of caterpillars, of which the butterfly had once been a member. Since 4-year-olds are prone to think more about particular objects than about classes (Kendler & Kendler, 1962), the child's confusion is not surprising. The teacher, by presenting states *A* and *A'* simultaneously (instead of offering the child some means to realize that *A* had been transformed into *A'* gradually) was unwittingly reinforcing some rather bizarre notions about origins. The child could have easily come away from this situation with the curious knowledge that a single organism can be preserved as a specimen at two different stages of development. This, incidentally, brings to mind the well-known absurd item in the Stanford-Binet test of intelligence "In an old graveyard in Spain they have discovered a small skull, which they believe to be that of Christopher Columbus when he was about 10 years old." Do current curriculum materials for young children, because of their static nature, decrease the child's ability to sense the absurdity of this Stanford-Binet item? More dynamic material, material that demonstrates a gradual change from $A$ to $A'$, would be more helpful. A filmstrip on the development of a butterfly, taking the caterpillar through its various stages, would certainly be better than a simultaneous presentation of caterpillar and butterfly.

Oppositional transformations are recommended not only when questioning children but also when presenting materials. Knowledge of the inverse adds power to the organization of thought. The child who knows how to undo $A'$, as well as how to do $A'$, is more likely to coordinate the invariant with the variant. Pouring four little cups of cola from one big bottle (a change from $A$ to $A'$) does not disturb the child who knows that all four little cups of cola can be recombined to make the original quantity (a change from $A'$ to $A$). The teacher should allow the children to explore both directions of transformation. Let them pour all their little cups of cola back into the large bottle again (of course, with no drinking allowed in the interim!). If the children think that a bent pipe cleaner is shorter than a straight one, encourage them to bend both pipe cleaners and to compare lengths as they go along. Doing and undoing helps children to organize their knowledge of objects into properties that change and properties that do not.

What is the disadvantage of merely identifying similarities and differences? In an earlier example, the teacher remarked that both the swan and the ostrich have long necks but the swan swims and the ostrich does not. This approach is static rather than transformational. This static approach that treats qualities as fixed runs the risk of separating form from function. A transformational approach is more likely to draw the child's attention to *why* the ostrich has long, strong legs and the swan has short legs and webbed feet. If the teacher asks the child to mentally transform the swan into a swan with ostrich legs, the relation between form and function will become more obvious. "He [the swan] would get stuck in the mud" the child might say. Putting swan legs on the ostrich might lead to "But then he couldn't run fast." Ultimately these types of mental games will help children understand that no organic system has an arbitrary structure. That form sets constraints on function and function sets constraints on form is a concept that students learn later on in biology. Form is not there without purpose, nor is one form unrelated to other forms. The student can better appreciate form $A$ by mentally transforming it into $A'$ and appraising the effects that transformation has on the function of $A$. Understanding the world about us involves, in part, understanding that events, forms, states, and apparently discrete materials are actually momentary points in time.

## Summary

This chapter began with a comparison between the copy theory and the constructivist theory of knowledge. The copy theory assumes that knowledge results from extracting information from an external world. This is done by attending to detail, making accurate mental images, and comparing objects on the basis of their physical features. The constructivist theory assumes that attention to detail is important but not sufficient for many cognitive tasks. Even features clearly discerned must be placed within a set of temporal and spatial relations before they can have meaning to the knower. Piaget's view about knowledge, particularly his concept of transformation, is an example of constructivist theory.

A transformation is more than the static state of a resting object. It is the process by which a static state became that particular state. A transformation is a process and not a product; but a transformation is bounded by end states $A$ and $A'$, which can be called the origin and the product, respectively. It is important for the child to consider how $A$ changes into $A'$ and, equally important, how $A'$ can be changed back into $A$. The chapter listed three advantages of teaching children to think about how objects change.

The child who thinks about how some current situation has become what it is now from what it was will be better equipped to discern certain perceptual illusions. For example, a perfectly dry cat runs behind a tree and through a lawn sprinkler and then emerges wet on the other side of the tree. To the observing toddler, the soaked cat looks like a completely different animal, but, by reconstructing the continuous movement of the cat, the child decides that this difference is only apparent. Thinking about transformations also helps the child to make inferences about how discontinuous states are related. By mentally ordering static states along a continuum of movement, the thinker can anticipate events that have not yet happened. If adding one ice cube to a glass of water causes the water to rise, a repetition of this operation will ultimately cause the water to spill over the edge. The child looks at the glass and, thinking about the reverse of this operation, reasons that, if the water ultimately spills over the edge, then adding even a sliver of ice must change the total volume inside the glass. Even though the increase that results from adding the sliver is imperceptible, if the child thinks about the whole range of this operation from many cubes to sliver, she can infer what happens when the sliver is added. Thinking about transformations also helps the child coordinate differences within similarities. A picture of ducks flying may not be seen as depicting the same class of animals as a picture of ducks feeding in the park. Labeling both pictures "duck" does not necessarily assure the concept. Seeing the ducks in formation land and begin feeding helps the child relate these different states within the constancy of the duck's form. Wings spread out in flight become wings folded while feeding, but the wings are still there. Seeing the feeding ducks rise in flight demonstrates this constancy.

It was pointed out that thinking about transformations has been a great advance in science and mathematics. The point here is that what is good for the total development of human knowledge is ipso facto good for the development of each individual child's knowledge. Therefore, the deliberate emphasis on transformational thinking in preschool education is no less than a concern for the further development of our species. We then suggested certain procedures for implementing transformational thinking in young children. Questioning style can be designed to engage the child in thinking about how objects change. Discontinuous material can be modified to provoke transformational thinking. The child can be presented with manageable conflicts that require transformational thinking for solution. These suggestions for classroom practices indicate that even the more esoteric concepts of a theory of knowledge have applicational value in the everyday world of young children.

## Suggestions for Further Reading

Kohlberg, L. Montessori with the culturally disadvantaged: A cognitive-developmental interpretation with some research findings. In R. D. Hess & R. M. Bear (Eds.), *Early education.* Chicago: Aldine, 1968. Raises some interesting points concerning the differences between Piaget's and Montessori's theories of knowledge.

Kuhn, T. S. *The structure of scientific revolutions* (2nd ed.). Chicago: University of Chicago Press, 1970. Some say that to fully understand Piaget's theory one needs to understand the history of science. This book is a good place to start.

Piaget, J. *The construction of reality in the child.* New York: Basic Books, 1954. A good introduction to Piaget's conception of knowledge as an act of construction.

# Section 3
# Development and Learning

# Chapter Four

# Stages and Dimensions of Development

In this chapter we will depart somewhat from our usual focus on educational practice in order to examine current perspectives on child development and, in so doing, define target terms that will recur in the chapters to follow. Since this book relies heavily on Piaget's theory of development (as well as on his theory of knowledge, as you saw in Chapter Three), we begin here with a brief coverage of that theory. Yet, we don't want to ignore all the fine work on child development that has other theoretical perspectives. We have, therefore, created a set of dimensions in order to organize in a functional way a wide range of research findings concerning the cognitive, social-emotional, and language developments of children from birth to age 7. We wish to remind our readers that, as we already stated in Chapter One, development is a continuous process and that the age-related changes that Piaget describes for each stage should always be integrated with those that take place in the preceding and following stages.

## Piaget's Theory of Developmental Stages

According to Piaget, the child goes through four stages of development: the sensorimotor stage (birth to 2 years), the preoperational stage (2 to 7 years), the concrete-operational stage (7 to 11 years), and the formal-operational stage (beyond the 11th year).

### The Sensorimotor Stage

During the first stage of development, from birth to the onset of the use of symbols (language and gestures), children deal with real objects at the perceptual level and in a very egocentric manner. They do not yet use an object as a representation, or symbol, for another object. The plastic spoon is something to be put in the mouth; it is not a "pretend" piece of candy. In this stage objects have meaning according to what can be done with them. The round block can be rolled, and the square block can be slid; but the round block is not treated symbolically as if it were a choo-choo train. (This comes later, during the preoperational stage of development.) During the sensorimotor stage objects are associated with actions and events but objects do not stand for actions and events. The sound of running water signals that someone is in the kitchen. The child goes to the kitchen to see. The sound causes the child in this stage to remember past events that have actually happened.

Piaget has made us aware of the complex nature of the "simple" task of remembering where something is. This task is much more than associating some particular sight, like a toybox, with the desired object (the toy inside the box). This task involves an awareness of the permanence of objects, of the fact that objects don't cease to exist when they are out of sight. In other words, in order to remember where an object is, the child must first understand that the object, although no longer in sight, still exists. This, in turn, means that the child must relate the movement of the object with the position of the place where the object is hidden; that is, the toy goes *behind* the walls of the toybox. If a child didn't understand that the toy still exists somewhere in space even though she cannot see it, she would not commit to memory the toybox as the signal to the toy's whereabouts. It is the concept of object permanence that gives the child a reason to make an association between two objects, which in itself is a rather simple task.

During the sensorimotor stage the child progresses in his ability to deal with several displacement situations—movements of an object or of himself. The child develops the mental wherewithal to organize the path that an object takes, even though some segments of the path may not actually be seen, as in the case of a ball that rolls under a piece of furniture (see Bower, 1974). Let's look in detail at several ways in which the sensorimotor child organizes object movement—what Piaget (1970) calls the *group of translations.*

We have already mentioned the *detour* situation. An object that can be reached by making a direct crawl from here to there can also be reached by going in many other and less direct paths from here to there. During this first step of development children show less and less difficulty with detour problems. In fact, they can even turn their backs on the desired destination for a moment while executing the detour. All of the segments of movement become organized into a closed system (what Piaget calls *the group*), which is no less than the space in which all these paths exist. All these paths lead to the same end point; that is, the segment from point $A$ to point $B$ plus the segment from point $B$ to point $D$ is one path (Figure 4-1a); the segment from point $A$ to point $C$ plus the segment from point $C$ to point $D$ is a variation of that path but still ends at $D$ (Figure 4-1b). In practical terms (but, of course, not in mathematical terms) $AB + BD = AC + CD$. The child can get to his chair either by crossing the carpet or, if that way is blocked, by going around the obstacle—in this case, the package.

The 1-year-old is capable of using *negation* in displacement situations. Piaget defines negation as the undoing of a transformation by the most direct means. If a child goes from $A$ to $B$ and then back to $A$, he has actually negated his advance by reversing his direction. This situation can be expressed with the formula $AB + BA = 0$. The child in the sensorimotor stage can also deal with displacement by using *reciprocity*. Reciprocity is an indirect means to undo a transformation. If a child rolls a toy on a string away from himself (movement $A$ to $B$), he can then undo that movement by either a direct or an indirect reversal. The direct reversal (negation) would be pulling the toy back to its original place—a movement from $B$ back to $A$. The indirect reversal (reciprocity) would be walking toward the toy—a movement

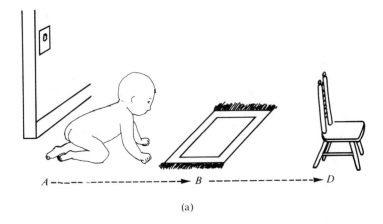

(a)

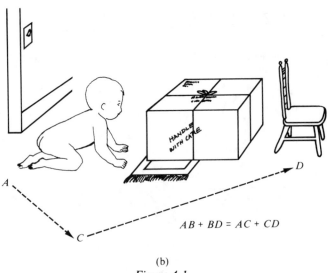

$$AB + BD = AC + CD$$

(b)

*Figure 4-1.*

from *A* to *B*. In both cases the separation between *A* and *B* is "undone." Figure 4-2 shows both forms of reversal.

    None of the displacement situations we have just discussed involved hidden movements, even though the desired object may have been temporarily hidden from sight (in the detour situation, for example, the chair was hidden by the package). But, as children approach the end of the sensorimotor stage, they learn to handle situations that do involve invisible displacement. These situations require children to mentally fill in (extrapolate) something they actually didn't see but that they

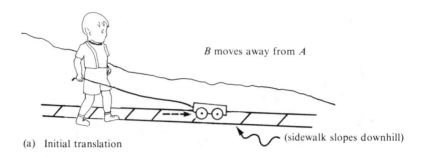

(a)   Initial translation

*B* moves away from *A*

(sidewalk slopes downhill)

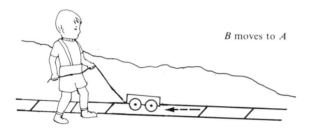

*B* moves to *A*

(b)   Reversal by negation

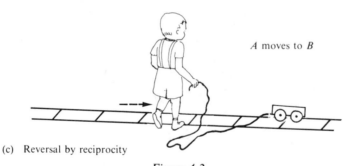

*A* moves to *B*

(c)   Reversal by reciprocity

*Figure 4-2.*

assume exists. When children begin to deal successfully with invisible displacement, they demonstrate that they are beginning to use symbols—mental representations of the hidden movement. Here is an example.

Keith puts a small doll into his pull wagon and pulls the wagon arouna tne room, watching his toy over his shoulder. For a brief moment the wagon is hidden from the child's view by an ottoman. After pulling the wagon a few more yards, Keith stoops over to lift out the doll. But the doll is not there in the depths of the wagon. Keith instantly checks behind the ottoman. Even though he didn't see the doll bounce out of the wagon behind the ottoman, he assumes that it must be there. He has more than a mental image of the doll; he has a mental image of the doll bouncing out of the wagon. When children are 2 years old, they can mentally represent translations (object movements); they can mentally coordinate movement, position, and object and come up with the mental image of the translation. This is a much more elaborate task than recognition, which involves a fairly automatic affair—that is, the mental image of the particular missing object. This higher degree of complexity explains why it takes about two years before the child can deal with invisible displacements of the type described above.

Invisible displacement involves an inference of sorts. If object *A* (the doll) is placed out of view in *B* (the wagon) and then object *B* moves behind object *C* (the ottoman), object *A* could be either in *B* or behind *C*—if not *B*, then *C*. Solving the problem presented by invisible displacement is an early form (a precursor) of the *transitive relation* in logic. In a transitive relation the child knows that if *A* is larger than *B* and *B* is larger than *C*, then *A* is necessarily larger than *C*. The learning encounters presented in Chapter Nine emphasize the concept of the precursor, particularly the analogy between sensorimotor problems of displacement and later problems that involve mathematical and logical thinking.

The mental representations of the sensorimotor period are limited to either the recall of the physical features of an object (recognition of form) or the construction of an individual, invisible displacement. Advanced levels of representation mark the beginning of the next stage of development, the preoperational stage. In the preoperational stage the child begins to understand how one displacement affects another displacement. As we said many times before, the mental structures the child builds in one stage make the mental structures of the following stage possible.

## The Preoperational Stage

This stage begins around age 2, with the acquisition of symbolic thought—the use of mental images and words to represent actions and entire events that are not present. It is called preoperational because it precedes the onset of logical operations. Children begin to imitate in some detail objects or events that they have seen in the recent past. One morning a 2½-year-old sees a seal in the zoo. That afternoon she does something that she had never done before. She bumps her wrists together and belts out several loud arffs. The child is evidently acting out a mental image that she recalls at the moment she imitates the seal, not presently in sight.

The child's new ability to represent the nonpresent event in gesture and in words helps her establish a relation between two events. In fact, the defining characteristic of preoperational thought is the child's ability to anticipate the effect of one action on another action. Piaget calls this type of relation a *function*. A function is a one-way relation between two events and can be direct or inverse. The rise of water in a glass is a function of the drop in the water level in the pitcher from which the water is poured. In this case we have an inverse function: as one level goes up, the other level goes down. The preoperational child understands at the practical level that more water in the glass means less water in the pitcher, just as he understands that throwing a ball down harder will make the ball bounce higher—an example of a direct function: the more of one action, the more of the other.

The preoperational child develops the mental competence to organize events into functional relations; he understands that a change in one factor causes a change in the other factor. This change can be an increase or a decrease; that is, it is a change *in a particular direction*—depending on the events involved. The child knows not only that throwing a ball down harder will make the ball bounce higher but also that throwing the ball down with less force will make the ball bounce lower. The concept of function represents more than the simple knowledge that $X$ leads to $Y$— like the infant's knowledge that kicking leads to release from his blanket. The concept of function involves the coordination of two *changes*, not just of two actions. An increasing change here leads to a decreasing change there (inverse function). An increasing change here leads to an increasing change there (direct function).

What is it then that the preoperational child does not yet understand? We defined the function as a one-way relation, and we said that the preoperational child can anticipate functions. But what the preoperational child cannot understand is the implication behind the fact that a function can be carried out in two ways. He knows that the water can be poured from the pitcher into the glass and from the glass into the pitcher, but he does not grasp the implication that those combined events carry for the concept of conservation. The preoperational child, therefore, could not answer the question "Do you have as much water now as you did before?" He can understand that more in $X$ means less in $Y$, but he does not yet understand that the change in $X$ is exactly compensated by a change in $Y$. He has reached the stage of understanding the *direction* of the change, but he does not understand the *quantity* of the change. Quantity in this instance does not refer to an absolute number of ccs but, rather, to the conservation of amount, since nothing was added or subtracted during the pouring of the liquid.

Children in the preoperational stage are deceived by appearance. You and we know that, if you push a blob of spinach into a compact heap, what the heap gains in height is exactly compensated by what the blob lost in circumference. In Piaget's terms, the quantity of substance is conserved despite changes in spatial distribution. When the 4-year-old looks down at the reduced circumference of his portion of spinach, he thinks that he has less to eat. (He may also think that he has more to eat, if he concentrates instead on the increased height of his portion of spinach.) Now this child may well understand that a decrease in circumference leads to an increase in height and vice versa. But he can think about these functions in one direction at a time only; he cannot integrate the two directions into a mental structure that has applications for conservation of quantity. His failure to make this mental integration leaves him open to errors of perception, such as thinking that he has more (or less) spinach to swallow. This inability is not surprising when you think that the child has just learned the function, which involves the coordination of two changes. Conservation of quantity, which involves the coordination of two coordinated changes, is a far more complex operation, and we will discuss it in greater detail when we talk of concrete-operational thinking. Now let's go back to the preoperational child and to what he can, rather than can't, do.

All functions are expressed by the general formula $A = f(B)$. This is read "A change in $A$ is a function of a change in $B$." By "change" we mean a directional difference—that is, an increase or decrease. As you read the following discussion, look at Figure 4-3 and keep in mind that the point of the discussion is to show that the group of translations of the sensorimotor stage is used by the child to understand

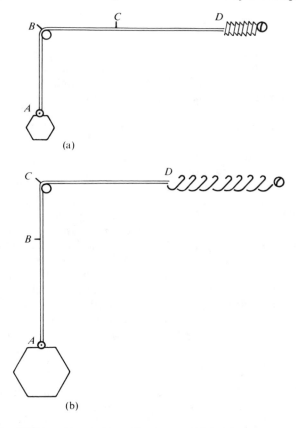

*Figure 4-3.*

functions in the preoperational stage. In Figure 4-3a a string is drawn over a nail hammered into the wall. End *D* of the string is attached to a light spring, which is itself anchored to the wall. A small weight is attached to the other end *(A)* of the string. The more weight is added to end *A,* the longer the vertical segment *AB* becomes; *AB* changes to *AC* (Figure 4-3b). At the same time, the horizontal segment *BD* becomes shorter; that is, *BD* becomes *CD.* The preoperational child knows that the length of the vertical segment changes as a function of the length of the horizontal segment: $V = f(H)$.

How have the translation problems of the sensorimotor stage helped the preoperational child to understand the function we have just discussed? Go back to Figure 4-1, which shows the infant solving the detour problem. In terms of practical action the infant knows that $AB + BD = AC + CD$; that is, both of these paths are variations of the same path from *A* to *D.* In Figures 4-3a and 4-3b the child understands that both situations (3a and 3b) are variations of the same span of string *AD.* The reason why *V* gets shorter as *H* gets longer is that *V* takes its length from *H.* It is all one piece of string. Even though the preoperational child does not yet understand that the gain in $V$ is exactly compensated by the loss in $H$, he knows where the additional length in $V$ comes from. He knows that the change from $AB$ to $AC$ (a gain) is correlated with the change from $BD$ to $CD$ (a loss). But he does not yet understand that $AB + BD$ equals $AC + CD$. In sum, the translation problems that the child solved in the sensorimotor stage help him relate the changes in the vertical and the horizontal spans as parts of one continuous space, but he has to go through the activities involved in preoperational thought before he can handle conservation of length. Right now he is perfectly willing to conclude that the string in Figure 4-3b is longer than the string in Figure 4-3a.

When asked the conservation question "Is the length of the string in Figure 4-3a the same as the length of the string in Figure 4-3b?" the preoperational child looks at segment $AC$ as we see it in Figure 4-3b and mentally compares it with his memory of $AB$, the vertical segment in its initial state as we see it in Figure 4-3a. Since $AC$ is longer than $AB$, the child concludes that the length of the string has increased. He has used the final product of the translation—the way segment $AC$ appears—but has not integrated this final product $AC$ into a total system of translations that includes the change of $BD$ as well. This concern with final products, the way things look, is called by Piaget *figurative knowledge*. During the next stage of development (the stage of concrete operations) the child begins to include in his thinking the very nature of translations and other transformations in general. The shift from thinking about static states to thinking about transformations plus static states characterizes what Piaget terms *operational knowledge*.

## The Concrete-Operational Stage

What is concrete about this stage, and what is operational about it? Somewhere around the age of 6 or 7, the child makes a shift in his ability to deal with change. The word *concrete* refers to the fact that the child is still dealing with concrete objects; when he deals with change, he deals with changing objects, not with change in the abstract. It should be clear that here the word *concrete* does not refer to concepts—more specifically, concrete versus abstract concepts. The concrete-operational child is quite capable of dealing with abstract concepts, although he deals with them in a concrete manner. As we shall see, he can, for example, integrate both directions of a function and conclude that quantity has been conserved. The word *operational* refers to the fact that the child at this stage of development does indeed create logical structures (mental operations) that allow him to conserve, albeit the data he uses to build these mental structures are concrete events. He does not deal with hypothetical assumptions, but he does go beyond the figurative aspects of things—the way things look at one particular time. We could say that the term *operational* denotes the outer reaches of this stage and the term *concrete* denotes its limits. The child in concrete operations can integrate (mentally combine) functions that pertain to concrete objects, but he cannot yet integrate two or more mental operations—an ability that he acquires in the next stage.

Let's use the problem of conservation of length illustrated in Figures 4-1 and 4-3 to see what the child in the concrete-operational stage can and cannot do. The sensorimotor understanding of the $AB + BD = AC + CD$ translation (Figure 4-1) helped the child learn that moving from $A$ to $C$, instead of moving from $A$ to $B$, can still lead to $D$ (Figure 4-1). As we stated in Chapter One, Piaget maintains that development builds on and includes the previous stage. How do translation and function combine to help the child understand conservation of length? In Figure 4-3a string $AD$ bends in a right angle at point $B$. In Figure 4-3b string $AD$ bends in a right angle at point $C$. In essence, the conservation question ("Is the total length of the string the same in Figures 4-3a and 4-3b?") asks the child to reason that $AB + BD$ (Figure 4-3a) is equal to $AC + CD$ (Figure 4-3b). Does this formula look familiar to you? Implicitly the child must understand that the imaginary segment $BC$ in Figure 4-3a is the same as the equally imaginary segment $BC$ in Figure 4-3b. In other words, segment $BC$ has been displaced from the horizontal segment $H$ to the vertical segment $V$—displaced, not added. The portion that the horizontal segment loses *(BC)* is the same portion that the vertical segment gains (again, $BC$). This means that $BC$ is contained within the total distance $AD$, just as the crawl $AB$ was contained in the total crawl $AD$ in Figure 4-1. The conservation problem is no doubt more difficult, but it does contain, embedded in the thought required for its solution, problems that have been solved in previous stages.

So why can't the sensorimotor-stage child or the preoperational child solve the conservation problem? The sensorimotor child could understand in some absolute sense that the two strings in Figures 4-3a and 4-3b are one and the same string. He knows that a change in the position of the string does not change the existence or the absolute identity of the string. He may even be able to learn how to make the vertical segment longer. But he wouldn't be able to relate the increasing length of $V$ with the decreasing length of $H$. The preoperational child, on the other hand, would be able to relate the increase with the decrease but couldn't go beyond that. In order to understand conservation, the child must be able to realize that segment $BC$ is *at the same time* a part of the vertical segment $AC$ and a part of the total length $AD$.

But how can something be a part of two different things? Can my nose be at the same time a part of my face and a part of your face? That's just the kind of question the preoperational child would ask. He knows that in the world of physical objects and actions one object cannot be in two places at once. What he fails to realize is that the conservation question does not ask about the position of an object but, rather, about the relation between segments, a relation independent of position. The concrete-operational child understands the distinction between a logical relation and a physical position. (In terms of logic, segment $BC$ can be both a subsegment of the vertical span and a subsegment of the entire string.) He can also understand other relations—for example, that 2 can, at the same time, be larger than 1 and smaller than 3. This relation is not confused by the concrete-operational child with a physical change, such as an actual change in size. In sum, the concrete-operational child has gone beyond the way things look at a particular moment in time (figurative knowledge) and has begun to understand how things relate (operative knowledge).

In the concrete-operational stage the "facts" are always a set of concrete objects or activities rather than a set of hypothetical assumptions. It is not until the final stage, which begins around age 11 or 12, that the child can deal with purely hypothetical propositions—that is, is capable of truly abstract thinking. A detailed treatment of formal operations would be beyond the scope of a book on early education. We must, therefore, confine ourselves to these few comments, which might clarify our discussion of concrete operations.

For example, we can say that in Figure 4-3 the concrete-operational child can conserve length because segment *BC,* a concrete object, is simultaneously a logical "member" of the vertical segment and of the total string, both also concrete objects. What he cannot do is make a verbal description of the relations between these classes and perform some mental manipulation of such relations. In the same way, the concrete-operational child could not perform in his head a multiplication of a multiplication—like $3 \times 4 = 12$, $12 \times 4 = 48$. The product 12 cannot be "seen"; it is the mere result of a mental operation (multiplication). If the child is then asked to perform a mental operation on a mental operation—that is, $12 \times 4$—he can't do it, simply because it is too much for him, even though he could do the first multiplication in his head.

In Figure 4-4 we have summarized the basic differences among the first three

a. Sensorimotor stage (0–2 years): Motor schemes
   $X \longrightarrow Y$: Action associated with action
b. Preoperational stage (2–6 years): Functional relations
   $X \longrightarrow X' \Longrightarrow Y \longrightarrow Y'$: Change correlated with change
c. Concrete-operational stage (6–11 years): Logical relations
$$\left.\begin{array}{l} X \longrightarrow X' \Longrightarrow Y \longrightarrow Y' \\ X' \longrightarrow X \Longrightarrow Y' \longrightarrow Y \end{array}\right\}: \text{Function integrated with function}$$

*Figure 4-4.* Basic differences among the first three stages of development. (The sign $\longrightarrow$ means "associates"; the sign $\Longrightarrow$ means "correlates"; and the double sign $\{\}$ means "integrates.")

stages of development to help you remember the main points of our discussion. In the sensorimotor stage (0 to 2 years) the child learns to associate one action with another action: a pull *(X)* on a string leads to a movement *(Y)* of the object tied to the string (Figure 4-4a). In the preoperational stage (2 to 6 or 7 years) the child learns to correlate two changes. This is called a *function:* as *X* changes to *X', Y* changes to *Y'* (Figure 4-4b). The child can relate the direction of change in one action to the direction of change in another action. However, he cannot yet understand the implication behind the fact that the correlation can run in both directions; for example, he cannot deduce the concept of conservation from the fact of physical reversibility. He knows that changing the weight from *X* to *X'* will change the vertical span from *Y* to *Y',* but he cannot integrate the initial state with the final state to prove that length has remained the same. In the concrete-operational stage (age 6 or 7 years to 11 or 12 years) the child can integrate the correlations in both directions (Figure 4-4c) to prove that length has remained the same. The concrete-operational child would say "I know that the string is the same length because, after all, you can put it back just as it was." He can now see the implication behind the physical reversal, because he has the mental ability to think about the two functions as variations of each other. Much of what can be done in the preschool classroom to facilitate thinking represents a precursor of concrete operations.

## Dimensions of Development

Our discussion of Piaget's theory has focused on stages of development and how each stage is defined by a particular structure of thinking. Development, however, as we have often pointed out, is a continuous process. Even though the stages differ qualitatively, certain dimensions of development describe the child's progress as a gradual change. We don't want to pigeon-hole children in any particular stage. The child is always growing, from the early phase of a stage to the later phase of that same stage and from one stage to the next. In order to capture the continuous nature of development, we have organized our review of the research on child development along three dimensions of change: reactive to active, empirical to logical, and absolute to relative. Although these dimensions reflect our Piagetian perspective, the research itself reflects a variety of perspectives.

We have made another division in the organization of this section, a division between two broad areas of development. Children develop in their ability to adapt to and understand (1) a social world and (2) a physical world. They become increasingly aware of the self-other and other-other relations (social world). They also become increasingly aware of the self-object and object-object relations (physical world). Here we are not referring to the source of knowledge, as we did when we discussed social and physical knowledge in Chapter Two. In this chapter we are referring to the product of knowledge—what the knowledge is *about*. The fact that we speak of division should not mislead you into thinking that the social world and the physical world, even as products of knowledge, are two separate worlds. In fact, as children mature, they learn more and more about the relationship between the physical world and the social world (see the discussion of the knower-known relation in Chapter Two). The main reason for our categorical system is to avoid the common split between cognitive and affective development. Cognitive development and affective development are actually two forms of cognitive development. Feelings come from the mind at work, just as do answers to academic-type questions. Feelings are thoughts that create emotional reactions of various degrees. We believe, therefore, that one should not separate a discussion of thoughts that create emotions from a discussion of thoughts (mislabeled "cognition") that supposedly do not cause emotional reactions. And the fact that there are no such emotion-free thoughts anyway is another reason to abhor the dichotomy between cognition and affect (see Baldwin, 1965).

Our discussion of developmental dimensions will not be concerned, as our discussion of developmental stages was, with particular ages. The dimensions we are dealing with should be understood as continua, as directions of change. We will identify particular points in the continua, but these points are meant to call attention not to stage differences but to the nature of the change, which is always a gradual process.

### Reactive to Active

Children begin life with certain built-in reactions to the environment, certain reflexes like sucking and grasping, that have great survival value for the infant. As infants mature, they gain greater control over themselves and their environment.

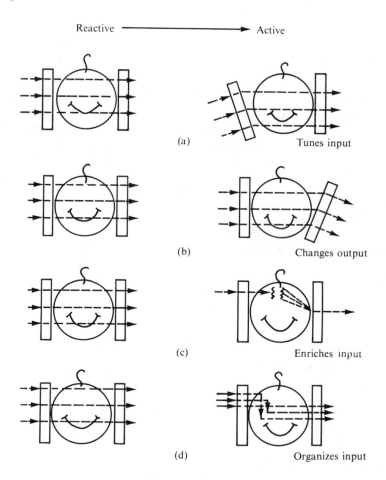

*Figure 4-5.*

They seek rather than wait. They anticipate rather than react. Figure 4-5 diagrams four different ways in which the developing child becomes more active in this sense.

The dashed arrows in Figure 4-5 move from the left to the right of each small circle, the child. These dashed arrows represent sensory and/or informational input. The dashed arrows leaving the circle are motor responses, answers to questions, and any other performance output. The developing child becomes more and more active, both physically and mentally, in how he treats the input. In Figure 4-5a we see that the younger child (left drawing) takes the input as it comes but that the older child (right drawing) adjusts his orientation to the input in order to better receive important information. Figure 4-5b shows the child becoming more active in the range of behavior he executes for the same sensory input; for example, he varies the speed at which he tosses an object, as well as the direction. Figure 4-5c illustrates the change from responding to the input as it comes in to enriching it with memory and fantasy. In Figure 4-5d the older child (right drawing) does not actually enrich the input, but he learns how to organize it for various purposes. In all of these cases the child adds more physical and/or mental activity to the input.

*The physical world.* During infancy a child does not passively wait for exciting things to happen. She gradually learns that a sound to her rear is quite likely coming from an interesting sight. She turns her head toward the sound, thus integrating two sources (sound and sight) that come from one object (Bower, 1974). Her treatment of the objects that surround her changes from unfocused looking and touching to deliberate exploration of all the effects that she can create with a particular object. She learns how to make interesting events reoccur and how to vary these events (Piaget & Inhelder, 1969b). As the child grows to ages 2, 3, and 4, the manner in which she observes the physical world becomes more active. Instead of looking at an entire object in a global manner, she begins to visually scan that object, as if she were looking for particular features. As she approaches 5 and then 6, her visual scanning matches the questions she has in mind ("Are these two pictures really the same landscape?"). She is no longer merely looking at; she is looking for (Vurpillot, 1976).

To the 3- and 4-year-old, objects cease to be simply objects. The child enriches them with all sorts of pretenses—the thimble is a pretend bucket for a pretend farmer—and the child is actively aware of the pretense. She laughs at her games, indicating that the thimble is not *confused* with a bucket; it is *used* as one. In other words, the object stands for the imagined object. This separation of the symbol from the thing the symbol represents is a most important step in mental development (Werner & Kaplan, 1963). True symbolic thinking is an active process, not the passive confusing of one stimulus with another.

Sights and sounds enter the child in disarray; but the child orders and categorizes them to suit her purposes. After she has mastered the basic skill of walking, she goes beyond practicing the walk. She actively integrates her movements with locations and pursues a particular destination (Knoblock & Pasamanick, 1974). She can organize and resequence a pull-then-grab into a grab-then-pull, as the situation demands (Bruner, 1968a).

Increased ability to organize information takes a more mental form as the child approaches 4, 5, and 6 years of age. If a 4-year-old has something to remember, like a set of instructions, sometimes she forgets, because she does not spontaneously rehearse to herself what she was told. Around 5 she can be taught to use mental rehearsal, and by 6 or 7 she does this as a matter of course (Flavell, Beach, & Chinsky, 1966; Conrad, 1971). Furthermore, if the information is not particularly well organized, the child can recategorize it or divide it into more natural groups—operations called *clustering* and *chunking,* respectively (Miller, 1956). By age 7 the child is doing much more with input than just reacting.

*The social world.* Children also become more active in their approach to the social world. As infants they accept all faces above them. But around 3 months, when they make the distinction between family and strangers, they actively seek familiar faces. Their ability to be selective continues to grow. As 2-year-olds they may treat most of their playmates with equal friendliness and/or aloofness. Between 3 and 5, children become more selective about their playmates and develop specific and persisting preferences (Fein & Clarke-Stewart, 1973). They also acquire greater ability to vary their behavior (Figure 4-5b). As infants and toddlers they cling and cry to get assistance. Beyond age 2 they begin to ask for help, and by age 4 they have developed rather sophisticated means of manipulating others to obtain what they want (Sigel, Starr, Secrist, Jackson, & Hill, 1971).

As children mature, they also enrich their social world. At first they watch an adult and try to imitate the adult's movements exactly. When they are 3, they pretend to be adults and show a certain amount of creativity in general sorts of mannerisms. By 4 the roles they play become more defined and differentiated—an angry adult, a nurturant adult. Beyond 4 they create new roles, new people, and imaginary playmates that satisfy in pretense those needs that are not satisfied in real life (Sutton-Smith & Sutton-Smith, 1974).

As children mature, their play increases in complexity.

Children's increasing ability to organize information means that their play with other children increases in complexity. The very nature of play changes from orientation to objects to organized themes of social exchanges (White, 1975). The social play of the 4-year-old has more continuity than that of the 2- and 3-year-old (Smilansky, 1968); it expands into longer and longer encounters, with parts and subparts (Garvey & Hogan, 1973). Yet, this increased ability to organize information has its negative effects as well. Children beyond 3 begin to hold grudges. Younger children are usually incapable of piecing together the many bits of a social encounter that would lead to the conclusion that they have been insulted; they cannot maintain in memory these subtle bits or translate them into the equally subtle reaction we call a grudge (Elkind, 1974).

This increasing ability to organize information also explains the change that takes place between the ages of 2 and 5 in a child's sources of frustration and, therefore, aggression. At 2 years aggression results from problems of possession—two children wanting the same object. By age 5, when children are capable of conceptualizing an organized plan, aggression more often results from differences in opinion. The disagreements of 5-year-old children take more thought to occur and more thought to solve, but then 5-year-olds have a greater capability to deal with complex problems (Bee, 1975). As they grow older, children do much more than just react to their social world.

*Empirical to Logical*

This dimension of development pertains to a gradual change in what the child uses to make judgments and conclusions. In the early years of life judgments and conclusions are based almost exclusively on the way things are and the way things have actually happened—that is, on empirical evidence only. Later on, children go beyond what they see and hear; they make inferences based on a combination of empirical inputs. One could discuss these changes as another example of the reactive-to-active dimension. We think, however, that this category deserves a separate discussion. We have already described aspects of this developmental dimension in the section on logico-mathematical knowledge in Chapter Two and in the section on Piaget's theory in this chapter. Here we want to carry the topic further and discuss it from a developmental point of view.

Figure 4-6 uses the same format as Figure 4-5. Figure 4-6a shows a child who

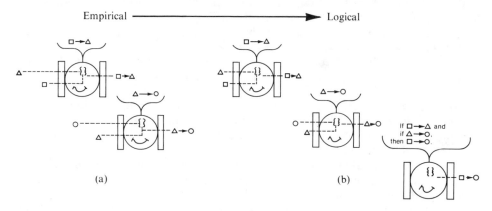

*Figure 4-6.*

receives two bits of information in a certain sequence: (1) a square followed by a triangle and (2) a triangle followed by a circle. The shapes represent any two bits of evidence in sequence—from two events, like push-leads-to-fall, to two facts, like addition-leads-to-more. The empirical child recalls the evidence and recalls the sequence as presented but does not make inferences beyond what is given. In Figure

4-6b we see that the child takes the empirical evidence and makes a conclusion based on a relation that he never saw in reality; that is, square-leads-to-circle. It is this attribute of going beyond the information given that defines the empirical-to-logical dimension. Inference and implication take different forms at different stages of development, as we shall see in the next section.

*The physical world.* It takes a few weeks of living just to become aware of separate events taking place in some regular order. When an infant does recognize that what she sees now did in the past signal an interesting event, she usually smiles broadly (Watson, 1972). She learns that an extended finger will probably lead to a tickle, a nipple to milk, and a face to a coo. Then she begins to integrate some of these inputs. A push leads to a fall, a fall to a crash; therefore, if I push, I will hear a crash. It is too early to call this type of response-chaining an inference, but chaining is a part of making logical inferences. We have already discussed how the child, by age 18 to 24 months, can solve a problem involving invisible displacement. This, too, is an early form of logical inference; but the invisible displacement refers to physical events and not to verbal definitions, as is true of logic in later years.

In the later years the child can answer questions that pertain to verbal definitions only. If a 6- or 7-year-old is told that *A* is longer than *B* and *B* is longer than *C*, he can answer that *A* must be longer than *C*. The *A*-to-*C* relation is fixed by the very meaning of the word *longer;* for example, objects do not change length when compared to different objects. The child can go beyond the information he has received and conclude, with perfect confidence, that *A* is longer than *C*. But even with the real objects before him, the 4-year-old cannot conclude that *A* is longer than *C* if only *A-B* and *B-C* were actually shown to him. "You can't say that, because you didn't show me those two" the 4-year-old insists.

We know that 3- and 4-year-olds have a very literal approach to the world. A 3-year-old hears that he was given his grandfather's name and then asks if grandpa is going to take it back. Another tells her mother that this is a picture of a bird. The mother replies "Yes, it is a robin." And the little girl gets angry because she knows that it is a bird, not a robin. The class-inclusion concept embedded in the mother's innocent remark exceeds the little girl's ability to think in terms of definitional relations. The first words that children produce and understand refer to witnessed events and tangible objects closely related to the children themselves (Frost & Kissinger, 1976; Beilin, 1975).

It is not until about age 6 that the child can reflect on a sentence itself as an object of thought (Beilin, 1975). At about that same age children establish logical, definitional relations. Before that age the words may be understood but are not used to improve inference making. For example, Holland and Palermo (1975) were able to teach preschool children the meaning of the words *more* and *less;* that is, the children could respond correctly when asked to place more apples here than there. They knew what the words meant. Yet, when given a conservation task that employed these words ("Are there more in this row, now that I have spread it out?"), they failed. Knowing a word or concept is not the same thing as entering that concept into a set of relations that make a logical inference possible (Figure 4-6b).

The 3- and 4-year-olds are also very literal in their attempts to represent the physical world. Early representational drawings portray "transparencies" (Piaget &

Inhelder, 1967). When a child draws the profile of a cowboy straddling a horse, he draws both legs. He doesn't really think that the horse is transparent, but he does know that a cowboy has two legs. He draws what he knows, not what he sees.

Here is another telling example of a preschooler drawing what she knew to be true. This child had recently finished eating a pizza and was asked to draw it. What she drew is shown in Figure 4-7a. What she actually saw would have been better represented by Figure 4-7b. The little girl knew that the pizza was made of several

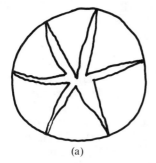     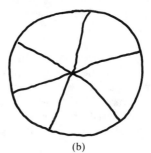

(a)     (b)

*Figure 4-7.*

pieces that could each be separated and eaten individually. Each piece had its own triangular boundary. Figure 4-7b would be quite unrepresentative of what the girl knew to be true, since the figure, if taken literally, shows only one edge for two adjacent pieces. It would be as difficult for this little girl to represent two edges with one line as it was for the other child to understand that one animal can be at the same time a bird and a robin!

The examples above explain how known relations interfere with the representation of reality. As the child develops, the known changes form and representational drawing improves. Take Figure 4-8 as an example. The child watches the fall of a

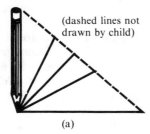

(dashed lines not drawn by child)

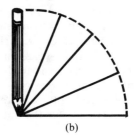

(a)     (b)

*Figure 4-8.*

pencil that had been held in a vertical position, point down. When asked to draw the descending positions of the falling pencil, the 4-year-old draws Figure 4-8a, while the 7-year-old draws Figure 4-8b. Neither child, of course, was able to actually "see" those positions, since the pencil fell too quickly. Each child had to infer what those successive positions looked like. The younger child, who (1) knew that objects generally fall in straight lines and (2) was centering his attention only on the erasure tip, drew successive positions as you see in Figure 4-8a. The older child drew Figure 4-8b because, despite her initial tendency to draw the lines as her younger companion did, she knew that such a drawing would contradict something she held inviolate: objects do not change their length when they change position. In this case, the inference improved the realism of the drawing. Even though the child could not see the successive positions, her drawing was a logical conclusion based on the premise that length is conserved.

*The social world.* Being able to go beyond the information given improves social relations. To the infant the information given might indicate that her mother is not present; but, as she develops object permanence, she understands that her mother still exists. The 1-year-old's ability to tolerate the separation from her mother can be described as an inference of sorts: mother goes behind door; mother reappears; therefore mother still exists when I don't see her (see Decarie, 1966). By age 3 and beyond, the child can use similar reasoning to make conclusions about the constancy of her mother's psychological support (Rheingold & Eckerman, 1970). Call this "conservation of affection." The 3-year-old who learns to wait for his turn is also using reasoning beyond the given. At some level he reasons "I want *X*. If I try for it now, I'll get *Y* [scolding]. If I wait, I won't get *Y*. Therefore I'll wait for *X*." Again, we point out that reasoning out a chain of real events is not a logical inference; it is a use of empirical facts in a form of thinking we can treat as a precursor of inferential thinking.

Communication with the social world would be greatly hampered if the child couldn't go beyond the reality of the given. In Chapter One we gave an example of how 3-year-olds find it difficult to abide by rules such as "Don't drive your cars on the grass." These verbal instructions are attempts to set constraints that are not actually present in the physical world. By age 4 or 5 the child gets better at using and processing language as a source of information that relates to the possible and not just to the usual. Strohner and Nelson (1974) found that 5-year-olds could act out a verbal statement appropriately even when the actions were improbable (for example, "The baby feeds the girl"), while 3-year-olds were more likely to do what was usual. The 4- and 5-year-olds' ability to think about the possible also contributes to social cooperation and to the reduction of physical aggression. As children mature, they use verbal aggression—which is a form of talking about possibilities—and consequently actual physical aggression diminishes (Bee, 1975). Reasoning in if-then terms greatly assists the child's social development.

## Absolute to Relative

The history of science is marked by epochal discoveries that have caused people to realize over and over again that absolute truths are in fact relative to one's perspective. Copernicus discovered that the sun's motion is an illusion of the observer positioned on earth. Einstein discovered that what appears to be a lunar orbit in a single plane is relative to how we measure time and space. What is is relative. Children, too, travel on a course of discovering various forms of relativity. They eventually learn that their perspectives, their experiences, their very language—all set limits on what they can know. As children become more conscious of the interaction between the observer and the observed, their knowledge of the physical world and of the social world improves.

In Figure 4-9 we have chosen a problem in spatial perspective to represent the

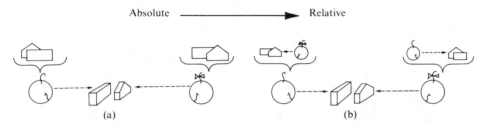

*Figure 4-9.*

general form of the absolute-to-relative dimension. This illustration could well be a metaphor for all sorts of problems of perspective, from understanding the listener's point of view to understanding the difference between cultural values. The child in Figure 4-9a looks at the world from his own point of view only and assumes that what he sees is absolute. He fails to consider that, from another perspective, another person sees a different world. The child in Figure 4-9b has his own view of things, but he can also figure out the other person's view from what he knows of the other person's position. As you might have anticipated, the higher forms of development on this dimension are a variation of the empirical-to-logical dimension. The observer may never actually experience the other person's view in the empirical sense, but he develops the competence to *infer* what that other view is.

*The physical world.* The first break with an absolute view of the world comes in the first year of life, when the child, instead of being one with space, becomes aware of himself as an object in space. When the child searches for a hidden object, he sees himself as an object as well. Instead of trying to make the hidden object reappear by blinking or wishing, he moves in space to retrieve the object. The child has discovered the permanence of objects; he now knows that it is not the object that has changed but his perspective. This fundamental discovery represents a milestone in the development of the child.

What is known is also determined by where one looks for information. The 2- and 3-year-olds in many elementary ways don't know where to look. They center their attention on one feature of a problem. For example, a 2-year-old will keep trying for minutes on end to position a large jigsaw-puzzle piece into a small hole, because the hole happens to have a single contour similar to one part of the piece. To use Piaget's term, children cannot "decenter" their attention to other features. The 4-year-old turns her wrist to look at a fly on the back of her hand, spilling the juice she is holding in that same hand. Decentration is a prevalent objective in preschool education, as attested by the frequent admonitions "Watch where you're going" and "How do you think he felt when you knocked over his tower?"

Piaget calls the child who has difficulty taking the point of view of another *egocentric*. This term has a purely physical meaning—for example, failing to see an object from another point of view, as in the case of failing to see that the jigsaw piece is too big for the hole—and does not mean selfish (as it often does in common parlance). There is nothing selfish about a child focused on a tiny curve of a jigsaw piece. But there is something self-centered (thus egocentric) about it. The child's preoccupation with his immediate aim to place the piece prevents him from backing away from this self-set goal long enough to see things from a different perspective. Having said this, we should also add that the behavior that parents and teachers label "selfish" does result from the same type of failure to decenter.

In some situations the child is asked to consider another person's view instead of simply expanding his own view. At what age can the child pick from a set of pictures the one that portrays the view of someone sitting on the opposite side of the table? Figure 4-9 shows how the view of the blocks of the child on the right is the reverse of the view of the blocks of the child on the left. When 4-year-olds are asked to choose a picture that shows the opposite of what they see, they tend to choose a picture that shows their own view (Laurendeau & Pinard, 1970). This egocentric approach changes between the ages of 4 and 7. As children acquire a more relativistic approach, however, they are likely to make certain mistakes that they didn't make when their views of objects were more absolute. For example, Maratsos (1973a) found that 5-year-olds thought that oblong objects were larger than equal-area round objects, while 3-year-olds, who took a more global view of the shapes, didn't make that mistake. The 5-year-olds were evidently comparing the relative heights of the shapes rather than their total areas, and the 3-year-olds looked instead at each shape as independent of the other.

Decentration from a narrow view of an object and from an absolute view of spatial arrangements improves the child's ability to deal with the physical world. This is true in the long run, even though, as Maratsos (1973a) demonstrated, children may overapply their newly acquired mental skills. The child's drawing the cowboy's leg as if the horse were transparent is another example of overapplication of inference—drawing what one knows rather than what one sees. These "regressions" are not only common but perhaps necessary to development (see Strauss, 1972) and are eventually replaced by higher forms of inference and decentration that incorporate the regressions. We can express this by saying that development is not a matter of ignoring the illusory but, rather, of understanding the illusion (see Inhelder, Sinclair, & Bovet, 1974).

*The social world.* The change from absolute to relative aptly describes social development. The entire socialization process, from the initial establishment of autonomy to the development of empathy and diplomacy, consists of an increasing ability to decenter from one's own personal perspective. At 6 months the child can look at the effects of his own actions and take pleasure in being their cause. This marks the beginning of self-awareness. Fear of strangers at 10 months of age is another form of self-consciousness. The child has become aware of himself as a person vulnerable to outside effects. At 13 months his increased mobility, through crawling and walking, expands his world and confronts him with a greater variety of effects, which, in turn, causes him to decenter from the world of the crib. By age 2 the child has developed a definite personality, with its own styles of coping, and at 3 he can accept his own limitations without bewilderment. The emergence of self is a process of decentering away from the proximal and the immediate (Murphy, 1962).

Around age 2 something occurs that causes distress to the adults about. Children become extremely negativistic. They frequently say no to requests, assert their will at great cost of energy, and become bossy and overbearing. This is another instance of overapplication of a newly discovered concept. Once the *me* is distinguished from the *you,* the child "practices" that distinction until it becomes solidly established. This phase, called "the terrible 2s," is crucial to the development of the child, who should never be denied the gains of this phase because of its negative expressions. Eventually, as children acquire higher forms of thinking, the struggle for control changes first into more prosocial forms of competition (Flapan & Neubauer, 1975) and then into an understanding and acceptance of the personal rights of others. It is only when the inflated sense of power that characterizes the 2-year-old is tempered with the mental competence that comes at a later age that the child can distinguish his own power from the power of the adults with whom he identifies—in other words, be able to assess his own power more realistically (Mahler, 1968).

Communication with the social world also involves a shift from the absolute to the relative. If the child does not consider the listener's point of view, he will fail to

Eventually the struggle for control shifts from physical force to verbal negotiations.

communicate effectively. When a 5-year-old tells a stranger in the neighborhood "Take me to Raymond's house," he is manifesting a failure to decenter. Yet, we are finding out that children are more capable of sensing another person's view than we had thought. Maratsos (1973a) found that, if the other person's view of an object is obstructed, a 3-year-old will point at the object. In more complex situations, however—like describing a picture to the listener—3-year-olds don't fare as well. A 3-year-old, for example, will try to explain which of four drawings he is referring to by using a description that is clear only to himself. He assumes that, when he tells the listener "It's the one that looks like crinkled bedsheets," the description is clear enough to eliminate all but one of the pictures. In fact, what looks like crinkled bedsheets to the child may look like everything but crinkled sheets to the other person, who, therefore, doesn't know which drawing the child is talking about. More conventional words, such as "three triangles in a row," would communicate the child's meaning much better (Glucksberg, Krauss, & Higgins, 1975). Eventually children learn that the meaning of a word is relative to a person's experience with that word and that, since we don't all have the same sets of experiences, the same word may mean different things to different people.

As children grow older, they become increasingly aware of the subjective states of other people. What someone does is relative to what that person feels. The 1½-year-old who pounded her father's foot with a small hammer is surprised at his eruption. Since she had not intended for her slam to hurt her father, she can't understand why he bolted from the chair. At a young age a child's subjective state is not sufficiently differentiated from the adult's subjective state. She doesn't even consider that the hit might hurt. Gradually the child will become more and more capable of recognizing the values and predispositions of others, and by age 5 she will have made giant steps forward (Martin & Stendler, 1953). At that age she will know that demands don't work as well as requests that take into account the adult's disposition at the moment. She will have learned that others might have their own plans and she'd better find out what they are before she is caught trespassing (Bowlby, 1969). All of these advances rest on the child's ability to consider the other person's point of view.

Social development in the preschool years evolves from egocentricity to companionship (Freud, 1965). At age 2, children direct, boss, and lead. When they are 3 and 4 they instruct, and by age 5 they are engaging their peers in conversation and explorations that work in social harmony. At 3, children can function occasionally in small groups, but by 4 and 5 they exchange ideas, contribute to a common cause, and offer suggestions (Flapan, 1968). None of this would be possible if children couldn't include in their decisions the desires and intentions of other people.

Healthy social relations are the product of a combination of autonomy and a sense of other. Children who are overly sensitive to the intentions and desires of others lack real social relatedness (Wenar, 1964). Others find such children difficult to predict, since they change at the whim of their group. Children who refuse needed help are instead overly autonomous and drive their peers away because of their own frustrations (Murphy, 1962). Children must learn to both resist and comply with influence—that is, to combine autonomy with dependency. In the absence of this compromise, the forever obstinate child is no less controlled by others than the forever obedient child (Piaget & Inhelder, 1969b; Aronfreed, 1964). The conflict between one's will and the will of others is necessary to assure a reconciliation between one's own point of view and that of others (Meers & Marans, 1968). The clashes over individual value (possessiveness) must occur as a grounds for learning collective value (empathy). The absolute will of the child gradually gives way to a will tempered by the needs of others.

## Summary

The discipline of early childhood education wouldn't exist if children between the ages of 2 and 5 were not appreciably different from older children. Obvious as this is, it points to the importance of these differences and to the need for teachers and child-care workers to become familiar with all of these differences—the gross as well as the subtle. Piaget's theory of development has contributed much to the understanding of these differences and, consequently, has had a great impact on education. The division of development into stages is perhaps the best-known part of Piaget's complex theory.

Piaget describes four stages of cognitive development. The age at which children move from one stage to the next is not as important as the following aspects of Piaget's stage theory. (1) The order of the stages is invariant. No stage can be skipped. Children may, and most likely do, go through stages at various speeds; but they move through the stages in the same order. (2) The development of the stages is cumulative; each stage builds and expands on the previous stages. There is continuity within discontinuity. Even though discrete stages with particular behavioral and structural characteristics can be identified, development is continuous, in the sense that each stage continues the development of the previous one(s) and prepares the way for the next stage.

The first stage of development is called the sensorimotor stage and encompasses the years from birth to 2. It is during this time that children come to understand their environment through their own actions. This is the stage of practical intelligence. Although not at the conscious level, a child of this age is capable of acting within the group of translations (the organization of object movement).

The second stage is that of preoperational thought. Here the child between the ages of 2 and 7 begins to use symbolic representation, including language, and begins to understand the operation of functions. A function is a one-way relation between two events—for example, the relation between the rise of the level of water in a glass and the decrease in the level of water in the pitcher from which the water is poured. It is important to note that functions during this stage are one way in nature. Because of this limitation, the preoperational child can think about the relation of one action to another and the direction of the resulting change but cannot grasp the implication that these changes have, for example, for the concept of conservation and cannot think about the quantitative aspect of the changes. The acquisition of that ability marks the emergence of the next stage.

The stage of concrete-operational thought, encompassing the years from 7 to 11, is marked by the child's ability to mentally reverse actions performed in the environment. This ability allows the child to move beyond the stage of mere perceptual appearances, which is typical of the preoperational child. At 7 or 8 a child *knows* that, when a ball of clay is rolled into a sausage, the amount of clay doesn't change. He knows because he can mentally reverse the process of transformation that the ball has undergone. This means that the concrete-operational child has gone beyond the mere appearance of things at a particular moment in time (figurative knowledge) and has begun to understand the relations between two states of an object (operative knowledge). Since most children in early childhood programs are chronologically preoperational children, the fostering of concrete-operational thought should be the long-term objective of these programs.

The fourth stage in Piaget's scheme is the stage of formal operations. It is during this stage, beyond age 11, that children begin to think about thinking and to perform operations on operations. Where the concrete-operational child's thought is tied to changes in concrete objects, the thought of the formal-operational child is involved with changes expressed in purely verbal propositions. Although not of direct concern to the early childhood educator, it is important to remember that, since these stages are cumulative, the experiences children have during their early years will have an effect on their formal-operational thought.

It is also helpful to look at development in another, slightly different fashion. As a general framework, children move along three dimensions in their understanding of and interactions with the physical and social worlds: (1) reactive to active, (2) empirical to logical, and (3) absolute to relative. These dimensions also describe various aspects of the stages Piaget has delineated, but, instead of serving as a broad perspective of a child's development, these dimensions provide a framework from which children's everyday behavior can be viewed and analyzed.

In terms of the first dimension (reactive to active), we see the child changing from simply responding to environmental stimuli to becoming more selective about the things he wants to look at, hear, touch, and so forth. He also begins to organize the input according to different networks of relationships. Whereas at first he may have reacted with joy to the appearance of his mother by his crib, he now begins to initiate the contact by cooing or crying. The 3-year-old begins to create novelty for himself by varying his actions on objects instead of simply reacting to fortuitous events.

The empirical-to-logical dimension is closely related to the difference between preoperational and concrete-operational thought. The child moving along this dimension begins to view the world with an understanding of how things must be given the organization of events. He no longer settles for just appearances. Returning to the clay example, if no clay was either added or taken away, there must be the same amount of clay in the sausage as there was in the ball. The child operates on the basis of logical necessity.

The dimension of absolute to relative is closely connected with Piaget's notion of egocentrism. As with notions in physics, the child begins to realize that one's own reality is based on one's own point of view. An object or group of objects may look different to people in different parts of the room, and something may be considered right or wrong by different people with different interests at stake. As young children become more relativistic in their thinking, they become more cooperative, can engage in group activities more easily, and begin to engage in social play. They can now do so because each of these activities requires the ability to understand another person's point of view, something children of 2 and 3 have a great deal of difficulty doing.

## Suggestions for Further Reading

Formanek, R., & Gurian, A. *Charting intellectual development: A practical guide to Piagetian tasks.* Springfield, Ill.: Charles C Thomas, 1976. A good introduction and guide to the tasks Piaget and his coworkers have used to investigate the stages of children's thinking.

Piaget, J., & Inhelder, B. *The psychology of the child.* New York: Basic Books, 1969. Although books by Piaget are generally difficult reading, this book is a concise and readable summary of his major ideas, including the characteristics of the different stages of development.

White, B. L. *The first three years of life.* Englewood Cliffs, N.J.: Prentice-Hall, 1975. An excellent source of information concerning the general changes in behavior children go through during the first three years of life.

# Chapter Five

# Behavior Modification and Conflict Inducement

In their efforts to facilitate learning in young children, teachers are continually faced with a choice between two approaches, albeit neither is ever practiced in pure form. These two approaches divide on the source of corrective information that children use to improve their performance. At times children learn what to do because their teachers, peers, parents, or someone else tells them how close or how far they are from correct performance. For example, the child applies the sponge to the spilled milk, moves it slowly from left to right, and looks to the adult, who quickly says "Nice job." The reinforcement comes from a source that is external to the performance itself. More precisely speaking, the source of reinforcement is *extrinsic* to the performance, since saying "Nice job" is not a continuation or a necessary consequence of the performance—in this example, wiping up the milk.

At other times children learn what to do because their actions create consequences or their thoughts create conclusions that suggest to them what is correct or incorrect about their performances. The source of the corrective information comes from and is a continuation of the performance and of the thoughts that accompany it; that is, the source of reinforcement is *intrinsic* to the performance—for example, the fact that wiped milk is absorbed more quickly when the sponge is moved slowly. In the research literature *behavior modification* is the term most generally used to identify teaching by means of *extrinsic* reinforcement. The literature covering *intrinsic* reinforcement is not as consistent in its terminology, but the term *conflict inducement* is often used to refer to teaching by means of intrinsic reinforcement.

This chapter compares learning that results from behavior modification with learning that results from conflict inducement. Our focus is on the nature of learning, but note that behavior modification and conflict inducement are methods of teaching—that is, things that teachers do. We feel that it is important to contrast these two methods in order to dissipate the doubt that may arise in the minds of the more behavioristically oriented readers that Piaget is denying the obvious. Piaget acknowledges the value of reinforcement provided by others—the hallmark of behaviorism and what Piaget calls "social knowledge" (see Chapter Two). But we also want the more Piaget-oriented readers not to throw out behaviorism with the bathwater.

We will make the case that behavior modification, as we define it, is an appropriate means to support the child's general pursuit of information but that it is not a preferred means to teach the child how to seek and use specific information to construct knowledge. Our definition of behavior modification is rather narrow. We have isolated, as the essence of behavior modification, the use of external (extrinsic) reinforcement. The other trappings, such as stop watches, response counts, base rates, and cumulative records, are embellishments of this central concept of extrinsic reinforcement; as such, we consider them irrelevant to the main issue.

Many early childhood educators, parents, and students have misgivings about this technique. They seem to have an intuitive feeling that extrinsic reinforcement for specific behavior is mechanistic and therefore less desirable. The behaviorists' retort to this objection is that behavior modification "works." But the feeling that something is not quite right remains. What we need is an explicit definition of behavior modification and an equally explicit definition of the criteria used to decide whether or not "it works." We hope to make clear in our discussion that many of the criticisms leveled at behavior modification are straw men, arguments based on a misunderstanding of the concept itself. We also hope that, by offering a comprehensive definition and a thorough review of the arguments in favor of and against behavior modification, we will substantiate our basic position that behavior modification can be used to improve the learning environment and support the learning process but that inducement of conflict intrinsic to the task at hand (see Schwartz & Shapiro, 1976; Walcher & Peters, 1971) is a better means to facilitate the actual construction of knowledge.

## Behavior Modification Defined

Our definition of behavior modification is a general one and includes only those elements that we consider essential to that approach. These elements can be expressed in the form of five principles, which collectively define the approach. One of the common mistakes that people make when they first read about behavior modification is to take one of these principles in isolation and use it to define behavior modification. For example, the statement of a behavioral objective (see Principle 1 below) does not, in itself, define behavior modification. Even the teacher who uses conflict inducement will want to clearly state just what constitutes evidence that the child has learned. How behavioral objectives are formulated and how they are used is another issue. To understand behavior modification, these five principles should be remembered collectively, not separately, and seen as five necessary steps in a progression.

1. The teacher defines, in explicit terms of observable behavior, an objective that he or she deems beneficial for the child.
2. The child enters the class with a set of responses, some of which approximate the objective and some of which interfere with the attainment of the objective.
3. The teacher provides positive reinforcement for those behaviors that approximate the objective and does not provide reinforcement for those behaviors that interfere with progress toward the objective.
4. Over a period of time the rate of on-target behaviors increases and the rate of off-target behaviors decreases.
5. Over a longer period of time the teacher fades out extrinsic reinforcement. In

this phase, control over the behavior is transferred from teacher-provided reinforcement to task-provided reinforcement—that is, reinforcement more intrinsic to success on the task.

Consider the following example as an illustration of how the above principles are applied. The teacher sets the behavioral objective "Gavin will be able to assemble a jigsaw puzzle." She selects this objective in part because she believes that puzzles have educational value and in part because she saw Gavin choose a puzzle a few days before. From that point on, her objective is clearly stated in the form of what behaviors the child will perform. This clear specification of behaviors becomes the criterion of success.

The next day Gavin picks up the puzzle again, and the teacher sits with him at the table. The child removes all the pieces from the box and then lifts one. But, instead of placing the piece into the form board, he begins to bang it on the table. The teacher is tempted to ask Gavin to gently place the piece into the form board; instead, she decides to use positive reinforcement. She praises those bangs that shake the table, but, at the same time, she gradually influences the child to change from banging pieces to placing pieces into the form board. After Gavin has discovered how the jigsaw pieces fit and blend with the other pieces and after he has begun to attend to the material feedback of the puzzle itself, the teacher fades out her (externally provided) social reinforcement.

In our example we have described a process of teaching that typifies behavior modification. Other examples would have done just as well, since it is the basic process of behavior modification that we are concerned with. But what is it in that basic process that elicits objections? Some of the objections rest on false assumptions. They are objections to poorly applied behavior-modification techniques rather than to behavior modification per se, or they are objections that stem from the uncompromising premise that control is inherently and invariably wrong. We regard these objections as mere straw men. Other objections, instead, concern the level of learning produced by behavior modification; since they deal with the essence of the question, these objections are at the root of true controversy. We will discuss the first kind of objections first, to dispose of the straw men.

## False Assumptions regarding Behavior Modification

### *Behavior Modification Is a Form of Bribery*

This criticism makes two assumptions. One is that the teacher's smiling or saying "That's good" when the child emits an on-target response is in fact bribery. The other assumption is that bribery is always bad. The problem with giving the child a reinforcement every time he emits *the* response is that, besides learning to make the response, the child is also learning how to build up a cash supply of M&M's, compliments, and smiles. The danger here is the chance that the reward may become the end in itself rather than a simple incentive to acquire knowledge. Like the mercenary soldier, who does not fight for the cause, the mercenary child may not respond in order to learn. What is wrong with this kind of situation is not so much that it doesn't help character building or that it is a corruption of "pure motives" but that it diverts the child's attention from the purpose of his behavior. Behavior is ideally a means of gaining new information, not a means for repeatedly receiving social reinforcement.

The behavior modifiers have several retorts to this criticism. The first is that the child is not being bribed, because bribery is promising to pay a person if he will perform a specified task and behavior modification reinforces the person *after* he has done something of his own choosing. This is a vapid retort because it simply ignores the time element. After a child has been reinforced once for making a response, the next opportunity she has to make that response carries the implication that, if she does it again, she will be reinforced again. If it weren't so, why would response rate increase? It is always the expectation of reinforcement that increases response rate; that is, the child is being bribed.

The second retort is directed to the assumption that bribery is always bad. Bribery may not be bad in the short run. If a child is not doing anything constructive, perhaps a temporary bribing to get him on target is preferable to doing nothing to get him off his random behavior. Once the child has been channeled into activities that have greater educational value, the reward can be faded out. It sounds reasonable. Yet, there is a problem, and that is the difficulty of deciding *when* the child is not doing anything constructive. This is an important point, and we shall come back to it later.

## Behavior Modification Ignores the Uniqueness of the Child

This criticism can mean one of two things. It may mean that the critic assumes that the teacher using behavior modification is ignoring the particular skills of each child—that is, his or her entering behavior. We have seen in the preceding example that this is not true. The teacher always starts with where the child is, even if it is banging a jigsaw piece on the table.

Alternatively, the criticism may mean that the kind of individualized instruction required for a reinforcement procedure is impossible. How can a teacher who has more than a few students to supervise be able to give each child reinforcement for each of his or her on-target responses? It seems to us that this is not a criticism of reinforcement theory but, rather, a criticism of large classes or perhaps of a system that does not provide sufficient technological support for truly individualized instruction. And the concern for lack of individualized instruction is a concern that all educators share, no matter what their pedagogical theory.

We must distinguish whether the behavior-modification approach has merit in terms of what it can do from whether it is currently feasible. If it has merit and all are convinced of that merit, schools will change so that the application of that approach will be feasible. We cannot reject a pedagogical theory simply because the status quo does not permit its implementation. We must reject a theory only if it has not lived up to its pedagogical objectives even when they are fully implemented.

In summary, the criticism against behavior modification based on concerns for the uniqueness of the child does not hold up under close scrutiny. The unique behavior of the individual child is always where the teacher begins. The logistic problems of providing reinforcement only attest to a school's resistance to applying behavior modification; it is in no way a test of its effectiveness once applied.

## Behavior Modification Is Too Mechanical

This criticism comes by and large from teachers who have just begun to apply contingent positive reinforcement in the classroom. The teacher turns to the child who is working quietly at his table and says "Look how quietly Irving is working." Since this is a new approach for both the teacher and the student and since the teacher may still have reservations about this approach, he feels that this reinforcement sounds stilted.

What does the statement "Positive contingent reinforcement is too mechanical" mean? Does it mean that the words *positive contingent reinforcement* sound too technical? If so, they can be replaced with warmer-sounding words, such as *praise, compliment,* and *approval.* Does it mean that uttering those words of reinforcement makes the teacher feel unnatural? Of course it does—as unnatural as trying for the first time to hold a pencil correctly. Does it mean that the technique is too deliberate? But how can deliberation on the teacher's part ever be a reason for criticism? Does it mean that it is too artificial? If this is true, then the problem may be no more than becoming comfortable with giving praise. As the teacher practices giving praise, its "practiced," artificial qualities will smooth into a more fluid naturalness as does any skill once mastered. Does it mean that it is too arbitrary, like a machine that is insensitive to subtleties for which it was not designed? If so, again this is simply a matter of the teacher's learning to include those subtleties in his repertoire as he becomes more proficient at giving praise. Perhaps praising Irving in front of the class makes the child uncomfortable and is therefore not positively reinforcing at all. The teacher does not abort his program of praising Irving; he simply looks to the subtleties of what is in actuality positive reinforcement for that individual child. Behavior modification through making positive reinforcement contingent on particular responses may sound mechanistic when described but need not be so when applied. If we are going to reject behavior modification, we must do so on the basis of the consequences that result from its best application and not from its poorly rehearsed application.

## Behavior Modification Is Too Authoritarian

This complaint most often comes as a reaction against such phrases as "shaping behavior" and "getting the child under stimulus control." The critic feels that the child's choices are ignored. While there is some truth to this criticism, there is also some misunderstanding. Reconsider the example of Gavin, the child working with the jigsaw puzzle. The child does have several choices, and the choices are honored. To begin with, Gavin chose that particular curriculum material himself. If he decides to abandon the puzzle, his choice will be honored, although the teacher will attempt to make working with it so pleasant that Gavin will not want to leave. The child's choice of pace is honored, as well as his choice of initial response to the curriculum material—for example, banging the pieces on the table. In fact, whatever the child does is ultimately his choice. It is his choice to engage in the behavior that leads to approval. However, leading a child forward with praise and pushing a child forward with threats may be equally authoritarian if one equates any act of direction with an act of authoritarianism.

Directing the child toward certain experiences rather than others simply cannot be taken as a prima facie case of authoritarianism. This is overharsh criticism and would make every act on the teacher's part, from bringing in gerbils to setting up a painting easel, an act of authoritarianism. Children learn better with a teacher around than they do without a teacher, and this is simply because the teacher directs in some fashion. The tricky part is the nature of that direction, and here we come to some substantive controversies regarding behavior modification.

## Controversy about the Level of Learning

### The Problem of the Criterion

The child may not really learn with the behavior-modification approach. This is not only the most severe criticism against behavior modification but probably the most relevant. The evidence seems to suggest that the criticism is unfounded. Behavior modifiers report remarkable gains. Children once mute are now speaking fluently; hyperactive children, once impulsive, are now reflective (Allen, Henke, Harris, Baer, & Reynolds, 1967; Becker, Madsen, Arnold, & Thomas, 1967). How can one say that behavior modification does not work? The answer rests in the criteria used to measure success.

Most anyone would recommend a schedule of contingent reinforcement to calm a hyperactive child or to elicit more verbal output from an autistic child or to increase attention to external events in a withdrawn child. The objective in each of these cases, however, is not to teach the child new information but, rather, to improve his means of acquiring any information. If a dysfunction in the motivational system (lethargy, distractibility, or withdrawal) prevents the child from receiving information in a usable form, behavior modification may well be the most expedient method to reset the child's general attentiveness. Behavior modification does work if improvement in orientation to information is the criterion (Blank & Solomon, 1969).

However, learning is more than acquiring the right orientation to information, even though the latter is necessary. Learning involves a process of discovering *what* information is necessary to solve a particular problem. Learning is indicated by a change in behavior, but its process is one of gathering information. Often this process is not observable. Effective teaching provides the child with the means to discover what information is necessary. The behaviorist typically does not focus on information processing but, instead, on the overt behavior, the performance. While the behavioristic approach has the advantage of explicitness, it has the disadvantage of a high rate of false positives—that is, assuming that learning has occurred, when in fact it has not (Kamii & Derman, 1971).

## The Problem of False Positives

Consider this example of a false positive. A 4-year-old girl is trying to place a jigsaw-puzzle piece into a vacant space in the jigsaw-puzzle form board. The piece is the only one that remains to be placed. The girl keeps jabbing the piece into the space with her right hand but doesn't rotate it to its proper orientation so that it will fit. After a number of stereotyped jabs, the girl stops, smiles, lifts the piece to her eyes, and begins to trace the contour of that piece with the extended finger of her left hand. At this point, it seems apparent that she is recalling a technique (contour tracing) that she was taught when she learned puzzle assembly. The context is correct: a piece will not fit. The behavior, too, is correct: moving the extended finger around the contour and visually tracking the finger. But does she *understand* what she is doing? Is she gathering the *information* necessary to solve her problem? As may be expected, as soon as she completes two rubbings around the contour of the piece, she starts all over again, with the confidence of Aladdin, her stereotypic, unrotated jabbing into the form board. It would be a false positive to conclude that this child has learned to relate the shape of the piece to the shape of the hole; she has learned only to move her finger over the edges of the piece.

A teacher concerned with changing the child's behavior may have difficulty understanding the very behavior he is trying to change. The behaviorist looks at the child's response as an indicator of what the child has learned rather than as an active attempt to gather information. The behaviorist is correct in insisting that one should never assume that learning has occurred unless some behavioral criterion is met. But the converse is also true; that is, one cannot invariably conclude from the observed behavior that learning has occurred. To this the behaviorist would reply that the problem of false positives can be easily solved by stating better behavioral criteria.

## Behavior as Product or Process

Even though the above reply suggests that the problem is simple enough, in fact, within a strict behavioristic approach, it is very difficult to establish better criteria to indicate when learning has occurred. The teacher must go beyond behavior and think about those mechanisms of the mind that operate in the process of gathering and organizing information. This means that the teacher must have some knowledge of the many different hypotheses that the child could be using during the act of making a given response. The response points at the process of learning itself, not just at the product. Speculating about the child's thoughts permits the teacher to decide what to do next and what variation on a theme might be beneficial. Making guesses about what external stimulus is controlling a particular behavior will not help. If the child is engaging in correct behavior for the wrong reasons, the teacher needs to know something about the development of young children's thinking if his next move is going to be a beneficial one.

If behavior modifiers say that these points are no more than the principles used in a well-written lesson, then they are only admitting that a focus on behavior is not enough. If the student answers that $4 \times 3 = 7$, the efficient teacher will branch the student into a review of the difference between the multiplication sign and the addition sign. Only by considering what the error means in terms of what the student is most likely thinking can instruction begin to work effectively (Blank, 1972). While there is no necessary reason why stating behavioral objectives should prevent the teacher from asking "what information is being processed," the focus on behavior as a product seems to have that effect in practice. The behavioral objective does a far better job in specifying the products of learning—that is, in representing the index of success—than it does in directing the teacher's attention to the process of learning.

Because these objectives specify products, learning is too often viewed as a short answer to a narrow question. The behavioral objective "The child will learn the names of the primary colors" gets translated into the classroom as "Andrea, what is the name of this color?" The teacher is even advised to take complex tasks and break them down into small steps. When learning is viewed as "a correct response," there is the risk that the child will be denied the opportunity to organize the confusion. When learning is viewed as a process of gathering the necessary information, teachers are less concerned about "errors" and are also less concerned with breaking down a task for the child.

## Smaller Steps or Easier Problems

In meaningful learning, the children themselves discover how to break down a task into smaller steps. But what does the teacher do when a child is overwhelmed by a complex task? In keeping with the constructivist philosophy of this text, we suggest that the teacher shift to an easier problem rather than fragment the complex task into isolated components. This easier problem is a whole, with a beginning and an end, and not an isolated component out of context. This simpler task prepares the child, no matter in how incidental a fashion, for the more complex task he cannot yet do.

Suppose that a child confuses the length of a row of objects with the number of objects in that row. When asked if the bottom row of five spread-out objects contains the same number as the top row of five objects bunched together, the child assumes that the longer row contains more objects. Therefore she says that the longer row has more, even though, when the objects in each row were matched up one to one, she said that the two rows had the same number. If the teacher has been trained in component analysis, he begins to break down this task into the simpler skills involved. In order to answer correctly, the child needs to look at the total length, consider the interval between each two objects, remember the initial state, and so on. The teacher decides to work on each component in turn. He places three objects close together and three far apart and asks the child to state in which row the objects are closer. The child learns to answer this question to perfection and over many variations. Then the teacher asks the child which row is longer. And the child learns to answer this question, and the related ones, quite correctly. She also learns to move either row into its original position, when asked to do so. The teacher concludes that the child can attend to the length and spacing of the rows and can remember the original state of correspondence.

At this point the teacher again presents the number problem, first with rows in correspondence and then with rows spread apart and bunched together. The child fails, as she had failed before being trained in the component skills. The reason for her failure is that the task requires a coordination of the concepts of length and density, not simply an awareness of their variation (Piaget, 1952). The child must come to understand that what the spread-out row gains in length it loses in density. And she must come to understand the implication of the reverse. This knowledge is more than simply remembering that correspondence can be reestablished. Training a child to focus on each concept as a separate component may actually postpone the development of this coordination.

Rather than training the student on each component in turn, the teacher would do well to discover games and tasks that the child can do and that have the incidental effect of developing prenumber concepts. The teacher asks the child to put one straw into every cup; she plays with clay, breaking it apart and putting it together; she asks the child if he has really eaten more of his pudding or just spread it around in his dish; she sets up a game in which the child discovers that his fireman's ladder is just as long lying down as it is standing up; and so on. All of these games play their role in developing number concepts; yet, none is an isolated, neat, academic exercise. Each requires a set of ideas that must be coordinated, but at a level of familiarity and continuity that the child can understand. Figure 5-1 gives a metaphorical rendering of the difference between teaching a component and teaching an easier problem.

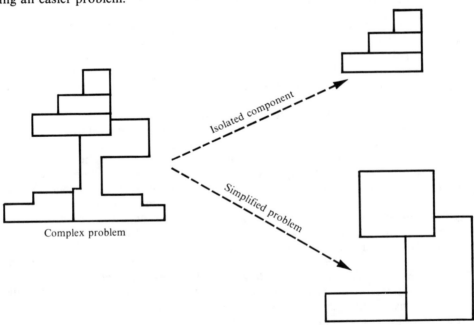

*Figure 5-1.*

*General Processes or Specific Behavior*

Stating objectives in terms of general processes rather than in terms of specific behavior can contribute to flexibility in teaching young children. Consider the child banging the jigsaw piece on the table. Recall that the behavioral objective was stated as "Gavin will be able to assemble a jigsaw puzzle." What if the objective had been reworded into a more general (process) format, such as "Gavin will be able to relate different objects in space"? Notice the difference between the word *assemble* and the word *relate*. The first refers to an observable action, the second to an unobservable mentation. The behaviorist would call the second word vague; we choose to call it general. It refers to a larger number of possible behaviors, and therein lies its power.

If the child is banging the piece on the table and the teacher is thinking about her objective "Gavin will be able to relate different objects in space," there is really no reason for her to shape Gavin's behavior toward the form board or, for that matter, even toward placing the pieces. Banging the piece can be a lesson in itself. So the teacher slips a small tin plate on the spot where the piece is being banged against the table, and the child notices the loud noise. Then the teacher slips the tin plate aside. If Gavin likes the sound, he may deliberately try to hit the plate with the piece. Many good things are happening here. For one, the objective is being met, in that the child is relating two objects (the piece and the plate) in space. For another, the reinforcement is intrinsic to the child's action rather than external, as a remark from a nearby teacher would be. Finally, the teacher feels quite comfortable in staying within the mode of action that the child naturally enjoys. Would specifying behaviors in detail have done as much?

## Intrinsic Reinforcement

*The Value of Intrinsic Reinforcement*

Why do we say that intrinsic reinforcement is better than extrinsic reinforcement? Does intrinsic reinforcement inform the child more quickly whether his response was correct or incorrect—in other words, is the difference between intrinsic and extrinsic reinforcement a matter of timing? Striking a tin plate does give instant information that the response was on target. However, in extrinsic reinforcement, too, the teacher could give positive reinforcement immediately after the successful response. The superiority of intrinsic reinforcement does not rest in how quickly feedback follows the response. Does it rest, then, in the fact that it is more effective in cueing the correctness of a response? The sound of hitting the table instead of the tin plate does inform the child that he missed. Yet, the teacher can provide the same information in an extrinsic form—that is, through her remarks. Therefore, the two types of reinforcement are equally effective in cueing correctness after the response has been made.

Is intrinsic reinforcement more effective in telling the child how he can change his response if the response was wrong? Actually, intrinsic reinforcement is less effective on this dimension. In extrinsic reinforcement the teacher can actually tell the child which way to move his hand, how close he is to the target, and so forth. In intrinsic reinforcement (intrinsic informative feedback), the child monitors his own actions and corrects his own errors without guidance from an extrinsic source. This self-monitoring takes longer to lead to correct responding than does being told by another person. But, when the child is told how to respond correctly, he is not learning what information he should use to correct his own behavior at some later time. All he is told is what he should do now. Thus, the real advantage of intrinsic informative feedback is its source, because the child is learning what information is necessary to solve the problem.

Intrinsic reinforcement tells the child what information is useful.

Consider the (not very likely) situation in which the teacher is so effective that the child can consistently hit an inch-square plate even while he is blindfolded. If he taps two inches to the left of the plate, the teacher instructs him to move two inches to the right and try again. Might not an approximation of this reliance on external feedback occur even for the child who was never blindfolded? The child in effect becomes oblivious to the spatial relation between hand and plate. While he may be *hitting* the plate, he is not learning *how* to do it. If the external reinforcement is removed, this hypothetical child would gather no information from a miss that could have led him toward a hit on the next attempt. He has not learned what information is necessary to the solution of the problem![1]

The above example represents an extreme form of external informative feedback. Not all shaping procedures are so exact. Furthermore, as indicated by Principle 5 in our definition of behavior modification, the external reinforcement is faded out in the last phase, allowing intrinsic reinforcement to play its proper role of self-direction. But the child often doesn't make this shift to independent learning. Consequently, it would seem more advisable to use an educational procedure that seldom uses external reinforcement and thereby obviate the problem of having to fade the reinforcement out. One such procedure, called *conflict inducement,* will be discussed later in the chapter.

## The Value of Using the Child's Preferred Mode

Banging the table with a jigsaw piece represents a different response mode than placing one piece next to another. Shaping the behavior from banging to placing may mean more than a quantitative change along a single dimension of difficulty. The very young child typically approaches material in an action-based mode. Shaping the motor response into a form that is not the child's preferred mode may be but another way of creating a separation between the motor act and the gathering of information. The child may learn to place the pieces gently, but he may be completely unaware of the relation among adjacent pieces.

Relating two blocks by placing them side by side occurs during spontaneous play at a much later age than stacking two blocks, and stacking occurs much later than banging two blocks at the midline (Forman, 1973). The earliest form of relating objects is through banging, alternately slamming them together and drawing them apart and then slamming them together again. The child may well be intrigued by the simple fact that the substance of one block cannot penetrate the substance of the other and vice versa. These early banging explorations may be quite important to the discovery of the physical limits of the object and have little to do with exploration of their more qualitative attributes, such as shape and color. Research indicates that even those children who have reached the stage of placing (rather than banging) do not realize that a puzzle made of 12 identically cut pieces can be assembled as a picture. They see the puzzle only as a game of inserting pieces and not as a game of making a recognizable picture (Forman, Laughlin, & Sweeney, 1971).

If the teacher is unaware of the value of the apparently meaningless banging, she will have no compunction about shifting the child from an action mode to a placement mode. She considers banging to be no more than a convenient place to start, since it approximates the preestablished behavioral objective. Once again,

---

[1]Note: If the teacher says "Watch your hand" instead of "Move two inches to the right," she is telling the child where important information will occur, information that the child can monitor on subsequent attempts. This type of guidance is not a type of extrinsic informative feedback. Rather, it is a general suggestion that orients the child toward the information that is essential for a variety of problems, not just for the correction of a single error. While this technique can often be used effectively, we still run the risk of telling the child to do something the purpose of which he does not understand, as we saw in the case of the 4-year-old girl finger-tracing the jigsaw piece without extracting any information from that operation. The timing of these orienting comments is crucial.

since the behavioral approach seems to create a mental set to think more in terms of responses than in terms of mental operations and to think more in terms of reinforcement than in terms of information gathering, placing is not considered to be qualitatively different from banging—only more modulated and more specialized.

When we look at the child engaged in spontaneous play with the materials, we cannot but draw the conclusion that action and placement are qualitatively different stages of development (Forman, Kuschner, & Dempsey, 1975a). Placing develops only after the child has learned that an object has substance (for example, that it can be picked up or that it can be slammed into another and offer resistance) and has begun to develop the notion that the object can have position (for example, that it can be placed in the ring, on the rectangle, and so on). Placing an object requires that one point in space be identified and remain fixed while the other point (the moving object) is put near that point. The child can cope with placement only when he can think about an object as having some spatial property (position) independent of his own ongoing action. When the child places two objects, their relationship continues to exist even after the hands are removed; but, when the child bangs two blocks together, the relationship (the product) disappears as soon as the action (banging) stops. Placement is indeed qualitatively different from banging in regard to what the placement requires mentally—that is, a greater dissociation of the object from the action of the hand.

If behavior is shaped away from the preferred mode prematurely, the hands may place the objects but the child may not yet be processing the relation between the objects he has placed. The child needs to continue in his preferred mode until he completely automatizes action and then, of his own accord, begins to notice the products created by his actions.

## Learning and Development

An approach that emphasizes specific behavior can blur the distinction between learning and development. Learning is a relatively permanent change in a behavioral tendency brought about by reinforced practice (Kendler, 1963). Learning is usually discussed in terms of a time span of a few minutes or perhaps a few days (to learn something, that is). Also, learning is usually discussed within a specific context—such as, "He learned to tie his shoes." "She learned to spell her name." Development, on the other hand, refers to a broader time span. Physical, social-emotional, and cognitive developments take years, not days, and do not refer to specific content. Cognitive development is generally defined as qualitative changes in the child's approach to problems in general (Zigler, 1963). These qualitative changes do not result from having particular responses reinforced but, rather, from having particular thoughts confirmed in a hundred different ways. For example, the thought that a change in an object's position is distinct from a change in the object itself is a general concept that develops slowly. To say that the concept of the permanent object is no more than a large number of reinforced responses is to miss the fact that the concept is not dependent on any particular context for its elicitation. If the child has developed the general concept of object permanence, he will search for an object he saw hidden—whether it be under a box, a leaf, or a washcloth—even though he has never seen that particular object or that particular hiding place before. Literally, he will leave no stone unturned.

Development is defined in terms of stages, and learning is defined in terms of the number of correct responses. Of course, the stages are themselves defined by overt behavior; but the focus, once again, is on the mental operations that a group of different responses represent. Knowledge of developmental theory gives the teacher guidelines for making critical decisions about which materials to present and which response modes to encourage. Learning theory, instead, does not give the teacher a means to classify a large number of specific responses. Thus, the teacher is less likely to think about different ways to accomplish the same objective. If the objective is worded in terms of behavior, the teacher has limited himself considerably. If the objective is worded in terms of information to be acquired, his alternatives are greatly increased. Most importantly, if the teacher has knowledge of developmental theory, he is less likely to shift the child to a level of complexity that the child cannot process.

Let's consider a 3-year-old playing by himself at the sandbox. The sand is moist, and he is making little mounds by overturning a cup filled with the moldable sand. Each time he makes a mound, he smashes it and smooths it flat. The teacher watches the child's activity and decides that it would be good if the child took longer note of the product he creates. Her rationale is that attention to product is necessary if the child is to begin making more complex sand constructions. So she states her objective as "The child will be able to describe the shape of the mound he has made."

The next day, the teacher provides cups of different shapes, and the child begins his play again. The first time the child makes a mound, the teacher asks him to name its shape. The child doesn't know what to say. So the teacher asks the child if he knows what to call the cup he is holding. He knows this. "Square" he says. The teacher places the plastic cup next to the sand mound that came out of it. "Are they the same?" the teacher asks as she points to the sand mound next to the square cup. "Square" the child sings out as if he had made a discovery. Just as the teacher's smile reaches its proudest width, the child smashes the plastic cup in an attempt to smooth it flat. At an early age, action defines a word more than some static property like shape (Ervin-Tripp, 1966).

Of course, it is almost impossible not to make wrong assumptions when working with young children. The task is to find an approach to education that at least minimizes these mistakes. Had this teacher paid more attention to mental processes than to behavior and more to developmental theory than to behavior-modification techniques, she might have engaged the child quite differently. The use of conflict may be an approach that minimizes mistakes.

## Conflict Inducement in Early Childhood Education

### *An Example of Conflict Inducement*

A child facing a situation that offers two possible correct choices can be on the brink of an important step in his learning process. It is at these moments that the observant teacher can learn a great deal about the child's level of learning.

If the child expresses conflict, he indicates that he knows enough to sense the apparent contradiction, and, what is more, he is less likely to learn some rote behavior. He will want to understand why he is confused (Smedslund, 1961). If the teacher can create a situation that causes the child to think that something is not quite right, the child will want to discover the relevant information in order to reduce the conflict. In this case, reinforcement (that is, satisfaction) and informative feedback are not dislocated as in extrinsic reinforcement; rather, they are one and the same.

Here is an example of the use of conflict instead of extrinsic reinforcement to motivate learning. The teacher senses that Daniel is on the brink of discovering the relationship between the shape of an object and the nature of its movement through space. The child is rolling a toy cart with regular round wheels across the table. The teacher rolls a different toy cart, this one with elliptical wheels, near the cart Daniel is rolling. Naturally, the teacher's cart rises and falls as it is pushed forward. As children are prone to do, Daniel takes the teacher's cart and begins to push it with one hand, while pushing his own cart with the other hand. The teacher, without any words, has effectively brought to the child's attention two events that are *discrepant*. The child's curiosity is aroused. He wonders why the two carts, which are both red with black wheels and are the same size, move in such different fashions.

Only when Daniel seems to hesitate or looks perplexed does the teacher ask "What makes this one go bump-bump?" Her question only expresses the child's thoughts. Daniel may say "Wheels." This does not necessarily mean that he understands that it is the shape of the wheels that causes the jerky movement. He could as

The teacher can use conflict to provoke thought.

easily be thinking that the wheels are round but the axle is off center or that the wheels are hitting some bumps in the road or that the cart itself is bucking. "Can you make this bumpy cart go smoothly like this other one?" The question could be too difficult, of course. But, if the child, through previous experience, has learned how to assemble and disassemble the cart, he may make the connection that some of those other wheels lying around on the table could change the nature of the cart's movement.

He may first try other things, like pressing more firmly on the cart to see if he can stop the bump-bump, or rolling it backward instead of forward, or tilting it up on only the front two wheels, or trying it on the floor instead of on the table. The exciting fact remains that he is perplexed, he has a problem he wants to solve, and he is using all the information-gathering skills at his disposal to reach resolution of the conflict. He may not persist, but that doesn't matter. The incompleteness will remain with him, and he may come back to the problem later in the day and then solve it. The effective teacher will know how to create conflicts of the appropriate magnitude, conflicts that arouse curiosity without overly frustrating the child.

The use of conflict inducement is quite different in practice and effect from the use of extrinsic reinforcement. For one, the child's behavior is not being "shaped" through a gradual process of successive approximations to some behavioral objective. In behavior modification every attempt is made to present the material in such small steps as far as difficulty is concerned that confusion is at all points prevented. Behavior modification even boasts of "errorless learning" when a program is well written (Ferster & Perrott, 1968). In conflict inducement the material is presented in steps that deliberately induce confusion. And children are encouraged to make errors in their attempts to reduce the confusion.

## The Value of Errors

The importance of confusion and errors has nothing to do with building "character" or teaching the child to cope. Confusion and errors are very relevant to what is learned about the problem under investigation. Confusion is important because it is the source of curiosity and prevents arbitrary reinforcement. Unless the child is curious about some apparent paradoxical situation, the wrong idea may be reinforced. This is an example.

If the child sees one cart ride smoothly and the other cart go bump-bump, he may or may not be surprised. If he is surprised (and the teacher should turn to something else if he is not), it is because he has contrasted the two events and these contrasted events have generated an apparent contradiction—what is often called *cognitive dissonance.* The only way this dissonance will be reduced is by discovering how the two events are actually similar in spite of their apparent dissimilarity. Both events follow the rule that the shape of the wheels contributes to the movement of the cart. In one case the round wheels make the familiar cart ride smoothly; in the other case the elliptical wheels make the cart ride jerkily. The reason why the child is initially perplexed is that he *sees* the bump-bump but *expects* the smooth motion. The importance of the initial confusion rests in the fact that the child will not feel "reinforced" until the seen and the expected are brought into harmony. This can be done only by considering the relation between shape and function, not the relation between the elliptical wheels and the teacher's comment; that is, reinforcement is intrinsic, not extrinsic, to the solution of the problem. If the teacher, by using extrinsic reinforcement, shapes the child to the point that he changes the wheels, there is no guarantee that the child has discerned the relation between shape and function. He could just as easily be thinking that the new wheels make the cart heavier and therefore less bumpy.

The behaviorist can reply that the well-written program of reinforcement can provide the child with experiences that extinguish the notion that the new wheels change the cart's motion because of their weight. The behaviorist can also say that all these incorrect alternative interpretations can be extinguished without the child even having to make a wrong guess about whether an alternative is correct.[2] While this is true in principle even if not feasible in practice, what are the consequences of errorless learning?

For one, children are not learning what questions to ask of the materials; they are not learning to test their own hypotheses. They are given the question full blown —a question they may have never considered. Of course, after the child is given the question, the answer becomes obvious, and learning has been short-circuited. This is why the so-called Socratic method is not pedagogy at its best (see Bugelski, 1964). If learning is indeed discovering what information is relevant to a particular problem, then learning to learn is learning to *discover* what information is relevant to a particular problem. The Socratic method and programmed instruction share the flaw that children are not given the opportunity to generate their own questions; that is, they are not learning *how* to learn. Skinner's reply to this criticism in *The Technology of Teaching* (1968) is that thinking, or learning how to learn, can be taught as a separate lesson, using programmed instruction. In other words, if the student is being taught how to generate relevant hypotheses, this objective becomes the content of the lesson on thinking. While Skinner's point may well apply to students capable of reflecting on their own thought processes and verbal propositions, his point does not apply well to children younger than 12 or 13 (Beilin, 1969; Kamii & Derman, 1971; Ausubel, 1969). Young children learning how to learn and developing strategies of discovery are best taught inductively within the context of real-life problems.

*Provoke Questions Rather Than Ask Questions*

We must distinguish two types of guidance, both of which emphasize learning by discovery: arranging potential conflicts and asking specific questions. When Socrates asks Meno's boy "Has not the diagonal of this square divided the square into two equal parts?" the student looks at the drawing and decides. It would have

---

[2]Note that a child can make a correct guess that something is wrong. For example, it is wrong to call a hammer a screwdriver. Well-written programs frequently present questions that require the child to identify a *negative instance* of some concept (in this example, the screwdriver is a negative instance of the class "hammer"). A negative instance is not to be confused with an error. An error is a wrong guess. A negative instance is merely a nonmember of the concept under study. When presented with negative instances, the child may still make an error, but he may also correctly identify it as a negative instance. Errorless learning does not refer to a program that fails to teach the exceptions to a concept but, rather, to a program that eliminates wrong guesses.

never occurred to him, however, to ask that question. He may be able to answer the question without understanding what information it provides with regard to the total objective—in this case, the Pythagorean theorem. Similarly, one could argue that had the teacher not placed the cart with elliptical wheels near the cart with round wheels, the child would have never thought of relating shape to motion. Both Socrates and the preschool teacher are guiding their respective students. Guiding is implicit in the function of teaching. The difference in the two approaches is that presenting potential conflicts carries a safeguard against rote learning.

The child with two carts is not given a question but a conflict that he may or may not sense. If he does sense the conflict, this is tantamount to saying that he understands the question—in his own words, "Why is this so?"

On the other hand, if he is specifically asked "What makes the cart go bump-bump?" when there is no attempt to produce a conflict or when he shows no perplexity if such an attempt is made, he may be able to answer "The wheels." But, like Meno's boy, the preschooler may not see how the answer to that question relates to the total objective—in this case, the relation between shape and function. If he does not sense a conflict between the motions of the two carts, answering the question about the one cart will not necessarily be relevant to the motion of the other cart and, more importantly, to all carts in general. The child has acquired an ad hoc association. Learning becomes a list of associations rather than an integrated system of understanding. Children must be allowed to ask their own questions, so that each step in the learning process can be assimilated to each prior step.

## Does the Child Sense the Paradox?

Teachers are often good about presenting the child with a counterexample as a means of testing understanding. This is the common "yes, but" approach to teaching. Characteristically, however, if the student does not come forth immediately with a suggestion as to why some event does not occur under certain circumstances, the teacher is all too quick to direct the student's attention to something more specific about the special circumstances. The teacher may forget to consider the possibility that the child can think of no reason why the special circumstances present a problem. In other words, the child may not sense the paradox that results when in one case $X$ leads to $Y$ and in another case $X$ does not lead to $Y$. Sometimes the cart rides smoothly, and sometimes the cart just bumps! The child may think about these two events as discrete, isolated occurrences, much in the same way that sometimes mother laughs and sometimes she frowns. And young children do attribute "will" to inanimate objects, which deters them from seeking common causes to discrete events (Piaget & Garcia, 1974).

Many events are in actuality unrelated and do not require reconciliation. The adult may casually note that the sports car has great pick-up power and the sidewalk trimmer does not. The adult does not see these two, in some way similar, events as paradoxical and does not search for the reason why the lawn trimmer is so slow compared to the sports car. The child, in a similar fashion, may treat the smooth motion and the bumpy motion of his cart as unrelated events, even though these events pertain to the same object. But it is not likely that the adult would fail to be surprised by a dragging dragster or by a runaway sidewalk trimmer—variations on the same theme. Why then do some events elicit a search for a common cause and others do not?

Surprise results when the person sees one event but expects another (Charlesworth, 1969). But surprise alone is not sufficient to elicit a search for a common cause of the seen and the expected. The child may be surprised that the cart goes bump-bump, but he may readily accept this novel event as a manifestation of the capriciousness of carts. It is not until the child thinks about the bumpy action as a *transformation* of the smooth action that he seeks to find out the means by which that transformation took place (see Chapter Three). Sensing the paradox is more

$$X \text{ applied to } Z \longrightarrow Y \qquad\qquad X \text{ applied to } Z \longrightarrow Y$$
$$X \text{ applied to } Z \longrightarrow Q \qquad\qquad X \text{ applied to } Z \longrightarrow Y'$$
$$\textit{Surprise} \qquad\qquad\qquad \textit{Paradox}$$

*Figure 5-2.*

than being surprised. Figure 5-2 illustrates the difference between surprise and paradox.

In Figure 5-2, $X$ refers to the action (pulling) and $Z$ refers to the object (the cart). The first time the child pulls the cart, the cart rolls smoothly *(Y)*. The second time he pulls the cart, the cart rolls bumpily. If the child is surprised but not roused to search out why, the observed event (the cart going bump-bump) is represented by the letter $Q$. Because of past experience $Y$ was expected, but $Q$ was observed—a discrepancy that leads to surprise. If the observed event is seen instead as a transformation of the expected event—that is, the child senses a paradox—the expected event is represented by the letter $Y'$. In this case the child is likely to search for the difference in $Z$ or $X$ that resulted in $Y'$ instead of $Y$.

## Use Conflict as a Diagnostic

How do we know if we have posed questions that fail to teach meaningful concepts? Principles of behavior modification tell us to check whether a child has had the necessary prior experiences to understand the question. If she has not, the instruction itself provides those necessary experiences in the form of numerous small steps that begin with responses that are already in the child's repertoire. The confidence that the behavioristic teacher places in his structured lessons results from his often naive assumptions regarding what "necessary prior experiences" are. Understanding what keeps the butterfly aloft requires more prior experience than feeling the force of the wind and flying a kite. In the case of the butterfly, relevant prior experiences include the thousands of interactions the child has had with objects of all varieties that gradually help her develop some understanding of air as a substance capable of giving support; the butterfly is but a special case. While the structured-lesson writer, by some Herculean effort, may assure that the child has indeed acquired these earlier concepts, the effort seems most inefficient. It seems more advisable to use conflict as the diagnostic. When children experience conflict, they are telling the teacher that they have had the necessary prior experiences, whatever those experiences may have been. By using conflict as a diagnostic for where children are in their understanding, the teacher can feel more confident that the students are ready to assimilate new information (Duckworth, 1973; Piaget, 1973).

*Know Important Conflicts*

Developmental theory can guide the teacher in creating conflicts for the child. Think back to the child building mounds in the moist sand. When the teacher first observed the child making and smashing sand mounds, she could have asked herself "What information is the child gathering by doing what he's doing?" and "What does developmental theory tell me about the thoughts of this young child?" Piaget certainly discusses the importance of reversibility at all stages of development. Reversibility at age 3 takes the form of doing and undoing, moving and moving back. One thing the mound smasher is learning is that the mound that is not there can be made to be there and then reversed back into nowhere. The fact that the smash is forceful may well be incidental to the delight of discovering that what was there can be made to disappear. The child even smooths the sand as if to accentuate the change of state $A'$ back to the original state $A$.

One is reminded of how children will place a jigsaw piece into a puzzle and slide their hand over the surface of the puzzle. The disappearance of the single piece, its blending flush with the larger surface, may be the most intriguing characteristic of the puzzle. The reversibility from here to nowhere to here to nowhere is a powerful notion. The ability of the child to learn that states that are apparently discontinuous are in actuality continuous, that they are actually variations of the same thing (what Piaget calls "invariance within transformations"), is an extremely important notion throughout cognitive development.

Having considered the information that the child was pursuing, the teacher thinks how she can enhance his experience, without having him depart markedly from that general theme of reversibility. Without saying anything to him, the teacher makes a sand mound next to the sand mound the child has made. Now, when the child smashes his mound, another mound remains standing. The presence of the standing mound may serve as a reminder of the first mound now destroyed. In this fashion the teacher has brought the contrast between the two states $A$ and $A'$ into a more nearly simultaneous comparison. In doing this, the teacher has probably kept in mind the importance Piaget places on the child's thinking about both the beginning and the end of a change (see Ginsburg & Opper, 1969). The second mound comes to represent the initial stage of the first mound and thus aids the child to consider both states $A$ and $A'$ in a more nearly simultaneous fashion. The child may eventually construct two mounds before he smashes one. If he does, the whole episode has brought him somewhat closer to the general concept of reversibility.

The teacher has not shaped the child's behavior. If the thought of building the second mound before destroying the first occurs to the child, he will do so. If the thought doesn't occur, the teacher changes to something else; perhaps she adds some dry sand nearby, sand that cannot be molded. But whatever comes next, the child leads himself according to what he finds interesting. What he finds interesting is usually something that provides at least a slight violation of his expectations—for example, "I smash $A'$ to $A$, but $A'$ still remains" (the other mound nearby). He explores the situation in an attempt to resolve the conflict and discovers something new about the situation (such as, "$A'$, my mound, is not one and the same as $A'$, her mound"). For the child this episode has been a nonverbal lesson on the difference between identity (one and the same) and similarity (identical in appearance but existentially different; therefore, not one and the same)—a lesson that results from different types of reversible actions (building and destroying).

The teacher cruises through the classroom with a general objective, such as facilitating the concept of reversible changes. He does not write out behavioral objectives, because he has no idea how he will work on the objective he has in mind until he sees the child in action. His general mission is to be a troublemaker. He sees a child pouring water back and forth between two cups, and he slips a cup with no bottom into the water. He sees a child rolling a car around a track, and he slips a second car on that track but faces the car in the opposite direction. He sees a child put a circle inside a ring, and he sits quietly by and puts a ring over a circle. Our teacher has a general objective and a keen eye. He does not shape the child's behavior. He gives the child an opportunity to sense some conflict and perhaps to experience the joy of reducing the conflict by making a discovery and inventing a solution.

## Behavior Modification Supports Conflict Inducement

As we mentioned earlier in this chapter, few people would object to a deliberate use of reinforcement schedules to increase the verbal output of an autistic child or to encourage the reality contact of an extremely withdrawn child. These are heroic cases. When should behavior modification be used in more ordinary cases? There are certainly times when the child's life is ultimately improved because the teachers have been consistent in saying "That's good, Stanley" or "Thank you, Trina." The use of positive social reinforcement changes the child's behavior in ways that are beneficial to both the child and the group in which the child lives and moves.

Positive social reinforcement is necessary to assure the safety of the children, to reduce chaos during group activities, and to improve the logistics of a transition from one classroom activity to another. Positive reinforcement is indispensable as a means to improve classroom management, and classroom management is indispensable as a means to improve the quality of the individual child's day. As Charles Madsen puts it, "catch the child being good" (Madsen & Madsen, 1968). Discipline problems and aggressiveness can be reduced in a program that takes into consideration fundamental principles of behavior modification. But let's not confuse the use of behavior modification as an *expedient* to make education possible with the use of behavior modification as a *means* of constructing knowledge.

Education, as we have defined it in this text, is more than a change in behavior. Education is also an increase in consciousness of self and in consciousness of the transformations regulated by self to construct what we call "facts." While behavior modification can prepare the child to take advantage of educational opportunities, behavior modification itself is not the best means to raise the consciousness of the child. In fact, through the use of behavior modification, adults can change a child's behavior without necessarily increasing the child's understanding of the knower-known relation. Yet, a teaching staff that refuses to schedule positive reinforcements may find that the class is too unruly to encourage the kind of reflectiveness required to construct meaningful knowledge. How can we have the best of both worlds?

First of all, we need to make a distinction between two kinds of child behavior: *support actions* and *exploratory actions*. Support actions place children in a position to profit from events that happen around them and from events that they might create. Support actions prepare children for unencumbered explorations of new information. Support actions increase the match between exploration and purpose of exploration. Exploratory actions, instead, are means to gather new information. Exploratory actions should be child-directed and teacher-supported. We have no objections to a teacher's saying "How nice, Debbie! I'm pleased that you made room for Eric." These positive social reinforcers support explorations without directing them. Classroom management techniques have the same effect. They support exploratory behavior. The teacher reminds an ebullient child that he can run outside later, but not now, inside the classroom. The sanction placed on this child supports the quality of the day for the other children, just as similar sanctions placed on other children support quality for this child.

The teacher supports the child's exploratory actions.

Social reinforcement does not necessarily have to come after a child's response. The teacher can just as well reinforce behavior by telling or showing a child what to do. Whenever a teacher says, in effect, "Do it this way," the child has no difficulty understanding the implication that "If I do, the teacher will be pleased." Even though the teacher's comment comes before the child acts, the child's behavior is nevertheless shaped by virtue of an anticipated reward—the teacher's approval. This brings into question the value of giving children direct instructions, if we assume that we are involving the child in the intrinsic joys of work. Yet, it seems overly stringent to eliminate direct instruction. When, then, is direct instruction appropriate?

The decision to directly tell or demonstrate depends on the function of the activity in question. Is the activity something that will support and amplify exploration, or is the activity a means of gathering new information? Support actions help the child explore materials. These actions are what the artist calls technique, what the scientist calls method, what the English teacher calls grammar. In preschool, support actions include such things as learning how to hold a paint brush, learning how to drive a nail, learning how to cut with scissors, and learning how to steady a tower of blocks. Support actions do not include painting a straight line, building a boat, cutting out paper dolls, or building a bridge with blocks. Support activities do not limit the products of actions, nor do they limit (in any significant way, at least[3]) the explorations the child makes. In fact, these skills amplify the number and types of explorations the child can make. The child who can hold a steady brush can compare self-created lines and curves. A child who can drive a nail can compare the motion of a board nailed and pivoting in the middle with a board nailed and pivoting near an end. Montessori was aware of the importance of teaching support activities to amplify explorations (Montessori, 1967).

Exploratory action is anything that the child does to test the limits of new materials. Spencer approaches a wooden mock-up of a toaster. He jiggles a lever on the side, sticks his hand into one of the slots, and in the process discovers that the lever on the side depresses a wooden stop inside the slot. At that point he places a square of wood inside the slot and makes it go up and down by pressing and releasing the lever on the side. Through his own explorations he has discovered the connection between the lever and the wooden stop inside and then has invented a use for this relation. Had a teacher shown Spencer how to use the toaster, the child may have never fully understood the relation between the lever and the rise and fall of a wooden square.

The ability to use a mock toaster is not a support skill. By a similar logic, is learning to cut with scissors not a support skill? Are we short-circuiting exploration by showing the child how to use a pair of scissors? How far can we take this distinction between support actions and exploratory actions? Are we hampering understanding by giving the child paint rather than having him invent it through a happy accident of mixing powder and water? Recall Dewey's lament that today's chil-

---

[3]It would be naive to say that support activities do not limit explorations at all. Their very power comes from the fact that they help improve the precision of movement by eliminating certain extraneous variations, like holding the brush between the elbows. We also grant that what is extraneous depends on the overall objective.

dren, who can just flick a switch and flood the room with light, are unfortunately deprived of the family chores that involved, among other things, the whole process of illumination. The early American child followed and often participated in the whole process, from killing the animal to boiling fat and making candles. The children of today are given fully developed processes and are deprived of opportunities to even observe these processes. To compensate for this lack of participation, we take children to the town powerhouse and say "See, this is what makes your lights burn—that generator over there." What chance does a preschooler have to understand the complicated set of relations involved in getting light from a powerhouse? There will be relations that we make available to the child outright, like telling her how to hold a pair of scissors. We instruct her directly now, and at some point later in her life we have her inspect the way in which the scissor blades "break" the paper. We give the child the advantages of our technology in a full-blown form, hoping that she will learn at a later age how things work. One important objective of early education is to teach young children *how to explore* new materials and new experiences. We show children support activities that increase their means to systematically explore, but we try to minimize showing children outright what new material does.

## Summary

There is certainly disagreement among educators concerning the value of behavior modification as a teaching technique. This disagreement also exists within the field of early childhood education. As with any controversial issue, we must be certain that it is the essence of the technique that is examined and criticized and not some extraneous points that are only incidental to the essential issue.

Therefore, the question is not whether behavior modification is directive, since all educational procedures are directive to some extent. And the question is not whether behavior modification can be applied to a class of 20 students, since that is a matter of technology and resources and as such concerns problems that can plague any educational method. Also, the question is not that the technique has a cold and mechanistic nature, since that problem can be overcome by experience and training. The real question is whether a behavior-modification technique facilitates and promotes the type of learning and development desirable for young children and, if not, whether there is a more viable technique of teaching.

The establishment of a behavior-modification plan requires five steps. First, the teacher must have a clear sense of the behavioral objectives that the plan is designed to produce. Second, the entering responses of the children must be observed and in some cases measured. Third, the teacher selects an appropriate positive reinforcement, one that he assumes will increase the occurrence of the desired response. The fourth step is the actual administering of the reinforcement contingent on the desired responses. The fifth and last step is the fading out of the rewards when the desired behavior is strong enough to continue on its own.

The basic problem with the technique just described centers around the location of the reinforcement. When a child is performing actions in the environment, he receives information and reinforcement about his actions from two different sources: external and intrinsic. External reinforcement, which is typical of behavior modification, is separate from the child's actions. Intrinsic reinforcement, instead, comes from the child's own actions, which provide both information and a feeling of accomplishment because of the successful completion of the task.

Why do we believe that intrinsic reinforcement is better? To begin with, it assures that what is learned is directly related to and integrated with the self-set task. With external reinforcement there is the danger that the child will be working for the praise of the adult rather than for the information that he can derive from his activity. Second, the child is learning what information is necessary in order to solve a problem rather than what behavior is necessary in order to receive a reward. An emphasis on information gathering is quite compatible with Piaget's theory of how knowledge is constructed. A final point is that an external reinforcement procedure promotes the learning of specific facts rather than the development of underlying networks of organized knowledge.

What type of teaching technique capitalizes on the use of intrinsic reinforcement? A procedure known as conflict inducement is based upon the principle that, when children sense a conflict in their understanding of the world, they will want to resolve that conflict. The resolution will in itself be rewarding. The teacher, then, armed with knowledge of developmental dimensions, observation skills, and familiarity with materials, can move through an early childhood program looking for opportunities to promote cognitive conflict. It is very important to note that, although the teacher can try to set the stage for conflict, it is the child who has to sense the conflict. If this doesn't happen, the teacher should reflect on the encounter and revise her plan. She must be sure that her actions capitalized on the child's preferred mode of action and that her aim is to provoke questions rather than ask questions.

The fact that conflict inducement is a more viable technique for facilitating the development of young children does not mean that behavior modification has nothing to offer the teachers of young children. Behavior modification can be effectively used in order to promote those actions that allow children to freely explore materials and, more generally, their environment. For example, restlessness may get in the way of the child's experience with language-arts materials. Behavior modification may be an effective means to produce or eliminate certain behaviors that prevent the child from interacting with the materials. However, once a child's attention is focused on the materials, he must be allowed to explore the materials freely in order to ask his own questions, sense his own problems, and search for the information he deems to be essential in order to answer the questions and solve the problems.

## Suggestions for Further Reading

Evans, E. D. *Contemporary influences in early childhood education* (2nd ed.). New York: Holt, Rinehart & Winston, 1975. This thorough analysis of different approaches to early childhood education contains a chapter on behavioral-analysis procedures with sections on research and criticisms.

Kamii, C., & Derman, L. The Engelmann approach to teaching logical thinking: Findings from the administration of Piagetian tasks. In D. R. Green, M. P. Ford, & G. B. Flamer

(Eds.), *Measurement and Piaget.* New York: McGraw-Hill, 1971. This very interesting article illustrates some of the pitfalls of using a behavior-modification procedure.

Sinclair, H. Recent Piagetian research in learning studies. In M. Schwebel & J. Raph (Eds.), *Piaget in the classroom.* New York: Basic Books, 1973. Some of the basic arguments in favor of a conflict-inducement procedure are presented in this article written by a frequent collaborator of Piaget's.

# Section 4
# The Practice of Teaching

# Chapter Six

# Entering
the Child's World

In the first chapter we emphasized that very young children need individual attention, autonomy, and freedom to act directly on materials. The special nature of 2- and 3-year-old children places special requirements on how the teacher approaches them. In Chapter Five we defined meaningful learning as an active, self-regulated process and explained how the shaping of behavior may interfere with self-regulation if shaping is used in more than an attempt to orient children to a problem. The need that children have to pace themselves through a problem and regulate a series of decisions also places special requirements on how the teacher enters the child's world. It is the discovery of these special requirements that we call the *problem of entry*.[1]

## The Problem of Entry

When children are 2 and 3 years old, they cannot be easily oriented to a lesson that is not of their own choosing. But, even if a child is compliant, we should still ask ourselves whether we should begin a learning activity right away. Probably not. A period of free play with new materials is needed. In the previous chapter we distinguished the actions that support and amplify explorations from the exploratory actions themselves. We also said that lessons on support actions are sometimes taught directly as techniques—cutting with scissors, holding a paint brush, or adding water to play dough. The teacher can also directly prepare the learning environment by displaying interesting materials in a central area. Still, a period of free play before any direct teacher intervention seems essential for several reasons.

Free play assures that new learning will build on past knowledge. Recall the case of Spencer engaging in the motor ritual of spinning the ring before trying anything new. Free play gives the teacher a means to diagnose his students' interests, so that he can more effectively build on the children's past knowledge. Without free play as a guide, the teacher might unwittingly pose problems for the children that exceed their abilities to structure goals and means. Free play gives children a sense of mastery and control that is necessary for the children to be receptive to the expansions on their play suggested by the teacher. Also, children will be more receptive to

[1] G.E.F. thanks his good friend Irving E. Sigel for this most descriptive phrase.

expansions if they see a similarity between what the teacher is doing and what they themselves have already been doing. This similarity makes a child feel that the teacher is playing with him on terms set by himself. He feels that he has a playmate who understands and who will not shift the play abruptly to something that is a diversion or to something that threatens him because he doesn't understand what the teacher wants from him. Therefore, a period of free play is essential. But how do we become a contributing part of the child's world once the child has begun his explorations?

To begin with, the teacher can ask the following questions as he watches the child explore materials and engage other children. From my knowledge of child development, what dimensions of development are potential in this current situation? What are the child's interests and objectives? How can I assure that the child will be stimulated by my expansions on his play? At what point should I make a direct entry into the flow of his play? It is to these questions that the following sections address themselves in the following order: the importance of a theoretical base, the importance of close observation, imitating the child as a means of entry, and sensing the critical moment.

## The Importance of a Theoretical Base

Good ideas seldom come from close observation alone. Seeing a child perform some particular action gains significance only if that action is related to some more general dimension of development. Lisa, an 18-month-old child, sweeps the floor with a dust broom by back-and-forth strokes within the spread of the sand on the floor, instead of sweeping in one direction. Her actions clear a space in the middle of the sand but in no way remove the sand from the floor. What does her action indicate? Or, to be more specific, what general dimensions of development can be related to this observed event? Paul, a student teacher, answers "Lisa has not learned to coordinate the actions involved in sweeping." True, Lisa is not pushing the sand forward, and we could probably teach Lisa how to sweep by modeling for her the coordinated actions in parallel with her own attempts. But the problem with Paul's answer is that it doesn't get us beyond the specific task of sweeping; it doesn't give us a source of curriculum ideas that can be applied in a variety of situations. In other words, that answer states Lisa's problem too specifically.

Helena, another student teacher, gives the more general answer "Lisa has difficulty with means-ends relationships." We agree with Helena that it is apparent that Lisa approaches the sand with the intention of sweeping it over to the large pile being created by the sweeping of an older classmate. The child makes a few back-and-forth strokes, looks at her more effective classmate as he sweeps the sand forward, and repeats her futile attempts to make the sand progress toward the larger pile. She does have difficulty coordinating means and ends. Yet, is Helena's statement of the problem helpful? Does her statement generate curriculum ideas, ideas for how the teacher might intervene?

Helena, in defense of her general statement, says "You can make the goal clearer by pointing to the pile of sand. The objective of making goals clearer can be used in a variety of situations." This suggestion is a good first round at what we mean by generating curriculum ideas by applying theory to specific observations of action. But the phrase "difficulty with means-ends relationships" is somewhat too general. Almost every problem the young child (and the adult, for that matter) has might be described as a difficulty with means-ends relationships. The first grader has difficulty with means-ends relationships when he wants to find his mother in the shopping center and wanders about rather than ask for help. The college student has difficulty with means-ends relationships when she wants to pass a course and runs about looking for old test questions rather than spend that time studying. *A statement of Lisa's problem should be phrased in a manner that accounts for the kinds of problems children of her age generally have.*

A third student teacher gets the message that the statement should be general but, at the same time, specific to the age range observed. "Well, we know that very young children have difficulty inhibiting action once it is initiated. We also know that children of this age love to repeat actions for the sake of actions. Furthermore, we know that the very young child's attention is overly focused on small details and small spaces. Piaget—if I remember correctly—calls this focus *centration*. Children need to *decenter* in order to solve problems. *Inhibition* of action, *repetition* for repetition's sake, and *centration* of attention may all be involved in this sweeping example!" the student exclaims at one fell swoop.

The general principles of development contained in this last answer help us decide how to approach the child. We know that words help children gain control over actions that continue without *inhibition* (Luria & Yudovich, 1959). As Lisa sweeps forward, the teacher might say "There!" thereby emphasizing the forward motion and, in effect, inhibiting the backward sweep. (If the teacher says "Stop!" the child might stop the sweeping altogether.) The teacher says nothing when Lisa sweeps the floor in the backward direction. *Repetition* of the same action can be reduced by making the consequences of one of the actions more prominent. As Lisa sweeps forward, the teacher places a dust pan in front of the sand. The sand strikes the metal pan, and Lisa's tendency to repeat the sweep in the opposite direction is reduced. She might want to create the sound of sand striking the metal dust pan, which makes the consequences of the forward motion more notable. The dust pan also helps Lisa *decenter* from the small spot that she is clearing and focus also on the accumulation of sand on one side of her sweep.

Not only have we discovered useful ways to enter Lisa's world at this moment in time and taught her how to sweep, but we have also thought of dimensions of development that we can use with Lisa in other situations. We notice that Lisa, like all children her age, makes circular scribbles with her crayon on the paper. Once again, we think of inhibition, repetition, and centration. As Lisa makes her circles, the teacher helps her make a straight line by giving her external supports to inhibit the backward stroke that makes a circle. A miniature house is placed at one end of the paper, and a crayon is jammed through the body of a miniature car. As the child "drives" the car toward the house, the crayon etches a straight line. The car and the house help the child decenter from her routine of just filling up space with circular scribbles. Although this game is probably better played with a child closer to 3 years of age, if it is played well, at some point the child makes the shift from filling up space to making a line in one direction—a great advance in conceptual development (Forman, Kuschner, & Dempsey, 1975b). This advance is facilitated by providing supports to inhibit actions not directed toward a particular goal, in order to bring about a shift in perspective from repeating actions to causing effects and a shift in attention from centration to coordinated decentration.

Here is another example of how a knowledge of child development—rather than observation alone—is essential in constructing curriculum objectives for young children. This example is from the social world of a 5-year-old. Arnie is being treated to a hamburger at Burger King by his father. Here is the dialogue between father and child.

> *Father:* Arnie, you wait here. I'm going to get our coats.
> *Arnie:* OK, Dad. (He promptly forgets his promise and runs across the floor, nearly crashing into a waitress.)
> *Waitress:* Oh, my! No running in the dining room!
> *Father* (returning quickly, coats in hand): Arnie, I told you to sit here, not to run across the room.
> *Arnie:* I wasn't running. I was just walking fast.
> *Father:* That's interesting. What's the difference between running and walking fast? (Arnie straightens his back and is about to slide out of his chair to demonstrate the difference. His father catches him in time, before he creates another traffic problem in the dining area.)
> *Father:* No, just tell me the difference.
> *Arnie* (after thinking for a moment): Well, walking fast is what I just did, and running is different.

On the basis of our knowledge of child development, what curriculum ideas are suggested by this anecdote? Focus for the moment on language development. Arnie was asked to describe an action in words rather than demonstrate it. One of the advantages of language as a social tool is its power to describe past actions or potential actions. We have seen in Chapter Four that young children use language egocentrically; that is, they have difficulty considering the viewpoint of the listener. Arnie may have had a clear mental image of the difference between walking fast and running, but his verbal description did not account for the fact that his father did not see his "walking fast." Now shift your focus to what we said about the development of self-knowledge. Young children have difficulty reflecting on their actions per se (Piaget, 1976). One way children gain greater consciousness of themselves is by describing their own actions in words. Arnie, even granting his awareness of his father's point of view, may not have been able to put his own actions into words. A 7-year-old might have answered "When you run, you sort of jump between steps." This level of linguistic representation (use of language) is more advanced than the level indicated by Arnie's answer. Arnie referred to his own mental image, but he did not translate that mental image into conventional words; that is, he did not symbolically represent (verbally describe) his own actions.[2]

If the dialogue we have just related had taken place in the classroom, the observant and theoretically prepared teacher could have developed it into a learning encounter. As the teacher listens to the child, she thinks about egocentrism in language and the development of conscious awareness through symbolic representa-

---

[2]To say that Arnie *could not* verbally represent his own actions would be an overstatement. This conclusion could be made only with further probing, as the observant teacher does in order to develop a learning encounter.

tion. She may take the opportunity to move the child further away from egocentrism and/or to increase development of representation of actions. The teacher, in a hypothetical sequel of our example, picks up after Arnie's last remark.

> *Arnie:* Well, walking fast is what I just did, and running is different.
> *Teacher:* I didn't see what you just did. Can you tell me exactly?
> *Arnie:* I scooted my feet. That's walking, not running.

Here the teacher's objective is to develop the child's awareness of the listener's point of view (or lack of view, in this particular case). The teacher's comment helps the child decenter from his egocentric perspective. Also, Arnie's answer indicates that the child is capable of representing his actions; he just hadn't felt the need to do so.

The learning encounter may take a different turn if Arnie is unable to verbally represent his actions.

> *Teacher:* I didn't see what you just did. Can you tell me exactly?
> *Arnie:* I bumped into the lady.
> *Teacher:* Yes, but tell me exactly what is the difference between a fast walk and a run.
> *Arnie:* I don't know.
> *Teacher:* That's all right. Let's walk together. (They do.) Now let's walk fast together. (They do.) Now let's run. (They break stride and run a bit.) OK. Let's walk. (The child is still enjoying the game, and he walks.) Tell me, Arnie, how do you feel when you run?
> *Arnie:* Bouncy!
> *Teacher:* And when you walk, how do you feel?
> *Arnie:* Not so bouncy.
> *Teacher:* That's interesting. When you run you feel bouncy, and when you walk you feel not so bouncy. Fine. Let's remember that. (End of learning encounter, at least until another naturally occurring episode to which this learning encounter can be generalized.)

Because this teacher was theoretically prepared, she saw the potential in the initial exchange. She knew that reflecting on actions is important for cognitive development. According to Piaget, reflecting on actions is an essential step toward the development of logico-mathematical knowledge. At first, Arnie was thinking only about the consequences of his actions ("I bumped into the lady"). The teacher identified the child's thinking process and decided to have him reexperience both running and walking. This had two positive consequences. As the child was walking and running, he was thinking about his actions. Also, remembering these actions was not difficult, since the teacher asked Arnie to describe them immediately after he had performed them. By reinstating the referent of the words and by reducing the load on memory, the teacher helped Arnie to reflect successfully on his actions and translate them into words. The teacher made a mental note, however, that Arnie's description of walking was merely the negation of his description of running ("Not so bouncy") rather than a description of walking. But at that point the teacher felt that Arnie had reached some success, and she didn't want to overtax him by pursuing the matter further. A more explicit distinction could be the objective for some other day.

Observing Lisa sweeping and Arnie running wouldn't have given the teacher any ideas for a learning encounter if she hadn't been able to relate immediately the "raw behavior" to general dimensions of development. As the teacher watches the children in her classroom, she looks for opportunities to enter the child's world through learning encounters that make use of the developmental concepts that are potential in the situation. The name of the dimension—decentration, representational competence, means-end coordination—is not important. What is important is that each be understood as part of a continuum of development, not as some once-in-a-lifetime problem. To see, for example, egocentrism as "a stage which the child will pass through" is to see it as a deficit that time will "cure" in its own way. If this were true for all developmental dimensions, the teacher's role would be reduced to that of a benevolent custodian. But these dimensions of development are just that—dimensions along which the child progresses with the aid of teachers and parents. In order to make use of developmental theory in early childhood education, we must know not only what stages occur in what order but also what methods are most effective in bringing about that development. These methods were discussed in Chapter Five and will be discussed again later in this chapter.

## The Importance of Close Observation

If one accepts the charge that education of the very young must be an individual, self-regulated affair, then one is faced with the challenge of having to know the child well enough to enter the flow of his own explorations. This means that the teacher of 2- and 3-year-olds will spend much of his time watching the children and doing nothing that can be properly called instruction for several minutes on end. It is not unreasonable for a teacher to sit near the water table for 10 or 15 minutes without any direct interaction with the group of children there. What he is doing is observing the three or four children nearby, looking for purposive behavior. When he observes it, he then spends a few more moments formulating an expansion of the children's play. But even when this has been done, the teacher still has to wait for the right moment to enter the play.

Skillful observation must be learned. The teacher's eyes are guided by questions such as: What most attracts the child's attention? What action schemes is the child repeating? What variations is he introducing in these schemes? What determines the variations? Have I seen this child do similar things with different materials? What consequences is the child producing with his actions? What does the child say as he explores? Is his language directed to an audience? What class of objects or events does this child describe in words? How does he cope with momentary distractions? Does he integrate the actions of others in his own play? These are some of the many questions that make the teacher's observations purposive. Their answers, of course, require close analytic observation.

Close observation is no less important when working with 4- and 5-year-olds. While the problem of entry may not be as great with older children, close observation is still necessary to understand the older child's patterns of thought. Once a learning encounter begins, the teacher must closely listen to the wording of a child's questions and analyze the strategies the child uses to solve a problem. Through their

Close observation is necessary for effective teaching.

"errors" children tell us what they know. Consider some of these questions quoted in Isaacs (1930, pp. 318–319).

| Age | Question |
|---|---|
| 3;6 | It [exit of a tunnel at a distance] looks very weeny. Why does it? |
| 3;7 | Why do ponies not grow big like other horses? |
| 3;7 | Why can I put my hand through water and not through soap? |
| 4;1 | Why is there no shadow when there is no light? |
| 4;3 | Why can't we see the stars in the daytime? |
| 4;5 | Why am I not in two all the way up? |
| 4;5 | Why does the glass look different in the water, but it doesn't if you just put water in the glass? The water can't really bend the glass, can it?* |

A teacher who regards these questions as simple manifestations of children's amusing curiosity is not listening closely. Each question is asked because some

*From *Intellectual Growth in Young Children, with an Appendix on Children's "Why" Questions by Nathan Isaacs*, by Susan Isaacs. Copyright 1930 by Routledge & Kegan Paul Ltd. Reprinted by permission of Routledge & Kegan Paul Ltd. and Schocken Books, Inc.

expectation held by the child has been violated, because something unexpected has been observed. Each question contains an assumption about the world held by the child. The teacher should listen beyond the question and hear the implicit assumption. Hearing the implicit assumption gives the teacher ideas for learning encounters.

Listen closely to these questions. We will rewrite them and include, for each of them, what might be the child's implicit assumption. We emphasize that these are only suggestions. Further probing by the teacher would be necessary to decide for sure why the child asked the question, and thus be in a better position to formulate a learning encounter.

We will label the general set of events with the letter $A$. We will label the child's expectation about these $A$ events with the letter $B$; that is, $A$ is the general set *horses*, and $B$ is the assumption *grow to be big*. The expectation can be expressed as: when $A$ is present, $B$ is present. However, the child sees a particular object or event $X$, which he identifies as an $A$; but the expected $B$ does not occur. For example, the object $X$ *(the pony)* is a member of the set $A$ *(horses)*, but $B$ *(grow to be big)* does not follow. The absence of $B$ is expressed as $\bar{B}$. The observed fact of $A$ followed by $\bar{B}$ violates the child's expectation of $A$ followed by $B$ ($AB$ versus $A\bar{B}$). We are maintaining that it is the conflict between $AB$ and $A\bar{B}$ that causes the child to ask a question. Now, let's take a few of the questions cited in Isaacs (1930) and rewrite them according to this formula.

This hole *(X)* is a tunnel exit for trains *(A)*.
Tunnel exits for trains *(A)* are big *(AB)*.
However, this tunnel exit is not big *(A$\bar{B}$)*. Why? *(AB* versus *A$\bar{B}$)*

This pony *(X)* is a horse *(A)*.
Horses *(A)* grow to be big *(AB)*.
This horse has not grown to be big *(A$\bar{B}$)*. Why? *(AB* versus *A$\bar{B}$)*

This bar of soap *(X)* is like water in many ways *(A)*.
One thing about water *(A)* is that you can put your hand through it *(AB)*.
This thing like water *(A)* does not allow me to put my hand through it *(A$\bar{B}$)*.
    Why? *(AB* versus *A$\bar{B}$)*

This shadow *(X)* is an object *(A)*.
Objects *(A)* can be seen when there is light *(AB)*.
This object *(A)* cannot be seen even when there is light *(A$\bar{B}$)*. Why? *(AB* versus
    *A$\bar{B}$)*

And so forth. The reader is encouraged to try a hand at translating the remaining questions into the $AB$-versus-$A\bar{B}$ conflict. Remember, $AB$ is the expected relationship, and $A\bar{B}$ is the observed relationship. When the *observed* conflicts with the *expected*, the child is provoked to ask a question. If the teacher can decipher the nature of this conflict and discover the child's assumptions that led him or her to ask the question in the first place, the teacher has a good guide for an on-the-spot learning encounter.

Take the last question analyzed above. It is possible that the child thinks that shadows are tangible objects, like other permanent objects. The teacher thinks of this possibility by reasoning backwards from the child's question "Why is there no shadow when there is no light?" The teacher asks himself "Why should there be a shadow when there is no light?" He pursues this line of thought and comes up with the possibility that the child may see a contradiction between permanent objects and impermanent shadows. He then begins a learning encounter, first with the objective of getting to the source of the child's question and then with the objective of helping the child work through the conflict between her expectation and what she observed. The teacher asks "That's true. Shadows are not there without a bright light. Why do you think that happens?" The child answers "I don't know. Maybe they are frightened away by the dark." It is becoming a little clearer now that the child thinks of shadows in the same way in which she thinks of physical objects—in fact, animate objects. Or, at least, the child doesn't know enough about the intangible quality of shadows to explain their absence in any way other than metaphorically.

The teacher, with a little more confidence in the source of the child's question, begins to work on the $AB$-versus-$A\bar{B}$ conflict. "Well, let's see. I'll turn the light back on. Here is the doll and here is the shadow. Now I'll turn the light off. What can you see?" The child answers "I can see the doll, but not the shadow." The teacher gets a flashlight. "Let's try it with this flashlight. Take it and shine it on the doll. What do you see?" The child says "The doll and the shadow." The teacher then asks "What happens when you move around the table with the light still shining on the doll?" This learning encounter continues through various steps of guided discovery. Eventually, with sufficient persistence, the child may discover that the shadow *is* the absence of light, or, as one 6-year-old put it, "The shadow is where the light cannot shine."

The course of this interesting and beneficial learning encounter was guided by the observant teacher's close analysis of the child's original question. Close observation and analysis of the child's behavior are essential to meet the challenge of individualizing the learning encounter. Of course, this highly verbal mode of teacher-child interaction is not appropriate for the 2- and 3-year-olds. In the next section we will discuss a means by which the teacher may enter young children's flow of behavior without turning them off with too many questions.

## Imitating the Child as a Means of Entry

Imitation is one of the basic ways in which children of all ages learn. The child's capacity to imitate begins to become apparent in infancy, when one infant's crying can stimulate another infant to cry. This capacity increases over time; at 2 or 3 months of age the child imitates acts that he has at some previous time already performed himself, and at 12 to 14 months the child will imitate acts completely new to him that he sees performed either by another person or by an object (Piaget, 1951). The amount of information children pick up just by watching increases further as they grow older. By 3 or 4 years of age the child observes another child receiving different types of positive reinforcement and decides which of the other child's actions will lead himself to the same positive consequences (Peed & Forehand, 1973). And, what is most important to our discussion, when an adult imitates a preschool child, the child, in turn, is stimulated to imitate the adult by increasing his output in the task at hand (Miller & Morris, 1974). This means that, by imitating the child, the teacher can enter the flow of the child's behavior and gradually shift the direction of the child's imitative pattern, so that the child begins to imitate the teacher.

By first imitating the child, the teacher can introduce new challenges into the child's play.

The objective of imitating the child is to lead the child beyond her current knowledge. The teacher imitates what the child is doing; the child imitates the teacher's imitation of her; and then the child continues to imitate the teacher when the teacher presents novel variations on the theme of play. This is an example. The teacher imitates a 2-year-old girl threading plastic spools on a string. The girl notices the teacher and continues to string spools. The teacher dangles his string by the end that is not knotted, and the spools stay on the string. The child tries to do the same, but she holds the knotted end, and the spools fall off. This signals the beginning of the learning encounter to discover why the spools fell off the string. If, instead, the child imitates the teacher exactly—and therefore the spools stay on the string—the teacher inverts the string so that the spools fall off. The child sees this, and a learning encounter begins to discover the different effects of holding the string in one or the other way.

Imitating the child is not difficult. It is easy for the teacher to cause the child to transform a shove into a gentle push, a throw into a toss, a bang into a tap, or a splash into a pat. These are all instances of *modulating the child's own actions,* a technique that is most effective when the teacher uses the same object the child is using. But imitating the child and then leading him beyond his current knowledge is much more difficult, partly because the teacher's expansion on the child's play cannot be too far beyond the child's own approach to materials. Here we are dealing with expanding the child's play by *shifting the product of the child's actions*—transforming a circle into a square, a stack of blocks into a bridge of blocks, or the phoneme *t* into the phoneme *p*. The younger the preschool child, the more probable that he will be attentive to the action itself (Forman, Kuschner, & Dempsey, 1975b).

Since children can imitate best those components of the world to which they are particularly sensitive (Uzgiris, 1972), it stands to reason that with the 2-year-old modulation of action will be more effective than modulation of product. Of course, the teacher, by modulating the child's actions, can lead him to discover new products; this occurs automatically, for example, when a circular movement of the crayon is changed to a back-and-forth movement, which results in a new product—straight lines.

Action has a force, a direction, a content, a product, and sometimes a target. The change from the action of slapping to the action of patting is a change in force but not a change in direction, content, or product (albeit the product does change in intensity). The direction remains downward, the content, which is the hand that meets the water, remains the same, and so does the product—the splash of water upon impact. Instead of changing the force, one could change the target of the child's action; for example, a slap at the water can become a slap at the bed of sand. The force is (more or less) the same, the content is still the hand itself, and the product's change is related to the change in target. A change in target is generally easier to accomplish than a change in force. This change from slapping the water to slapping the sand requires very little inhibition of the ongoing behavior—only a slight shift to the right or to the left. A change in content is more difficult than either a change in target or a change in force. Let's say that in order to expand the action, as the child slaps the water with his hand, the teacher slaps the water with a spoon. Again, the effects are different, but here, too, that is related to the change in content. If the child tries to imitate the teacher, he must grasp the spoon before he slaps the water; that is, he must inhibit slapping while he is in the process of grasping the spoon. This, as we indicated above, may be more difficult to accomplish.

Finally, the teacher may make an attempt to change the product directly. The content—in this case, the child's hand—remains the same. For a while the teacher imitates his slapping the water, and then she begins to make waves instead of splashes. She knows that making waves requires a change in both the direction and the force of the child's original action, but she hopes that the child's interest in this new product will cause him to construct for himself the necessary changes in force and direction. He does, and it is no small miracle. The actions used to produce a wave are complexly different from those used to produce a splash. This becomes quite obvious when we watch a 1-year-old trying to make waves in the water by a glancing splashing action. He must grope in order to structure the means that will result in this new product.

A teacher more attentive to the products of actions than to the actions themselves may expand the child's play beyond the child's ability to imitate. Let's take a case that can be considered typical of a 3-year-old child. Fern is looking intently at a spider web clearly defined by the morning dew. "What is it, teacher?" The teacher answers "That is a spider web, Fern." Later Fern is drawing with a white crayon on blue paper. After making several circles with her crayon, she pauses for a moment and then says "See, teacher, a spider web." The teacher takes a white crayon and a piece of blue paper and begins to imitate Fern's web. After a few marks, the teacher makes a perfect web with straight lines radiating out from a hub, itself circled by concentric spans of thread. Fern sees the teacher's web and acknowledges that this one looks very much like the one they both saw earlier in the garden. However, the teacher's changes are too great for Fern to handle. All the child can do is to draw a few straight lines on top of a host of circles. The teacher's expansion on Fern's web was too complex, because the teacher was overly attentive to the product of action. Another tactic could have been more successful.

The teacher imitates Fern's scribbles. Then the teacher says "I want to attach my web to these two twigs. So now I draw these four threads all the way to the twigs. See? Now my web can hang on the twigs." The budding artist stops and inspects the teacher's web. Then, imitating the teacher, she adds four threads to her own web. One could say that not only has Fern learned something about representing a spider web but she has also learned the function of different parts of the web. By relating the parts of a web to their respective functions, Fern will have a better chance to remember these parts. The total product of the web design was not seen as important as keeping the actions of the expansion simple. Another plus for this learning encounter was the teacher's use of the function of objects to determine their shape and position.

When the teacher begins to imitate the child, something interesting happens. The teacher, perhaps for the first time, begins to feel what it is like to be a child again. Imitating the child is an excellent way to gain insight into the child's intentions, style, and problems. As the teacher begins to make the same moves—and, consequently, the same mistakes—as the child, the actual movements influence her thinking. The teacher not only imitates the child but begins to reflect on her own movements. The child's use of repetition, his difficulty with simple motor coordinations, his lack of foresight, his attention to action, and his sensation of movement while watching—all make a greater impact on the teacher when she is imitating the child.

In a graduate course one of us (G.E.F.) had students watch videotapes of 2- and 3-year-old children playing with geometric blocks. As the graduate student watched the child, he or she mimicked "exactly" what the child was doing. These imitative movements of the graduate student were themselves being videotaped. Then both the tape of the 2-year-old and the tape of the graduate student doing the "same thing" were played back simultaneously on two monitors side by side. The difference between the fine motor coordination and subtle adjustments of the adult and the lack of anticipation and absence of adjustments in the child was fantastically revealing. The adult employs all sorts of concepts about balance, symmetry, continuity, and other components of premeditation that the 2-year-old does not possess. These "anachronisms" exist even when the adult is deliberately trying to behave like the young child. Through their efforts to physically imitate children's actions, teachers can improve their understanding of the minds of young children.

Will the child become dependent on the teacher if the teacher continually expects the child to imitate his expansions on the child's play? Yes and no. Let's take the no answer first. As the child grows older, the teacher develops many more methods of stimulating the child's thinking. Sometimes the teacher asks the child a question outright; for example, Fern's teacher might ask "What could we add to the web so that it hangs from these twigs?" Or, if the child is a 5-year-old, the teacher might ask "Where do you think the web's thread comes from?" These are expansions on the child's initial interest in spider webs.

Now let's take the yes answer—that the child will become more dependent on the teacher. But is that a cardinal sin of preschool teaching? All we mean here is that the child will learn to look at the teacher as a source of information. That is not the same as looking at the teacher as a source of answers. The information provided by the teacher could be in the form of a challenge. Every challenge contains a certain amount of information, and often children need that certain amount in order to be provoked into their own, self-directed problem solving. This is particularly true in the case of very young children, for whom everything is new and who tend to be easily distracted away from a task. The teacher's expansions of the child's play help the child build a set of understandings around a common theme instead of seeing them as isolated, episodic facts. Children look at the teacher as someone who can help them see the world in new and varied perspectives and help them gain control, either physically or representationally, of these perspectives and variations. Children look to the teacher for interesting challenges, without depending on the teacher for answers. The ultimate objective for any teacher, however, is to have the children develop to the point of creating their own interesting challenges instead of just responding to the challenges that are met accidentally and then solved by trial and error. The "educated" child is one who can deliberately construct the challenge of a particular task, one who can transform a vague problem into a challenge that is so well conceived that its solution can be systematically discovered.

## Sensing the Critical Moment to Enter

When should the teacher enter, or not enter, the child's world with a challenge? This decision is based so much on the particular child and the particular situation that we feel very hesitant about making general comments that might apply to a range of children and situations. On the other hand, if we don't make these comments, how can we speak of a theory of curriculum and method? So, at the risk of being simplistic, we do offer a few suggestions, with the reminder for the reader that, in the final analysis, clinical judgment and intuition make the difference between success and failure.

Perhaps one time not to intervene is when a 2- or 2½-year-old has just discovered a new scheme of action. Let the child go through several repetitions of the new scheme. Let her consolidate the new scheme until it becomes fluid and deliberate. By this time, you will have had a chance to both imitate the child and decipher the child's objective. Sometime just after the child has completed one of her repetitions, you can initiate your expansion of the scheme. The child may or may not follow suit. This is the child's prerogative and should be honored.[3]

The action schemes of the 3- and 3½-year-old are not as repetitive as those of the 2-year-old. The play of the 3- and 3½-year-old often contains a long series of nested actions, actions that are themselves different but that relate to a common goal. A 3½-year-old making a train with a row of small chairs is not repeating a

---

[3]We are not suggesting that the teacher never initiates actions. Some children are not spontaneously exploratory. For an excellent treatment of such cases see Blank (1973).

single action scheme as a 2-year-old does when he keeps turning the derrick on a toy truck. The teacher watches the child add the chairs to make the train and anticipates that, when the child has added the last chair, she will begin to role-play the part of the engineer. Just as the child adds her last chair, the teacher says "Let me on your train, please. I must get to my grandmother's." The little girl nods permission. The teacher says "I would like to sit in the back of the train, please. I like to look out the back window." The teacher remembers that this little girl likes to sit in the back of the school bus for that very reason. The teacher waits for the girl to direct him to the back of the train. "Sit there" she says, pointing to the back chair. The teacher pauses. "OK, but how do you know that this is the back of the train?" he asks. Amazed that it isn't obvious, the child answers "Can't you see the train is going that way?" and points toward the first chair in the row. The teacher sits and then waits a while for the child to create a new theme. After some choo-choos and chug-chugs, the train gets underway, and the teacher and the child share pretend sights as the train passes the countryside.

This teacher has effectively created a challenge, the challenge to decenter from the personal perspective. By asking "How do you know that this is the back of the train?" he has confronted the child with the reminder that other people may not see things that are obvious to the child. His request to sit in the back of the train has confronted the child with a challenge to think about the structure of the train in relation to its pretended direction of movement. With an older child, the lesson could have focused on why seats in a train usually face forward or what kind of cars the train needs in the front and in the rear. The critical moment of initial entry was when the child had completed one of the phases of her play and was about to begin another. After successful entry, the teacher waits a few moments for the child to reestablish her own momentum of play. They then share pretend sights. This pretense stimulates the child's imagination and improves her understanding that language can be used to refer to the nonpresent.[4] All of these objectives are deliberately and carefully constructed by the teacher.

Great moments for teacher's intervention occur when a child engaged in purposive behavior is ready to expand his scheme of action. These are the moments we described in Chapter Five when we discussed conflict inducement. Anticipating the child's goal, the teacher slips in an obstacle. The obstacle creates a mild degree of conflict, sufficient to cause the child to generalize his scheme and to accommodate to the requirements of the situation as changed by the teacher. The critical moment occurs immediately before the child activates the initial components of an action scheme. The teacher changes the environment at this time, and the child repeats the action scheme only to discover that what he expected to happen does not happen; as a result, the contradiction between $AB$ and $A\bar{B}$ provokes thinking.

Just before the child pieces together a jigsaw puzzle for the second time, the teacher rotates the form board 180 degrees. Just before the child begins to build with blocks on the table, the teacher shims up two of the table legs, creating a slanted surface. Just before the child reaches for the ball to roll it down a small incline, the teacher hands the child a cube. Just before the child repeats her bouncing on a foam rubber mat, the teacher replaces the mat with a peat-moss cushion.

---

[4]This pretense is an example of what Sigel (1972) calls *distancing*.

The contrast between the expected $AB$ and the observed $A\bar{B}$ is likely to generate exploration.

It is not enough just to have the child remove the obstacle or change the environment back to what it was before. If the teacher rotates the form board 180 degrees, the child may simply rotate it back to its original position. This is the child's prerogative, and it is fine; but the teacher can still encourage the child to reflect on his own actions. The child has, in fact, *negated* the teacher's change. The teacher asks "What did you do?" The child says "Turned it back." Although this situation has not developed into a learning encounter of any duration, the teacher has elicited some reflection on action-as-a-reversal—an important theme of cognitive development. It might be helpful at this point to see how the several suggestions made so far can be put to use in an exemplary learning encounter of greater duration. Such an encounter is discussed in the following section.

## An Exemplary Learning Encounter Using Sand Play

Eric is building a mound of sand. The sand is moist enough to hold the shape the child creates. Shortly after building the mound, Eric smashes it flat with his hand, smooths it out, and begins to build the mound again.

### Comment

As we indicated earlier when we discussed a similar situation, the child here is learning, among other things, that what can be created can be destroyed and, most importantly, can also be recreated. By his own actions Eric has taken a flat bed of sand (state $A$), transformed it into a mound of sand (state $A'$), and then reversed that mound back into its original state (state $A$). The cycle repeats itself, perhaps identical to the first, perhaps with some variation.

It is quite likely that the child is amazed that the mound can be reversed into "nothingness." Now the mound is here, now it is not. When the mound is gone, it can be made to reappear. The young child treats these transformations with the same interest an older child shows as he watches a magician pull a rabbit from thin air. The fact that the transformations are produced by his own hands helps the child understand all the intermediate steps between no mound, mound, and no mound again. Knowing how the mound was created is an important experience for Eric, because it eventually helps him understand that shape can be changed by redistributing small parts. The grains of sand are the same, but their distribution has changed. Eric learns that the flat bed and the mound are the same sand, because he can level the mound to its original state of flat bed.

### Entry

The teacher observes Eric engaged in his cycle of building and leveling mounds of sand and recognizes the situation as an opportunity to enter the child's world. She is cautious not to interfere with the child's self-set goal. She approaches the sand table, careful not to violate the child's personal space. She begins to make sand mounds near enough to Eric for him to see, but not so close that he feels he is about to be pressured into an interaction with the adult. The teacher proceeds to build mounds, without offering any comment. Periodically Eric glances over to see what the teacher is doing. After all, teachers often have interesting ideas, and this teacher is gentle and unobtrusive.

After making several mounds, the teacher begins to evolve a new approach. Instead of smashing the mound down, she places her hand on the top of the mound and presses firmly and steadily, holding her head to the side in exaggerated inspection of the mound while the mound is *in the process* of changing shape. Again, she does this without making any comment, without encouraging the child to do the same. If Eric sees anything interesting in what the teacher is doing, he will choose to do so himself. If he doesn't see anything interesting in what the teacher is doing, he should not be asked to imitate her by rote. The teacher recognizes the importance of the child's need to ask *his own* questions. Only if children ask their own questions about the physical world can we be relatively certain that the results of their actions will be related to their existing understanding (Duckworth, 1973). If the teacher is the one who always asks the questions and directs the course of action, the results of the action may not bear any relation to the knowledge the child currently possesses. Eric's interest in this new approach to the sand is the teacher's cue that he is ready to learn from the experience.

The teacher unobtrusively introduces a new way to dig in the sand.

Suppose that Eric does modify his smash to make it more like the teacher's firm and steady press. Then the teacher can feel free to make a specific comment about the action at hand. She may say "The sand is getting flatter," for example. The best time to say this is when teacher and child are pressing at the same time. But, while making her comment, the teacher looks at her own flattening mound. If the remark is clearly directed at Eric, he is quite likely to shift his focus from the action he is performing to the words of the adult (see Montessori, 1967, pp. 112–119).

The teacher focused her comments on the transformation of the sand rather than on the child. If she had said instead "Look how flat you are making it," Eric could have interpreted the remark as an indication that he had done something wrong (something like "Look how you ruined it") and felt quite apprehensive about it. By doing the action herself and by addressing her comments to her own actions, the teacher is less likely to threaten the child. The fact that her comment comes at a time when she and the child are doing the same thing facilitates the development of cause-and-effect relations in the child's thinking. He hears the teacher's words while he is acting and, quite naturally, makes the association between his action and the effect that is being simultaneously described, seen, and felt. The focus is always on the interesting consequences. The child himself is not being praised (Hawkins, 1974). His reward comes automatically from sensing that he is the agent of change: he made the interesting event occur.

If the teacher makes comments such as "That's good," all sorts of problems arise. First, the child has not been given a vocabulary that he can use later when he tries to solve other problems. The "that's good" comment does not help him identify the nature of the change he is producing; it does not facilitate the generalization of this knowledge to other situations in which things can be made flatter. Second, the "that's good" comment, despite its good intentions, takes the child's attention away from the physical consequence of his action and redirects it to himself as a person being evaluated. It makes no difference that he is receiving positive evaluation. The point is that he is being evaluated. The comment "That's good" throws the child into thinking about things that are good and things that are bad. Consequently, he will want to flatten the sand mound not because the change of shape is interesting but because he has learned in an instant that this is a way to have the teacher reaffirm that she likes him.

The comment "The sand is getting flatter" keeps the focus instead on the transformation. The child's improved self-concept will come automatically from his realization that he can effectuate interesting changes. The improved rapport with the teacher will also come naturally, because she has done nothing to make the child anxious and has very cleverly given him something interesting to play around with.

What was the teacher's purpose in modifying the smash into a gradual press? While the smash obviously satisfies Eric's need for a quick result, it changes the sand from state $A'$ back to state $A$ too fast. The child is more likely to understand that the process of leveling is actually the reverse of the process of building if he slows down the act of leveling. To the degree that building and leveling are performed at about the same speed but in different directions, the child is more apt to see state $A'$ as a potential state $A$ and vice versa. Thinking about state $A$ when seeing state $A'$

requires a small amount of reflection. If the child is busily smashing, he doesn't give himself enough time to reflect on the future state of the sand. The more modulated method of leveling the mound helps the child *bring into consciousness* not just the action when it occurs but, equally important, the consequence that has yet to happen. It is only by a consideration of the action and of its future effect that the end states *A* and *A'* are eventually seen as the opposite ends of a continuum and not just as two disjunctive states.

*Variations*

Variations can be introduced for the 3- and 4-year-olds, depending on what activities these age groups find interesting. Compared to the 2-year-olds, the 3- and 4-year-olds are more likely to be engaged in constructing several mounds than in simply building and destroying a single mound. This increased complexity indicates an increase in the ability to think about several, discrete objects at once. The child is doing more than changing the state of a single object. He begins to consider the size, shape, and position of several objects. The teacher should discover ways to facilitate the generalization of the child's knowledge to several objects simultaneously.

Suppose that the teacher observes Hillary making two sand piles side by side and then driving a toy car through the gap between the two piles. The car barely passes through the gap. The teacher plays in parallel with the child for a while, and then he sees an opportunity to enter the child's game. He tries to drive a large truck through the gap. But the mounds are too close together. "I would like to get this truck to the other side," he says and waits for the child's response. If Hillary waves the teacher away, he plays in parallel with the child again. She may look carefully at the size of the truck but continue her own play with the small car. If, instead, she seems to acknowledge the problem posed by the teacher, he may ask "What can you do to help me get this truck through these mountains?" With this question the teacher is asking the child to make a judgment regarding the size of the truck and the size of the gap. Furthermore, the child has been implicitly asked to change something about the sand in order to accommodate the new object, the truck.

The interested child can respond in several ways. She may crash the truck through the sand, she may burrow out more space between the mounds, she may detour the truck around the mounds, or she may lift one of the mounds entirely and displace it to create a wider space. The problem posed by the teacher causes the child to think about the relation between two objects and how to change that relation to meet the demands of a particular situation.

The space between the two mounds may have been made without much reflection. It just so happened that the toy car would neatly fit through. The teacher's request asks the child to reflect on that space. The child can give deliberate thought to a relation by thinking about what the present conditions could be rather than what they are at the moment. Thinking about changing the distance between the two mounds is the same thing as thinking about distance as a relation, as a continuum of movement. If all the objects in the world were the same length, we would have no need for measures of length. Thinking about variation carries with it a bringing into consciousness of the dimension of length itself (Piaget, 1976).

# Summary

This chapter poses a series of questions that the teacher can consider before beginning a learning encounter with a child. What are the special problems of entry into this child's world? What theoretical principles are relevant to the behavior I am observing? What details about the child's behavior am I noticing? How can I influence the child to go beyond his current knowledge? When is the proper moment to intervene?

Since the 2- and 3-year-old child is by nature self-directive, a period of free play with materials is essential to ensure continuity between new learning and existing knowledge. Free play also makes the child more receptive to new ideas from a teacher in parallel play nearby. Free play gives the teacher more thinking time and a better indication of the child's natural inclinations and approaches.

To develop good curricula, watching children is not enough. The raw observations need to be translated into theoretical statements that are neither so general that they lead to no concrete suggestions nor so specific that they lead to no hints for generalization to other content areas. To say that Lisa's problem with sweeping is an inability to relate means with ends is too general; to say that Lisa has not learned to sweep is too specific. Cognitive concepts like inhibition, decentration, and language representation—which are general yet specific to an age range—help teachers create useful learning encounters for young children.

A teacher must often spend 10 to 15 minutes observing a small group of children at work before he gets an idea about how to enter the flow of the children's work. A hasty entry could destroy the momentum that the children have established or divert the children from an objective. Close observation reduces the probability of creating diversions. When accompanied by sensitivity to the implicit assumptions behind a child's questions and approach to a task, close observation can greatly help a teacher facilitate the child's quest. Observation can be improved if teachers ask themselves these questions:

> What most attracts the child's attention?
> What action patterns is the child repeating?
> What variations is the child introducing in these patterns?
> What determines these variations?
> Has the child done similar things with different materials?
> What consequences is the child producing? Is the child aware of these consequences?
> What is the child saying while he works? Is the child aware of an audience as he talks? Does he assume that he is listened to?
> What class of objects or events does the child describe most often?
> How does the child cope with momentary distractions?
> Does the child integrate the actions of others into his own play?
> Does the child reflect on his own actions? If so, by looking or by verbal description?

These questions actually help the teacher see more and look at child behavior with greater purpose and organization.

Imitation is one of the essential ways in which very young children learn. By first imitating the child's free-play explorations, the teacher can shift the direction of imitation, causing the child to observe and imitate him, the teacher. In the process of imitating the child, the teacher often discovers the purpose of the child's actions. One should not be overly concerned about the possibility of the child imitating the teacher blindly. The child will choose either not to imitate the adult or to imitate those parts of the teacher's modeling that he can understand. The model provided by the teacher serves as a sort of end point toward which the child strives. As the child approaches a task with a modeled objective in mind, he goes through a great deal of trial and error. The teacher becomes a source of challenge and a model for systematic exploration. The skilled teacher refrains from the kind of modeling that prevents the development of problem-solving skills in the child.

At some point the teacher makes a definite attempt to provoke thought in the young child. Sensing the correct moment to make this provocation is a delicate matter. Just after the child has discovered a new scheme or a new variation on a scheme is not a good time for a challenge. A much better time is just before the third or fourth repetition of a scheme. Pauses in play, just before the child shifts away from one theme of play into a new one, is another time likely to yield good effects. Under some circumstances, the teacher can change the environment at the very beginning of the child's approach, thereby creating a surprise effect that will heighten the child's interest and lead to renewed and varied explorations. With 4- and 5-year-olds, the teacher listens closely to the child's questions and notices the child's pauses. The observant teacher can often time his or her intervention so exactly as to ask the very question that the child is pondering but that he cannot quite articulate. Good teaching is a matter of close observation, breadth of theory, good entry techniques, and sensitive timing.

## Suggestions for Further Reading

Carew, J. V., Chan, I., & Halfar, C. *Observing intelligence in young children: Eight case studies.* Englewood Cliffs, N.J.: Prentice-Hall, 1976. A very interesting description of how the close observation and analysis of children's behavior and interactions with the environment provide crucial information concerning children's development.

Hawkins, F. P. *The logic of action: Young children at work.* New York: Pantheon, 1974. Many interesting examples of how a teacher enters the world of children's play are reported in this book based on the journal of a teacher of young children.

Rowen, B. *The children we see: An observational approach to child study.* New York: Holt, Rinehart & Winston, 1973. A good, comprehensive source of information concerning theory and techniques of child observation.

# Chapter Seven

# Expanding and Generalizing the Learning Encounter

Because of the child's nature, learning encounters will be more episodic with 2- and 3-year-olds than with older children. However, the fact that any one learning encounter may be short-lived is no reason why the child's total classroom experience should consist of bits of scattered and disjunctive events. The teacher has the means to establish some continuity between different encounters and to relate learning encounters that take place a few hours or a few days apart. The distinction we are trying to draw here is between episodic learning and disjunctive learning. Episodic learning does not need to be disjunctive and unrelated to a broader base of experience. This chapter discusses means for expanding the learning encounter in progress and generalizing the gains of that encounter to future ones.

## Expanding the Learning Encounter in Progress

### Thinking while Teaching

In order to be able to increase the duration of a learning encounter, the teacher must have an objective in mind. Only by defining an objective can the teacher outline the procedures needed to meet that objective. In addition, having objectives in mind gives the teacher reasons for *not* doing, as well as doing, certain things. For example, if the objective is to develop the child's awareness that taking a block tower apart is the inverse of putting it together (an inverse relation), the teacher will not build a complex structure next to the child's tower. Or, if the objective is to develop a sense of empathy between two children, the teacher will not, at that particular point, shift the conversation to fantasy, because it is reality, not fantasy, that can foster a feeling of empathy between the two children. Having a clear objective in mind permits the teacher to be aware of the many things that would not be beneficial to the encounter and thus makes it easier for the teacher to choose what to do to keep the encounter going.

The sources of objectives are countless. But usually an objective is the result of the teacher's knowledge about a particular child *and* about child development in general. As the teacher observes the child at play, he thinks, among other things, about stages of development, sources of knowledge, dimensions of development, and the nature of knowledge construction. He watches, thinks, enters the child's world, notes the effects of his entry, plans his next entry, and then enters again. The teacher is not dismayed when his entry doesn't work in the expected manner. In a broad sense, all entries work, because all entries give the teacher information about the child. That information is then used to make the next entry work better. Let's now watch a learning encounter in progress and follow the teacher's thoughts as the encounter develops.

Janine, a 2½-year-old, has a way of dealing with others that generally gets her what she wants—and she knows it. Her way of manipulating others is by making a fuss. If by screaming and yelling she can get the seat closest to the teacher or the largest piece of play dough, that's what she is going to do. Her tolerance for frustration is among the lowest in the group. The interesting thing is that she knows that her being noisy has an effect on others, but she doesn't seem to know that she can have an effect on others by being quiet. Watching Janine, one gets the impression that, when she is quiet, she feels invisible. The teacher is quite aware of this and of Janine's frustrations.

Janine approaches a table where several children are playing with play dough. The teacher notices Janine standing by the table and, with a slight upward inflection, says "Janine would like some play dough?" This is likely to be Janine's own unexpressed thought. Janine acknowledges the teacher's comment, and the teacher hands her a small portion of play dough. The child begins to roll, bang, and press the play dough. Just before speaking to Janine, the teacher thought:

> Janine is standing quietly near the table. Probably she is not aware that her presence is noticed by anyone, since, in order to feel noticed, she usually creates a disturbance. I will acknowledge her presence.

Thus the teacher has established the objective of helping Janine become more aware of her effect on the group when she is working quietly. By talking to Janine, the teacher has already helped in one way; she has let Janine know that Janine's subjective state (her desire to play) was anticipated by the teacher even though Janine did not create a ruckus.

Now Janine is one of four children actively involved at the play-dough table. The teacher thinks:

> Children at this age have difficulty thinking about another child's point of view. Most of the time their world is one absolute perspective—their own. Perhaps when Janine, in her characteristic style, snatches something from another child, she is not aware of the other child's feelings. She knows that snatching nets her the object but cannot simultaneously think about the other child's feelings. Perhaps, if I convey Bobby's enjoyment to Janine now, before she snatches his play dough, she may become aware of Bobby's feelings.

The teacher enters the children's world with the comment "I think Bobby is having a fine time." She says this softly to the group at large, knowing that Janine, too, will hear the comment. Janine stops momentarily, looks at Bobby rolling and pressing, and then snatches all of Bobby's play dough! What went wrong?

Instead of losing faith in the value of her theoretical knowledge, our teacher rethinks her particular use of that knowledge and, more generally, of her knowledge of children. These setbacks, because of the opportunities they offer for improving teaching strategies, are among the most useful experiences teachers can have. As the teacher returns the dough to Bobby, she thinks:

> Very young children are likely to see things as they appear and have difficulty making inferences. Perhaps all I did with my comment about Bobby's fine time was to direct Janine's attention to Bobby's play dough. Once she noticed his play dough, she wanted it for herself. She didn't integrate my comment about Bobby's enjoyment with her desire for the play dough. Perhaps an older child would have concluded "Bobby feels good when he plays with the dough; without the dough he wouldn't feel good; therefore, snatching the dough would make Bobby feel bad." Unfortunately I directed Janine's thoughts only to Bobby's play dough and not to the *implied relation* between Janine's snatching and Bobby's feelings!

The teacher realizes that her first approach required Janine to make a rather subtle inference. So the teacher simplifies her entry by making a more direct comment. Immediately after Janine has snatched the play dough, the teacher says "Bobby is very upset that you took his play dough. Please, think about how Bobby feels when you do that." By saying "Bobby is very upset," the teacher has given Janine a simple and effective description of an event (Bobby's anger) that was obvious in Bobby's frown and in the mounting tenseness of his body. Perhaps now Janine knows how people look when they are angry. She may have to transgress a number of times before she begins to anticipate Bobby's reactions—or anyone else's, for that matter. Over the next several weeks Janine will probably snatch other objects; but each time she does so, the teacher will promptly describe the other child's subjective state and ask Janine to return the object to its rightful user. Thus the teacher gradually leads Janine to anticipate the consequences of her actions. "What must you do if you take Lemar's cup?" the teacher asks as she sees Janine eyeing the handsome plastic cup in Lemar's hand. "Give back" she says. The words that the teacher has been using during the past several months to comment on Janine's snatching *after* it had occurred work their way into the child's mind to help her realize the consequences of her actions *before* the actual events take place. Over time Janine (and other children like her) will be able to use mental imagery and language to predict consequences and inhibit or reorganize her behavior in deference to these anticipated effects. This ability to select and organize present information to make predictions is part of the developmental progress from a reactive to a more cognitively active approach to the world.

"If you can't play without fussing, I'll have to take you from the table" the teacher reminds a child with kind firmness. These words are later paraphrased by the child when he says to a friend "Play right, or you're gonna hafta leave." The child now enters the present events into a cause-and-effect scheme—if $X$, then $Y$. The child goes beyond the immediate givens: he develops from a reactive to a more cognitively active person.

## Summarizing for the Child

There are no final exams, end-of-week reviews, or chapter summaries for the 2- and 3-year-old student. An average learning encounter ranges from five to ten minutes for young children and often doesn't have a clear-cut ending. The teacher doesn't know if the child "got it" or if the child expanded his base of knowledge. Nevertheless the teacher feels the need to help the child solidify the learning that may have occurred in even the most episodic of encounters and is aware of the importance of summarizing the lesson contained in the encounter. But when should the summarization take place? And what form should it take? Finally, is summarization inconsistent with a commitment to child-directed education?

Summarization is not something that is done just at the end of a child's contact with a task, since few tasks are so simple as to have only a single component. The teacher is continually summarizing—or, should we say, *reviewing*—the child's process of exploration at each component step. As Peter, age 3, works on a jigsaw puzzle, the teacher notices that he is trying to insert a piece backside up. Peter has been rotating the piece for several seconds and has tried the piece after each rotation, but he hasn't flipped the piece over. Every so often the teacher says softly "Peter turned the piece around." After a full minute of rotating the piece, Peter places it in his left hand, and, as he passes it back to his right hand, he turns the piece over. Sensing that Peter is not quite aware of having turned the piece, the teacher says "Peter turned the piece *over*," emphasizing the word *over*. Now, after a few more attempts, Peter succeeds in seating the piece. The teacher quietly summarizes the action by saying "Peter turned the piece over, and then the piece fit." She says this more to the aura of concentration that surrounds Peter than to Peter himself, to the point of even deliberately avoiding eye contact with the child. She is talking directly to Peter's thoughts and is not trying to engage him in conversation, which would divert him from his task (see Chapter Six, "Entry"). The teacher believes, however, that Peter has internalized her words and that her words will improve his reflection on his own actions and his actions' consequences.

With children younger than Peter, summarizing can take the form of momentary emphasis rather than of verbal comment. Teachers almost reflexively say things like "Weeeee!" when a child is running or going down a slide. The teacher may clap his hands together once as the child jumps to the floor from a small height. The teacher makes his lips buzz as the child blows on the paper pinwheel or rotates his hand round and round as the child watches the gerbil on the activity wheel. Through these nonverbal codes children are influenced to notice events in their environment that our culture has chosen to emphasize in its language and in its science. The world to the completely naive and unbiased mind is a continual flux with no particular anchor points. But through the nonverbal and, later, verbal influences of adults, the world of the child becomes at first a punctuated flux and then crystallizes into a series of conventional starts and stops, which exist more in the child's mind than in the raw flux of reality. The teacher, either unwittingly or wittingly, contributes to this process of adding points of reference to the child's world view.

Sometimes, when the teacher punctuates the child's play, she does so from the adult's, rather than the child's, point of view. These kinds of summarizations may actually work against the child's attempts to construct a useful world view. Here is an example, which is based on the observation of a group of children on the playground of a preschool in Massachusetts. A teacher was pushing a 3-year-old boy sitting on a swing. Every time the boy started to move forward from the top of a return swing, the teacher made a "weeeeee" sound of rising inflection (Figure 7-1a).

(a)                                      (b)

*Figure 7-1.*

(These noises are almost universal among adults playing with children.) Every time the boy made a return swing, the teacher reversed the noise, starting with a high inflection and ending on a low pitch as the child completed the return swing (Figure 7-1b). The teacher probably believed that her sounds were representing (summarizing, in our terms) the child's swinging movement. But do you see how mistaken she was? The illustration shows that the teacher was using herself as the point of reference, while the child was quite likely using the ground as the point of reference. If the high pitch was supposed to represent height away from the ground, the teacher was misusing that relation. The teacher actually used a low pitch at the completion of the child's return swing, a time when he was once again high from the ground. Evidently the teacher was using pitch to represent the child's distance from herself and not from the ground.

It would seem that this teacher was being egocentric in her attempts to represent (or, perhaps, we should say in her attempts to have the child *review*) the trajectory of the swinging movement. She used the child's proximity to herself on the return swing rather than his distance from the ground. Had the teacher herself been swinging next to the child, she might have made the appropriate pitch changes: pitch falling, then rising, then falling, then rising again. This is another testimony to the value of the teacher's imitating the child's play so that she can enter the child's world as the child sees and feels it (see Chapter Six).

These forms of in-progress summarizations do not signal the end of an encounter. Other forms, instead, do signal the completion of a task. These forms are used to compress, in a sense, the object of the learning encounter and, at the same time, suggest that a new task should be addressed, such as cleaning up the materials, going to wash hands, or preparing for snacks. How does a teacher meet the demands of the daily schedule without violating the principles of child-directed learning? What are some good ways to terminate a learning encounter?

There will always be "times"—clean-up time, time to go home, nap time, and so on—that interfere with the child's decision to continue or stop a learning encounter. These unavoidable terminations can be anticipated by the teacher, and conflict can be minimized by giving the children explicit signals. Ringing a triangle to signal clean-up is better than making the vague statement "In a few minutes we will stop and wash our hands." The more explicit the cue, the less trouble young children have in realizing what behavior is now appropriate. These are merely common-sense approaches that minimize the problem of the transition from one activity to another.

*Leaving a Task Unfinished*

What we just said applies to those situations in which, for one reason or another, the teacher must terminate a learning encounter. The reason may be a disturbance that requires immediate attention or simply not enough time to finish the encounter. There isn't much to say about teacher-initiated terminations, except that most of the time they are unavoidable. A more interesting issue concerns the best way to handle those children who, as we have often heard teachers say, "flit about from task to task." Should a teacher discourage a child from leaving a task unfinished?

When dealing with 2- and 3-year olds, we think that the teaching staff should let the children flit. As we stated earlier, at that age learning is episodic anyway. Often children move around from area to area and then settle down to a task for a few minutes. Teachers station themselves in activity areas and serve as good models for the children. A teacher involves himself in some activity and waits for the children to enter as they choose. Members of the teaching staff brief one another after the children have gone for the day. They exchange ideas and make decisions concerning methods for adding continuity to a child's learning, even when that child characteristically moves from one teacher to another.

When there is more than one teacher in the classroom, it is a good idea to have one teacher stay away from the activity areas. This teacher watches the floaters, gently directs them to activity areas, and monitors the overall quality of the classroom—noise level, traffic patterns, frequency of conflicts, and so on. This teacher is usually the first to anticipate conflicts and the first to move in to arbitrate. His function is to support the objectives of the teacher(s) stationed in the activity areas. He cannot be tied up with the one or two problem children. It is a good idea to recruit student volunteers or parent volunteers to spend extra time with those children who have particular difficulty in coping with classroom rules. In our own classrooms we have had great success with our use of a one-to-one relationship between a child and an adult to increase the child's prosocial behavior.

If a child decides to leave a task incomplete, it is probably because she is frustrated, bored, or distracted. If she is frustrated, she will leave and perhaps come back to the task later, when she feels less negative about it. If she is bored, she should leave the task. At the ages of 2 and 3, children need not be taught that they must continue boring tasks. It is better that they regulate themselves according to their own interests. Children who learn this lesson well may be in a better position to resist boring and irrelevant education later in life. If the child is distracted, there is no reason to assume that the new task to which she shifts is any less educational than the one at which she was working before.

If the child leaves materials scattered around, she can always come back at the end of the free-play time to help put these materials away. Forcing the 2- or 3-year-old to put away materials immediately before she is allowed to pursue her shift of interest has the effect of inhibiting her interest. When the child is 4 or 5, she is better at planning shifts of interest and maintaining a new interest while she puts away materials that no longer interest her. As we mentioned earlier, the tasks of managing and distributing materials and protecting the individual child's work space are often obstacles to smooth-flowing, goal-directed child behavior, especially for 2- and 3-year-olds. A teacher who is overconcerned with building "good work habits" may make cognitive demands that exceed the 2- and 3-year-old's ability to maintain one goal in mind (the new interest) while working on another goal (completing the current task). The developmental approach to early childhood education helps the teacher appreciate the cognitive capacities of children at different ages and organize the learning activities accordingly.

## Reflecting on What the Child Learned

At some point the learning encounter terminates for any of a variety of reasons: the child leaves the teacher's area, the daily schedule calls for a change in activity, or the child stays with the teacher but shifts to a completely different task. The teacher should pause and reflect a half minute or so on the encounter that has just been terminated. What did the child learn? Teachers develop the ability to reflect on the immediate past while, at the same time, maintaining contact with the present. The ability to reflect on an encounter improves with practice, especially if the teacher uses some useful categories, such as the four types of knowledge we discussed in Chapter Two.

Even when the teacher has no clear feedback, it is probable that the child has learned something. Each encounter with objects and people nets some increment, no matter how small, of knowledge—physical, social, self-, or logico-mathematical. The teacher quickly reviews the encounter and speculates on it. She will then use the product of her speculation to expand and generalize the child's knowledge.

As you read the following account of Derrick's adventures with his snowsuit, imagine that you are his teacher and review the series of events keeping in mind the four categories of knowledge. Don't choose among them. Just speculate on how they all might be involved in the encounter.

> Derrick (2 years, 8 months) marches toward the clothes cubbies in the hall, tugging at his one-piece snowsuit to remove it. He manages to pull his arms out of the sleeves and is confronted with the more challenging task of getting out of the leggings. He sits on a bench and pulls and pulls at the leggings, which stubbornly refuse to give, since they are held firmly in place by Derrick's own weight. Enter Meg (3 years, 6 months), who, after removing the sleeves of her snowsuit, pushes the suit down below her hips and then sits on the bench and nonchalantly pulls the suit off her legs by grabbing the leggings' cuffs.
>
> Derrick has watched the whole speedy performance, and now, thanks to Meg, he knows how to solve his own problem. Still sitting down, but omitting to first push the suit down below his hips, he grabs the cuffs of his leggings and tugs and

tugs. Since his weight is still pinning the suit to the bench, the new approach produces much frustration and no positive results. Derrick then stands up, pushes his suit down below his hips, and—without sitting down!—bends over and again starts tugging at the cuffs of his leggings. Naturally, this strategy doesn't work either. At last, by raising his right foot and then his left foot a few times and shaking his feet vigorously, he succeeds, and the snowsuit—by now a tangled ball on the floor—finally releases its grip from a frustrated Derrick.

What did Derrick learn? (The question does not imply that Derrick learned anything in a complete and final form.) Derrick was faced with a problem. What type of problem was it? Even though the learning was incomplete, facing the problem gave Derrick a reason to apply certain types of knowledge, albeit at a rudimentary level. As we stated in Chapter Five, the occurrence of problems stimulates cognitive and social development. We make the assumption that, if the child makes even rudimentary attempts to solve a problem, because of those very attempts he learns something about that type of problem.

Let's see how in this particular example the areas of knowledge interact. *Self-knowledge* and *physical knowledge* interact quite clearly. Derrick's primary problem was the failure to consider his own body as an object in space, an object with which he had to contend. By watching Meg, he probably came closer to understanding that the weight of his own body obstructed his goal. The two acts of tugging his suit while sitting down and pushing his suit below his hips while standing up may have increased his *body awareness*. He was also learning a physical *sequence*—that is, first push snowsuit down below hips and then tug off leggings. Once Derrick has learned this sequence completely, he will have coordinated *position* with *movement* (the position of his body with the movement of pushing down the snowsuit).

Keep pretending that you are Derrick's teacher. Now that you have analyzed this learning encounter, what can you do to facilitate Derrick's body awareness and his ability to coordinate position and movement? You may decide, for example, to put mirrors in the hallway near the cubbies; also, you may want to ensure that older children arrive at the same time as younger children, so that imitative learning can occur. Finally, once Derrick has thoroughly mastered the removal of his suit, you may decide not to remove his boots, as you usually do, in order to add a new element to the sequence. These ideas will come to you as a result of your reflecting on the areas of knowledge that are involved in the encounter between Derrick and his snowsuit.

Before going on to discuss another topic, let's analyze another encounter to increase your practice with this very useful technique. The encounter takes place at snack time.

Jill (2 years, 9 months) holds up a plastic cup to Mrs. R., her teacher, puts her finger in the cup, and asks "What happened in dere?"

Mrs. R. understands that Jill probably means "What goes in there?" or "Where is the juice that belongs in there?" but decides to take Jill's words literally. She bends over to look into the cup, but Jill has moved slightly away, making it difficult for Mrs. R. to see inside the cup. "I don't know what happened in there. Let me look inside" the teacher says.

Jill repeats "What happened? What happened?" making no accommodations to Mrs. R.'s moves to see inside the cup.

"Jill, if you let me look inside, maybe I can tell you what happened in there" Mrs. R. says.

Jill's voice gets stern: "Happened to juice! Juice!"

Mrs. R. replies "Oh, what happened to your juice. I haven't poured it yet. Here it is" and pours the juice.

In this learning encounter between Jill, her empty cup, and the teacher, we can see at work knowledge of social conventions and knowledge of logico-mathematical relations. Knowledge of social conventions involves learning the use of certain words. The teacher, as an agent of the culture, provokes Jill to consider the difference between "happens *in X*" and "happens *to X*"; that is, she provokes the child to become more aware of different word meanings. We are not saying that, because of this exchange with her teacher, Jill has constructed a full understanding of these different meanings. But this opportunity, together with a hundred others, will eventually lead Jill to make these mental constructions.

As mentioned in Chapter Two, logico-mathematical knowledge pertains to the coordination of actions. In this example the actions in question relate to determining if anything is in the cup. Jill puts her finger in the cup as a way of finding out, while Mrs. R. wants to look inside the cup. This is a case of two different actions having the same goal and centered on the same object. Continuity, then, is represented by the goal and by the object of the actions. In order for Mrs. R.'s actions to be successful, however, certain adjustments need to be made in the position of the cup. For Jill the position of the cup in relation to her body is immaterial, since she is using her finger as the method of exploration. Reflection on the coordination of these actions results in logico-mathematical knowledge—that is, an understanding of the relationship between means for achieving a goal and the goal itself.

Reflecting on a learning encounter according to the four areas of knowledge gives the teacher new ideas for subsequent encounters with the child. In Jill's case, the teacher may look for opportunities to use words such as *where, what, when,* and *how.* Also, more generally speaking, the teacher can be sensitive to those confusions that are typical of children in a particular stage of development—for example, confusion about the relationship between one's own perspective and that of another person and confusion about the relationship between changes in appearance and changes in identity. Heightened sensitivity increases the teacher's chances of spotting critical moments of entry in future encounters.

## Generalizing Learning across Encounters

In order to generalize to future encounters the gains the child makes during one encounter, the teacher should be able to judge why an encounter was successful and which were its optimal features. The teacher doesn't want to carry over into future encounters excess baggage. Not everything about the presentation, the materials, and the motivational state of teacher and child contributes to learning, nor could these elements ever recombine in an identical way during some future learning encounter. Perhaps the following *systems* view of learning will help you decide what factors influence the child's learning.

*Factors That Influence Learning Encounters*

Many things besides the child's developmental level influence the success of a learning encounter. Among them are momentary states of the environment, of the teacher, and of the child; specific bits of information above the child's general level of competence, which are therefore unfamiliar to him; and specific limitations that are placed on the child's performance by the structure of the task rather than by the child's lack of knowledge. These factors have been organized in Figure 7-2 to

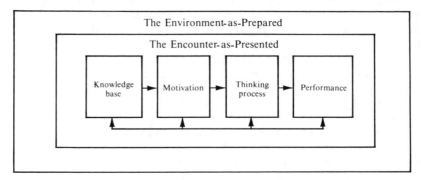

*Figure 7-2.* Factors that influence learning encounters.

include six categories. Each of these six categories influences the others. Think of the child as consisting of four systems: knowledge, motivation, thinking, and performance. These four systems—our whole child—operate within a larger system—the particular encounter with the teacher and/or materials. The encounter as a system operates within an even larger system—the environment as prepared and as it globally exists.

The child comes to a learning encounter with a *knowledge base.* He already knows a certain vocabulary, certain rules of conduct, and certain facts about the physical world, the social world, and himself. The child already has a wide range of expectations, such as that balls roll, nuts screw on bolts, spoons are for soup, teacher protects from harm, teacher asks questions and waits for answers, Stanley is rough, and small places are fun. The child also comes to a learning encounter with a level of competence that is not specific to a particular task—for example, the ability to think in two directions, to think about both similarities and differences, to remember more than a few items, and to link discontinuous events. The knowledge base and the *thinking process* are presented as two different categories in Figure 7-2. The knowledge base refers to what the child has already learned. The thinking process refers to how the child goes about acquiring new knowledge.

The distinction between knowledge base and thinking process can be made only in relation to a particular learning encounter. It should be obvious that at the conclusion of a particular learning encounter the knowledge base increases as a result of thinking. Sometimes a learning encounter goes poorly because the child doesn't have the sufficient knowledge base. At other times the child has the sufficient knowledge base (vocabulary, rules of the game, and so on), but the demands of the task exceed her thinking competence (memory load, combinatorial thinking, coordination of contrasts, and so on). The reverse is also possible; the child does poorly because she doesn't understand what is expected of her or doesn't know the meaning of certain key words in the teacher's request or in another child's question. After a brief clarification or a simple rephrasing, the child proceeds without difficulty, indicating that the initial problem was in knowing rather than in thinking.

Between the knowledge-base box and the thinking-process box in Figure 7-2, there is a box representing *motivation*. Motivation encompasses all the emotional components of learning, such as the child's interest, fear, drive, conflict, and boldness. The learning encounter is in large part a matter of motivating children to use their knowledge base in the process of thinking. All those factors that influence the child's interest—attention, persistence, ability to delay gratification, and ability to cope with ambiguity and frustration—are a part of the motivational level of the child at the time of the learning encounter. Some of these motivational factors are general traits of the child's personality (for example, proneness to anger, exuberance, restlessness, and enthusiasm for novelty). Other motivational factors are, instead, situational (for example, fatigue, illness, and excitement after seeing something special, like a circus). All these motivational factors, from those that relate to general personality traits to those that are specific to certain situations, contribute to the success or failure of the learning encounter.

Assuming that the child has an adequate knowledge base and is sufficiently motivated to engage his thinking processes, he still must express what he has learned before an observer knows that the child knows. The very act of *performing* a response may imply certain requirements that make it difficult for the child to express his knowledge. If a child can't draw a circle, it may be because he has difficulty holding the crayon (a problem of performance) or because he can't end the loop where he started it (a problem of knowing). If the child is given a "trainer crayon" (an extralarge crayon with a sculptured plastic grip), he may be able to draw the circle and thereby prove that his problem was at the response end rather than at the knowing end of the task. Once again, these distinctions are clear only in context with a particular learning encounter. If the teacher sees circle drawing as the objective of an encounter, the child's inability to hold a crayon is a performance problem. If, instead, the teacher identifies crayon holding as the objective, the child's inability to hold a crayon is a problem of knowing. Although arbitrary, the distinction between knowing and performing is not without value, and thinking about it may help the teacher structure the objective of a learning encounter.

With very young children the distinction between performance and knowing is important, since very young children seem to know more than they can do. Recall, for example, the case of Lisa (Chapter Six), the little girl who wanted to sweep the sand toward a pile but didn't know how to do it. In very young children the sweeping *is* the problem; that is, the problem is frequently a matter of not knowing *how* to do something, even though one may know *what* needs to be done. A 2-year-old wants to build a five-block stack but doesn't know how to do so without knocking it over before it is done. A 3-year-old sets out to reconstruct a pattern with mosaic tiles but doesn't know how to go about it, even though she can recognize that her attempt doesn't match the model.

To summarize, the child enters a learning encounter with a *knowledge base* that is relevant to the task at hand. If the child is properly *motivated,* he will engage his *thinking processes* in the most competent way he can. He then expresses the result of his thinking processes—the use of his knowledge base—in some overt *performance.* The entire cycle continues and repeats itself during the whole span of the learning encounter. At times motivation increases or decreases, and this, too, influences the encounter. Also, the child's own performance gives him new information that increases his knowledge base, which in turn affects his motivation and thinking processes.

Not all of the factors that determine fluctuations of the child's knowledge base and motivation are the result of the child's own thinking and performance. Some of these factors come from the teacher, from other children, from the structure of the materials, and from the environment at large. Indeed, knowledge, motivation, thinking, and performance are embedded in the context of a particular encounter, and the encounter is embedded in the immediate physical environment with all its bright lighting, noise, warm colors, and good ventilation. These inclusive systems— the encounter-as-presented and the environment-as-prepared—also influence the course of the learning encounter.

The *encounter-as-presented* may be determined by the foresight of a teacher or by the whimsy of another child. An encounter can lead to greater knowledge if what the teacher does motivates the child, improves his knowledge base so he can begin the task, causes him to reflect on the situation and engage his thinking processes, and allows him to respond in his preferred mode. The teacher can do this by adding a single word of instruction, by promising pleasant consequences if the child persists in his task, by giving him new materials more suited to his preferences, by slowing the pace, and by directing the child's attention to pertinent information —that is, by doing all the things that teachers do to improve the quality of learning.

The *environment-as-prepared* includes the physical setting, the materials, the work surface, and all those fixed aspects of the physical environment that bear on the progress of the learning encounter. It is interesting to note that this system of influence also includes those parts of the environment that, although fixed, are not necessarily prepared to facilitate the particular learning encounter, such as the shape of the room, the position of the windows, the amount of open space, the locks on the doors, and a score of other things in the physical environment that may determine the success or the failure of a learning encounter. The momentary states of the environment, like the shrill of a passing siren, an outburst of fighting, or the crash of a falling limb outside, are not part of the environment-as-prepared. They may become part of the encounter-as-presented if the teacher chooses to incorporate them as the topic of an encounter. Otherwise they are simply unpredictable distractions. If, for example, the teacher knows about the felling of a tree a day in advance, he can make sure that the children are near the window at the right time, so they can watch this event. Then the crash of a limb becomes part of the environment-as-prepared. While it is true that momentary states of the environment influence the success of a learning encounter, since they are unpredictable and outside the teacher's control, they don't warrant a discussion beyond the simple acknowledgment that they happen.

*Applying the six systems of influence to a learning encounter.* As you know, Figure 7-2 is used to identify factors that facilitate or impede the progress of a learning encounter. Here is the account of a learning encounter that took place among Jimmy (3 years, 2 months), Beth (3 years, 5 months), and their teacher, Mrs. G. As you read this account, reflect on the success and failure of the encounter by applying the six systems of influence we have just described and that are diagrammed in Figure 7-2: (1) the child's knowledge base; (2) his motivation, (3) his thinking, and (4) his performance; (5) the encounter-as-presented; and (6) the environment-as-prepared.

| | |
|---|---|
| 1 | Jimmy, Beth, and Mrs. G. enter a small room (12 × 12 feet) |
| 2 | with two windows, a high ceiling, and a one-way vision screen |
| 3 | in the wall. The floor is linoleum. A long bank of fluorescent |
| 4 | lights hangs from the ceiling, and over that dangles a microphone, |
| 5 | about three feet above a table. The table is covered with tightly |
| 6 | stretched green felt. The children and Mrs. G. go to the table |
| 7 | and sit in three chairs, each on one side of the table. Beth, |
| 8 | Jimmy, and Mrs. G. have been coming to this room for "tutorial |
| 9 | sessions" about twice a week for the past two months. The table |
| 10 | has been prepared with a toy-train track in the shape of an |
| 11 | ellipse (actually, a rectangle with rounded ends). The track |
| 12 | is made of red plastic strips that can be joined in a jigsaw- |
| 13 | puzzle fashion with tongue and groove. The strips are eight |
| 14 | inches long; some are straight and others curved. The sides |
| 15 | of the ellipse are made of three straight pieces bounded by |
| 16 | a curved piece at each end; this forms two semiellipses that |
| 17 | are joined to make the complete ellipse. Two toy-train engines |
| 18 | and four cargo cars rest on the felt. Also on the felt lie |
| 19 | an assortment of little wooden people that can fit inside the |
| 20 | cars. At one end of the track a papier-mâché tunnel covers a |
| 21 | portion of the track. The tunnel is long enough to conceal an |
| 22 | engine attached to two cargo cars. |
| 23 | Jimmy and Beth each take an engine and two cargo cars, |
| 24 | attach them to form a train, and drive them around the track— |
| 25 | Beth going clockwise, and Jimmy going counterclockwise. As both |
| 26 | children reach the curved ends opposite each other, Mrs. G. says |
| 27 | "Beth, Jimmy, what will happen to your trains?" Beth pauses; Jimmy |
| 28 | continues to move his train in a counterclockwise direction. Beth |
| 29 | lifts her train, rotates it, and continues her play, this time |
| 30 | going counterclockwise. |
| 31 | After the children have made a few circuits, Mrs. G. removes |
| 32 | one of the curved end sections of the track, places it on the |
| 33 | felt nearby, and exclaims "Oh my! We have had damage to the track. |
| 34 | It needs to be fixed before the people can ride the trains." At |

35    these words Jimmy gets a few of the wooden dolls and places them
36    in his cargo cars. Beth looks at the track and reaches for the
37    detached piece. As she attempts to fit it in place, Jimmy drives
38    toward the broken section. Beth warns Jimmy "No!" Jimmy continues
39    to drive his train off the track, onto the felt, and then onto the
40    track at the other side of the gap. Some of his dolls fall out in
41    the process.
42         Mrs. G.: "Look, Jimmy, your passengers were thrown from the
43    train because the track was broken." Jimmy retrieves his passen-
44    gers and returns them to his cargo cars. He places one passenger
45    in each car and one in the compartment behind the engine.
46         In the meantime Beth has made two attempts to mend the track.
47    On her first attempt the two tongues were facing each other, and
48    she had to rotate the piece she held in her hand 180 degrees,
49    so the tongue would be opposite the groove. Now, on her second
50    trial, the track fits nicely in the groove, but the piece is curving
51    in the wrong direction. To solve this problem and close the gap,
52    Beth must flip the piece over and then fit tongue to groove. She
53    is getting frustrated when here comes Jimmy again. "No! No!" Beth
54    says menacingly to Jimmy. As the boy continues his journey toward
55    the trouble spot, Beth pushes Jimmy's train away. The teacher
56    intervenes: "That track does need to be fixed. Jimmy, let's watch
57    Beth work." As Mrs. G. says these words, she gently hugs Jimmy in
58    such a way that they both can see Beth. While Beth keeps working
59    at the track, Mrs. G. speaks softly to Jimmy: "Beth is trying
60    to fix the track. The curved piece doesn't fit at both ends.
61    Only one end fits. What can Beth do? What can she do?" Finally
62    Beth, after a few more attempts, flips the piece over and rejoins
63    the track at both ends, tongue to groove here and groove to tongue
64    there. Once the track is repaired, Beth and Jimmy return their
65    trains to the track and begin to drive them round counterclockwise.
66         Mrs. G. says "Now that the train has been fixed, Beth, I'll
67    bet Mommy, Daddy, and Baby will want a ride in your train." These
68    are names that both Beth and Jimmy have used to refer to the wooden
69    dolls in past sessions. Mommy and Daddy are tall; Baby is smaller.
70    Mommy is blue, and Daddy is red. Beth places one doll in each com-
71    partment—Mommy first, Daddy second, and Baby in the caboose.
72    Jimmy, too, places one doll in each car (the cars can hold only
73    one doll). In Jimmy's train Baby is first, Mommy second, and Daddy
74    in the rear. As Beth's train passes Mrs. G., the teacher says
75    "There go Mommy, Daddy, and Baby." When Jimmy's train passes
76    Mrs. G., she says "Here come Baby, Mommy, and Daddy last." The
77    children make one complete circuit, going through the tunnel.
78         The second time Beth approaches the entrance of the tunnel,
79    Mrs. G. places her hand at the exit, obstructing the train. Beth
80    moves her train all the way into the tunnel. She can't see any of
81    the little people. The teacher says "The tunnel is closed for a
82    minute. Do you know who will come out of the tunnel first?" This
83    is the first time Mrs. G. has asked this question. Beth pushes
84    on her train, but the teacher's hand prevents its exit. Mrs. G.
85    asks again "Who will come out first?" As Beth starts to back her
86    train out of the tunnel, Mrs. G. removes her hand. When Beth sees
87    that the tunnel is clear, she pushes her train forward again. Just

88    as the nose of the train appears outside the exit of the tunnel,
89    Mrs. G. exclaims "Oh, Mommy is coming! Mommy is coming!"
90        Jimmy hears the noise of children in the next room. The small
91    room that Beth, Jimmy, and Mrs. G. are using is next to the regular
92    classroom. The children in the classroom are singing "All fall
93    down"—a favorite game of Jimmy's. Jimmy runs to the door that
94    leads to the classroom and tries to turn the knob. After several
95    obviously futile attempts to reattract Bobby to the tutorial
96    session, the teacher decides to end the session for both children.

This is an average learning encounter—not the best, not the worst. As we suggested earlier, let's reflect on the success and failure of this encounter by using the six systems of influence. What is the knowledge base of Jimmy and Beth? From observation Mrs. G. knows that both children realize that their trains can travel in two directions. Also, since the children have crashed trains on this track before, Mrs. G. assumes that both children realize that each train needs to make some sort of adjustment to the other. This leads Mrs. G. to ask them to think ahead (line 27). Mrs. G.'s objective here is to stimulate anticipatory thinking. The teacher's question does affect Beth's thinking, and the child reverses the direction of her train (lines 28–30). Jimmy, instead, is so absorbed in his own activity that Mrs. G.'s comment doesn't affect his behavior at all. Therefore, it is hard to tell if his failure to respond is due to poor thinking, poor motivation, a poor knowledge base (vocabulary), or even a good knowledge base (he *knew* that Beth would move her train).

In the section from line 31 through line 65, the teacher structures a problem by creating an obstacle to a goal that, as Mrs. G. knows, the children share. The activity of fixing the track is placed in the context of the children's self-set goal of driving the train on the track. The encounter-as-presented is coordinated with the motivational system of the children (see Blank, 1973, p. 126). In lines 66–89, the teacher tries to provoke thinking about serial order. Perhaps the reason it doesn't work is that solving the problem—that is, anticipating who will come out of the tunnel first—is not really instrumental to the goal that Beth has set for herself. In this case the match between the encounter-as-presented and the motivational system is less than sufficient.

We can see Beth's thinking process at work in lines 46–64. We can also identify her anticipatory thinking as she warns Jimmy to stay away. As it turns out, part of Beth's problem is a mechanical one; tongue and groove fit too snugly. This problem falls in the area of the environment-as-prepared. Jimmy's encroachment on Beth is, instead, part of the encounter-as-presented, since it affects Beth's motivation. Mrs. G.'s restraining Jimmy supports Beth and, at the same time, helps Jimmy learn by watching. The teacher's support is also part of the encounter-as-presented.

We get a glimpse of Jimmy's thinking process in lines 34–36. At Mrs. G.'s comment "It needs to be fixed before the people can ride the train," Jimmy reaches for the little wooden people. It is likely that Jimmy has picked up only the key word *people* and has not integrated the entire sentence with the situation of the broken track before him. Beth, instead, has seen the implication of the broken track even before Mrs. G. makes her comment. Therefore, the teacher's words are related in Beth's mind to the focus of her attention—the broken track. Although Beth may have begun to mend the track even without Mrs. G.'s comment, the comment is internalized by the child. Once Beth has internalized these words, Mrs. G. can use them in future sessions. Mrs. G. uses a similar technique in lines 74–76, by describing a scene in the hope that her words will serve as a vehicle for staging the objective on serial order. The environment-as-prepared includes the constraint represented by the fact that each car can hold only one doll.

The six systems of influence can be applied to other aspects of this encounter. What about the influence of the environment-as-prepared on the success or failure of the encounter (lines 1–20 and 90–96)? What improvements can be made before the next tutorial session? Regarding the encounter-as-presented, what does the teacher do to provoke thought (line 89), support the encounter (lines 55–58 and 86–89), increase Jimmy's and Beth's knowledge bases (lines 60 and 89), and motivate the children to continue their activity (lines 94–95)? What could have been done more effectively? What have we learned about Jimmy and Beth? Which child has a greater sense of the problem (lines 34–37)? Will Beth be better prepared for future tasks dealing with serial order (lines 78–89)? Would it have been wise for the teacher to request Beth to predict a backward order when the child began to reverse the train out of the tunnel (lines 85–86)? Assuming that Beth could predict which doll would emerge from the tunnel first, would she also have been able to predict which one would be the second to emerge? How much of Beth's problem in dealing with serial order is a matter of motivation, of thinking, or of knowledge base? Has the teacher ever heard Beth respond correctly to similar questions?

An accurate diagnosis of a learning encounter is instrumental to good decisions about future learning encounters. The diagnosis is the basis for the prescription. How can the children apply later what they have learned now? How can they apply to other areas what they have learned in a particular situation? More generally, how can transfer of learning be facilitated?

*Facilitating Transfer of Learning*

Each learning encounter has an objective and a content. The objective is the general cognitive demand in an area of knowledge. The content is the particular task that confronts the child in the encounter. In the preceding example one of the objectives was anticipatory thinking (line 27) and the content was the problem of two trains moving toward each other. In order to provide transfer of learning, we maintain the objective (anticipatory thinking) and change the content (from trains to balls, for example). Beth rolls a ball down the slide. The teacher asks "Will it hit the box or the chair, Beth?"

Another objective in our example was serial order (lines 78–89). The next day in the classroom Beth strings three beads of different colors on a knotted shoelace. The teacher hands her a cardboard tube. Beth pulls the string of beads through the tube. Mrs. G. asks "What color will come out of the tube first?" Jimmy places three wooden quoits, each of a different color, over a post. "Which one did you put on first, Jimmy?" the teacher asks. Jimmy points to the topmost quoit. The teacher notes that Jimmy confuses *topmost* with *first placed*. Still another objective was to have Jimmy sense another person's goal (lines 56–57). The next day in the classroom Mrs. G. turns to Jimmy and says "Can you help Trina" or "What do you think Trina is trying to do?"

One way of making teaching more continuous from one day to the next is to define objectives clearly, even though, as we said in Chapter Five, this doesn't imply

Transfer of learning can be facilitated by using different objects in similar ways.

that one must define specific behavioral objectives. Knowing that Jimmy needs to work on integrating what he hears with what he sees (lines 34–36)—this problem has occurred many times before in other learning encounters—sensitizes the teacher to the need of looking for opportunities to improve this skill. Seeing that Jimmy confuses *topmost* with *first placed,* which is actually a special case of confusing *first* with *nearest,* encourages the teacher to look for opportunities to work on this distinction—for example, in a line of children, in a line of pull toys, in the order children come down a slide, and so on. Sometimes the teacher will prepare the environment to increase the probability that the child will be provoked to think about key distinctions. Sometimes the teacher will just be on the lookout for a means to convert spontaneous play into a challenge that provokes the child to consider these key distinctions. Whichever way transfer of learning occurs, it can occur by the deliberate design of the teaching staff.

Please remember these words: the primary function of the preschool teacher is to facilitate transfer of learning. The qualitative shifts that involve the development of the child as a whole, such as the transition from preoperational thinking to concrete-operational thinking (Piaget & Inhelder, 1969b), should not be a direct concern of the teacher. The teacher can facilitate transfer of learning, but the child does the brunt of the work that leads him on to the next stage. The teacher can make a direct contribution to the child's learning but only an indirect contribution to the child's development (see Furth, 1974). The distinction between learning and development is an extremely complicated one; and the scope of this book does not allow an in-depth discussion of this complex topic. Here we confine ourselves to saying that the teacher should be less concerned about qualitative jumps in the child's thinking competence and more concerned with a "horizontal" expansion of the child's ability to apply his or her knowledge. Through a complex internal process that Piaget calls *equilibration,* the child eventually synthesizes huge segments of learning and develops new ways of asking questions and solving problems (Piaget & Inhelder, 1969b). According to Piaget, this type of synthesis cannot be taught with any direct "let's practice $X$" method. It is somewhat the "American problem" (Elkind, 1969a) to speed children from one stage of development to the next. When we speak about transfer of learning, we do not advert to this approach.

Earlier we referred to transfer of learning in terms of shifting the content while maintaining the same objective from one learning encounter to another. There is another way to facilitate transfer of learning and thereby increase the breadth of learning: providing the child with general procedures for learning. If the child learns how to explore new situations in general, his or her breadth of learning automatically expands. The child who has learned how to explore and seek information has learned how to learn. The teacher's role in helping the child do this is slightly different from the role of directly attempting to transfer learning across analogous tasks. In this second approach the teacher tries to improve the child's art of seeking information.

*Teaching 4- and 5-Year-Olds How to Explore*

In Chapter Five we made the distinction between support activities and exploratory activities. Support activities assist and improve exploration but are not the exploration itself; they guide in asking questions but are not the questions themselves. In this section we deal with the exploration itself—more specifically, with techniques that can help children improve exploration. Children who know how to seek information are in a good position to generalize newly acquired knowledge from one encounter to a future one. The following is a list of general techniques that support exploration and increase the yield and transfer of a learning encounter:

1. Identify parts.
2. Look from different angles.
3. Contrast with familiar objects.
4. Relate structure to function.

We will define these techniques by presenting a learning encounter in a class for 4- and 5-year-olds. Then we will explain how more elementary forms of these techniques can be used with 2- and 3-year-old children. The reason for the distinction is that the highly verbal content of this first situation would not be appropriate for the younger children.

Before the students arrive, place in the center of a large table an unfamiliar but interesting-looking object—for example, a periscope. You have found out, by asking their parents, that the children have not had first-hand experience with a periscope. The children arrive and begin to explore the unfamiliar object. Allow them to turn, look into, rub, or whatever they want to do in this initial hands-on phase. Periodically ask the children "What do you think this is? What can you do with it?" This sets the general goal. After the children have satisfied their need to touch and manipulate the new object, you start to help them probe more selectively.

*Identify parts.* Young children have a natural tendency to name the entire object. "It's a pipe" exclaims a 4-year-old. "It's a mirror" another says, somewhat less sure of himself. Lead the children onward: "That's true, it does have a mirror. *Part* of this thing is a mirror." Then: "What other parts do you see?" With these few words, and quite casually, you have made the basic distinction between the whole object and a part of it. "There is a mirror at both ends!" a third child discovers with delight.

*Look from different angles.* The object is passed around and looked at from different angles, so that the children can discover parts and features theretofore unnoticed. "It's hollow" one child says poking her hand in one opening. The children take turns at poking and probing, with each child occasionally adding a descriptor. You keep a record of each descriptor mentioned by the children.

*Contrast with familiar objects.* "Have you ever seen anything like this?" Of course, each time the child offers a word to describe the object, the child is telling you what this new object reminds him of. The question "Have you ever seen anything like this?" is the teacher's way of getting children to synthesize the various descriptors. In order to avoid a restatement of the all-inclusive designations mentioned earlier (such as "a pipe" or "a mirror"), you can remind the children of some of the parts or features they have listed: "It's hollow," "Has a mirror at both ends," "Has a handle on each side." By doing so, you encourage the children to accommodate their knowledge of the total object to what they now know of its individual features. "It looks like a telescope because that's [the telescope] hollow too."

All teachers eagerly await such moments. The child has compared a periscope to a telescope. There happens to be a telescope in the toy bin nearby. You make a dash to get the telescope. The two objects side by side generate a three- or four-minute discussion about their differences. "The tel'scope makes things look big" volunteers one child. "And what about this other thing?" you ask. "It's just a mirror" one of the quieter children joins in. "But it's crooked. I can hardly see myself" a frustrated child observes. Yet the general idea that the periscope may also be something one looks through has emerged.

*Relate structure to function.* "For what reason are the two mirrors crooked, Irene?" This will bring to the child's attention that these mirrors are crooked for a reason. How often do children take things the way they are, as if they were so by a law of nature—for no particular reason they can see? How often do children think that, if something is not the way they expect it to be, someone must have made a funny mistake? But even thinking that someone has put the mirrors in the periscope in a crooked position by mistake is a terrific indication that the child senses that someone had a *choice* regarding the mirrors' placement. And if someone had a choice, then it is possible that someone had a purpose. It is the object of these lessons to give children the necessary skills to see purpose in a static object. And in order to see purpose in a static object the child must get to the point at which she is capable of imagining that mirror *in the process* of being positioned.

Irene answers "They're just turned funny." Instead of leaving it at that, you probe a little: "Do you think that the person who made this thing wanted the mirrors this way?" The question is too much for the child. So you take another course: "Let's see what happens if I change the position of this mirror." If you have a periscope with fixed mirrors, you are sunk. Solution: plan ahead.

By transforming the object—rotating the mirrors, removing the mirrors, and more—the children may eventually discover the relationship between the angle of the mirror and the purpose of the periscope—that is, the relationship between structure and function. Children can be given two small pocket mirrors with which to experiment. You may start them off by modeling an uncommon use of the mirror: walking backwards and seeing where you are going by looking into a mirror held in front of you slightly above your right shoulder. The children watch how you are able to avoid objects *behind* you by looking into the mirror *in front* of you. While it is true that this is an example of showing the child how to do rather than how to explore, we think that once in a while this kind of demonstration can be of help in encouraging exploration. Seeing the teacher do the rear-view-mirror-walk could start the children on a whole series of more elaborate explorations. Another justification for this outright demonstration lies in the fact that no deliberate effort to demonstrate the purpose of the periscope has been made.

With your rear-view-mirror-walk you have indeed given the children a big idea; you have helped them realize that mirrors can be used in a less egocentric fashion than the usual one. Instead of looking at *oneself* in the mirror, one can look at *other objects* in the mirror. From this the children may piece together the relations that ultimately lead to the discovery that one mirror can reflect the objects already reflected in another mirror.

In sum, a deliberate attempt to identify parts and to look at the object from different angles increases the likelihood that critical information will be gathered. Contrasting the new with the familiar encourages guesses regarding the purpose of a new object. The approach that structures are rarely arbitrary and that most of the time they are designed that way to serve a particular function guides the child's thinking. Descriptors of parts and characteristics of the whole are no longer a list of static features but an indication of the function of the object. The child can think about what the object is, what the object is not, and why the object is not what it is not. Why weren't the mirrors in the periscope placed in such a way that one could easily see one's own face? It is important to teach children that the object as it is now is a momentary arrangement of parts that were once in different positions (see discussion of transformations in Chapter Three). The object was positioned and shaped the way we see it now by someone who had a definite purpose in mind. At times the teacher may model an exploratory activity, if that modeling is likely to lead the children to make more sophisticated explorations on their own. These instances of priming the child to explore are often useful in the initial stages of a learning encounter but should be discontinued as soon as possible.

*Increasing Exploratory Behavior in Children 2 to 3 Years of Age*

How can the teacher help 2- and 3-year-olds improve their explorations? Asking the 2-year-old, and perhaps even the 3-year-old, to name the parts of an unfamiliar object would probably frustrate the child. Children this young must touch, twist, probe, and otherwise manipulate new objects. But there is touching and touching. Some touching is no more than a confirmation of the physical existence of an observed object. Some touching is more clearly a search for information—information about the boundaries, the weight, the limits of movement, and countless other characteristics of that object. This skilled manual and visual exploration becomes increasingly sophisticated with age (Zaporozhets, 1970).

One might wonder if general support techniques can be taught to the very young child. It is true that we might be effective in helping a child discover the delight of some particular object, but do we, in the process, improve the child's general ability to accommodate and assimilate? Perhaps we shouldn't be too concerned with the level of generalization at such an early age. Everything is so new to the 2-year-old, anyway. Perhaps we should proceed on the belief that, in the process of discovering how to right an overturned pull toy, the child also learns something about how to explore problems. Extra drag on the pull string indicates that something is wrong. This causes the child to look for the source of the resistance. Whether or not this routine of "looking at the end of the string" generalizes to the point that the child simply assumes that "physical resistance indicates an obstacle somewhere" is not our primary concern with such young children. After countless experiences of this kind every day, the more general problem-solving strategy will develop naturally. Learning is much more an inductive process in the early years than in the later, more verbal years. Consequently support activities cannot be the primary content of an encounter with 2- and 3-year-olds. As Piaget's theory suggests, children this young will not be able to reflect on their exploratory behavior. They are attentive to specific objects and to specific actions of objects but have difficulty looking at their own actions as a general pattern that can be studied, improved, or modified. Recall, for example, the difficulty of the little girl (Chapter Five) who had been taught to trace the contour of a jigsaw-puzzle piece but was not reflecting on that action as a means to gather information.

If support activities cannot be taught directly to very young children, what can the teacher do to improve exploration? Perhaps the answer is simply to ensure that children spend time exploring. The teacher's role, as we have defined it in Chapter Five, is to stage problems for the children—give them a reason to explore. A capable teacher with a good sense of timing can do a great deal to give the child practice at exploring parts of an object, looking at it from different angles, contrasting the new with the old, and discovering how changes in structure can change the function of an object. But when the children are very young, teacher and children explore more in action and rely less on verbal descriptions of the exploratory process itself.

*Explore parts.* You can stage problems that increase the young child's explorations of the parts of an object. Throw a cloth over half of a familiar object. Does the child recognize the object by seeing only part of it? Remove a part of an object. Does the child recognize the part as belonging to what is left of the object? Or does he instead try to adjoin the part to a second, whole object—for example, does he try to add a third arm to a whole doll? Can he locate the missing smaller part when he sees the larger remainder? Can he also work the other way and find the larger remainder when presented with only the smaller part?

These techniques may or may not improve the child's understanding of the functional relation among parts of an object. Other, more advanced techniques focus more on function. For example, will the child notice that the rubber band is missing from the wind-up propeller plane? The missing rubber band does not make the object look odd, like a doll without a leg, but it does keep the object from performing its function. In teaching children to notice a missing part, it is better to have them notice it because the object acts funny than because it looks funny. We agree that the car looks funny without its wheels; but the teacher should accentuate that the wheels are missed because now the car cannot roll. In other words, a missing part is missed because its function is missed.

The fantasy play of young children can be useful to learning. But teachers who try to use fantasy to improve support activities are often disappointed. Here is a child using a pencil as a pretend airplane. As he is buzzing and diving, the teacher exclaims "Oh my! How can that plane stay in the air. Something is missing," thinking that the child will make pretend wings. The child looks incredulously at the teacher, as if to say "Well, after all, teacher, it *is* a pencil." Furthermore, not many 2- or 3-year-olds think that it is the wings that keep the plane up. Even older children think that it is the pilot who keeps the plane aloft (Piaget, 1969). The point is that, by their very nature, pretend objects have missing parts. Pretend objects don't need to suffer from the constraints of real objects. There is no real need to add "missing" parts. It takes a rather sophisticated child to build pretense on pretense by thinking that something is missing when its presence is not in any real sense essential.

*Look from different angles.* Very young children don't sit still for long. Therefore, they will naturally explore materials from different angles, or, at least, they will see materials from different angles. There are things the teacher can do to increase the chances that one view will be coordinated with another view of something. If the child's activity involves a particular object and the child looks at that object first from above and then from the side, the two views are more likely to be related as two views of the same object if the activity in question continues across both viewings. We have seen 3-year-old children look at a table-top village from above and then bend their torsos to the side to capture the on-line perspective. The bird's-eye view presents the total outlay of miniature streets and houses, while the on-line view presents an almost realistic perspective of the closest objects. An on-line view of a miniature house seems to elicit more thematic play and imaginary dialogue between imaginary household members than does the bird's-eye view. The bird's-eye view, on the other hand, seems to elicit more orientation toward total arrangement of streets and traffic from house to house. If the teacher models the different ways of looking at something—sometimes from above and sometimes from the side—he may facilitate more than a change in visual angle. He may also facilitate a change in the cognitive set the children assume toward the material—for example, a neighborhood in one case and an individual family in the other. While these two visual perspectives are not coordinated hierarchically into class (neighborhood) and subclass (family), it is quite possible that the alternation between these two visual perspectives is essential to later classificatory skills (see Chapter Two on logico-mathematical knowledge).

Look from different angles. Here is finger painting seen from under the Plexiglas table.

*Contrast with familiar objects.* As we said earlier, when we were discussing older children, problem solving involves thinking about events and objects similar to the events and objects defining the problem at hand. The periscope reminded one child of a telescope; that association suggested to the child that the new object might also be something one looks through. We cannot ask younger children to tell us what an object reminds them of, but we can increase the likelihood that such association will be made. If a child is painting with thick paint, the teacher puts a jar of diluted paint in the easel tray. If the child is building with blocks whose weight is balanced about their midline, the teacher gives her blocks with an asymmetrical distribution of weight. Sometimes the teacher provides a contrast with something that is more familiar, sometimes with something that is less familiar; but either way the child is given an opportunity to contrast the familiar with the unfamiliar.

If the material is quite unwieldy, like the play space in a sand table, contrast can be provided by rotating the entire material. A table on casters or, better yet, a table with a lazy-Susan top can solve many of the logistical problems of changing material or changing the position of children standing around a table. If the rotary top is sectioned into large play spaces, a child standing in one position can easily compare the modeling properties of moist sand with the fluid properties of dry sand. A rotary surface also allows for interesting contrasts between two children's points of view. A child who places a toy house in front of a mound of sand sees how the house disappears as he rotates the play space 180 degrees toward his friend.

Relate structure to function. Here the curved board makes the toy car rock back and forth.

*Relate structure to function.* Once again we remind you that young children's way of thinking is more practical than representational. A 2-year-old may know that she can rock in this chair with the funny legs but that she cannot rock in that other chair. However, the 2-year-old cannot represent in words or even in a mental image the relationship between the curved rockers and the chair's movement. She will sit in the rocker and shift her weight to start rocking; she will also realize the futility of doing this in the kitchen chair. This means that she can make the basic discrimination about when to do what; but this is a much simpler understanding of the structure-function relationship than the understanding of the mechanism by which that relationship operates. The 5-year-old might say "The legs are bent, and that makes it [the chair] fall and fall." Although this explanation lacks precision, it does verbally represent the relationship between structure and function.

We may catch a glimpse of the 2-year-old standing near the rocking chair, swaying back and forth in unconcerned rhythm. The child is representing the function of the object through body movements similar to the actual rocking of the chair. The teacher, who has observed the child, imitates the child in parallel play, and then they both sit in their respective rocking chairs. Teacher and child approach the seesaw and dip their knees up and down a few times. They approach the steering wheel mounted on a wooden box and make a few mock spins of the wheel together. They look at a whistle and blow air through their pursed lips. Movement and gesture are excellent vehicles of expression to represent the function of objects, especially with the 2- and 3-year-old. And, as we stated before, the better the child can represent his world, the better he can control the relations necessary to understand his world.

## Summary

Although much of what a teacher does in a preschool classroom may appear to be episodic and fragmentary, this is true only from the perspective of traditional curriculum building. With young children it is very hard to guarantee that each day's activities will flow smoothly and exactly into those of the next day. This, however, doesn't mean that teachers of young children should not strive to achieve some degree of continuity between learning encounters. It is the nature of this continuity that is in question.

The goal of continuity is supported by a framework of general objectives that the teacher uses all the time to observe and analyze children's activities. Naturally, teachers relate the behavior of individual children to certain basic concepts of child development. As the teacher observes the children's activities, he reflects on the meaning of these activities from the point of view of the four areas of knowledge we discussed in Chapter Two; this process of critical reflection is as vital to the activity of teachers as it is to the activity of children.

In the process of deciding how to expand on learning encounters, teachers are likely to make mistakes. This is to be expected and in many ways welcomed. Very often mistakes can provide important information that should not be overlooked. Instead of regretting that a particular encounter didn't work, the teacher should eagerly look for the information about the children, the materials, and teaching in general that each mistake yields. There is really no such thing as wrong information —only wrong use, or no use, of information.

The primary function of teachers of young children is to facilitate the transfer of learning from one content area to another. This doesn't mean that children should be systematically drilled in the use of different materials so that they learn how to apply the various concepts they have learned. What it does mean is that the teacher needs to be aware that children are constantly involved with certain general areas of knowledge and processes of learning and that, in observing the children at play, he or she needs to use this awareness to identify opportunities for meaningful interactions with the children. Piaget's conservation tasks are a good illustration of what we are talking about. These tasks were never intended to be teaching techniques or curriculum activities; yet that is how they are used in many preschool programs. This is not to say that teachers shouldn't be exposed to the conservation tasks and that they shouldn't have experience administering them. These tasks should serve as a tool the teacher can use to notice and recognize when children are grappling with the concept of conservation in their regular play.

Teachers need to continually monitor all the factors that influence a child's engagement with a particular learning encounter. These include the child's knowledge base, motivation level, thinking process, and performance ability. As suggested very strongly by psycholinguists, a child's performance and his competence may not necessarily be comparable. In addition to those factors that center on the child, learning encounters may be affected by the environment within the classroom and by the way in which the encounter is presented, which comprises fixed elements, such as the shape of the room or the number of children present, and variable and controllable elements, such as the materials used and the method of presentation.

The true test of how well learning is transferred from one content area to another is not how well a child does on an exam but how well a teacher identifies general principles in individual children's activities and, therefore, how well she is able to guide the children's experiences toward these general principles. With 4- and 5-year-olds this may be done verbally by suggesting that they identify parts and features of an object or look at the object from different angles. With younger children the teacher cannot rely on verbal suggestions. She encourages and improves exploration by modeling, by showing genuine interest in the activity at hand, and by indicating, through her actions, that many interesting things can be done with the object or activity in question.

## Suggestions for Further Reading

Hawkins, D. The triangular relationship of teacher, student, and materials. In C. Silberman (Ed.), *The open classroom reader.* New York: Vintage Press, 1973. This article speaks to the question of how materials should be used in the classroom. It takes the position that the materials and activities should be a focus for *both* the teacher and the student.

Hawkins, F. P. *The logic of action: Young children at work.* New York: Pantheon Books, 1974. This is a journal kept by an experienced teacher as she worked with a group of deaf preschoolers. It contains many examples of how children learn through their activities with concrete materials and of how important it is for teachers to observe these activities carefully and speculate about their meanings.

Sponseller, D. (Ed.). *Play as a learning medium.* Washington, D.C.: National Association for the Education of Young Children, 1974. This book offers a fine collection of articles on different aspects of children's play, as well as numerous descriptions of children's play. It can serve as a good source for staff discussion about potential learning encounters.

# Chapter Eight

# *Improving the Quality of Teaching*

If we want to improve the quality of teaching, we need clear educational objectives, good techniques for monitoring teacher behavior, openness to constructive criticism, and explicit prescriptions for change. Before staff members can help each other improve, they need to discuss their respective basic assumptions about how children learn. We pointed out in Chapter Three that the copy theory and the constructivist theory are based on two very different assumptions about how children learn and lead to very different methods of teaching. A teacher who values extrinsic motivation and the teaching of specific concepts may find himself at cross-purposes with a colleague who values intrinsic motivation and the teaching of general processes of learning to learn. When we are not fully aware of our basic assumptions, we cannot effectively communicate with others and, what is even worse, with ourselves. It is to this crucial issue of becoming aware of our basic assumptions that we devote the first part of this chapter.

## Discovering Basic Assumptions

Our assumptions about a child's growth are not limited to learning but extend to all areas of child development—social, motor, moral, and cognitive. Our assumptions about one area influence our assumptions about each and all other areas. If, for example, we assume that moral development occurs as a result of internalizing specific sanctions, this may influence our view of other areas of development. One teacher states "Moral development is knowing what to do when—knowing what is right and wrong." Another teacher counters "Moral development is knowing how to determine what is right and wrong and then doing the right thing." These two statements are a clear illustration of the essential split between content approach and process approach. And, although the two teachers are discussing right and wrong, it is very likely that their different approaches will be applied to areas that have very little to do with moral development—for example, to motor development. "Learning a dance rhythm is learning the specific body movements and when to make them" the first teacher explains. The second teacher counters "Learning a dance means first of all being able to better determine body position—an increase in general body awareness."

Teachers need to discover their own basic assumptions regarding child development.

Are these truly different assumptions, or are they simply different ways of describing the same practices? We believe that these are essentially different approaches and that they do lead to real differences in classroom practices. We have discussed some of these differences earlier in the book. In Table 8-1 we review the different classroom practices we have discussed and add a few more. The column on the left lists practices more common to programs that assume that development occurs by the accretion of specific concepts. The column on the right lists practices more common to programs that assume that development occurs by laws of construction that are as internal to the child as a biological system. We said "more common" because no program uses—or, at least, should use—only one of these approaches. Each program should include elements from both, depending on the situation (see the last section in Chapter Five). These assumptions and practices are presented in Table 8-1 in exaggerated terms to emphasize the contrast.

Our basic assumptions not only determine how we approach theoretical issues but also guide our interactions with the children. Basic assumptions are the source of our intuitive feeling that one approach "just isn't right." Basic assumptions are hard to identify because they are so pervasive. They can go unchallenged

*Table 8-1.*

| *Assumption 1:* Development occurs by learning specific concepts that are reinforced extrinsically. | *Assumption 2:* Development occurs by learning processes of discovery and invention that are reinforced intrinsically. |
| --- | --- |
| *Practices consonant with Assumption 1* | *Practices consonant with Assumption 2* |
| An error is a cue that the lesson has been poorly presented. Break lesson into smaller steps. | An error is a cue to how the child has organized information. Engage the child in the subprocess that is causing him difficulty. |
| Knowledge is a repertoire of facts. To evaluate the success of the program, ask the child specific questions. | Knowledge is a system of understanding. To evaluate the success of the program, observe the child solving new problems. |
| Information should be presented in the proper order. Be careful to sequence a lesson properly. | The organization of information is gradually constructed by the child himself. Learning encounters can be episodic. |
| Transfer of learning occurs only between concepts that are quite similar. Be sure to present various forms of the same materials and games. | Transfer of learning occurs across materials of widely different content because of common processes of thinking. Be sure to analyze the cognitive demands of each category of materials and games. |
| Poor memory indicates that the child has not learned the facts well enough. Use more drill and repetition. | Poor memory indicates that the child has not organized his thoughts well. Help the child develop ways of relating new knowledge to old knowledge. |
| Lack of attention indicates that the child is not motivated. Increase your enthusiasm and praise. | Lack of attention indicates that the child is not motivated. Allow the child to shift to a more interesting task. |
| Learning is knowing what response to make. To assess the child's level of learning, measure the frequency of correct responses. | Learning is knowing why we make a response in a given situation. To assess the child's level of learning, identify the pattern of responses across a variety of situations. |
| Learning to learn increases with practice. Make learning difficult, increase praise, and the child will learn by virtue of the struggle. | Learning to learn increases with awareness. Encourage the child to reflect on the processes of solving problems, even easy problems. |
| Development is advanced by knowing which goals to pursue in a given society. Approach the child with a particular goal in mind, and praise his working toward that goal. | Development is advanced by knowing how to structure goals from ambiguous and conflicting information. Allow the child to structure his own goals, and support his overall efforts. |

for years, mainly because so many people share the same set of assumptions—the same "environment." It takes deliberate effort and systematic analysis to clarify values, outline our own implicit learning theory, and uncover our own views about human nature and fundamental objectives for the good life.

Following are a few (stereotyped, we wish to emphasize) examples of how different assumptions affect a teacher's behavior and explanations of behavior. See if you can correctly identify the basic assumption regarding human development that underlies the teacher's approach in each example.

Mrs. T. saw Leroy hit Trina from the rear. Trina had not provoked Leroy in any direct way; she was simply standing by the sandbox, a place usually occupied by Leroy. Mrs. T. saw Trina get very angry. Retaliation promptly followed, with Trina bopping Leroy in the head with her fist. Leroy gasped in surprise and then began to cry. He left the sandbox area and didn't attempt to join the other children for the rest of the free-play period. Although Mrs. T. had anticipated Trina's retaliation, she had decided not to intervene.

Tony, age 3, was having a great time going down the slide. After going down three times on his seat, he began to negotiate the slide on his tummy. Mr. B. stopped him and explained that he might get hurt doing it that way. Tony persisted, and Mr. B. firmly told him to stop going down on his tummy. Tony stood up on the top of the slide and yelled out across the room "Get away! I hate you!" Mr. B. removed Tony from the slide and told him that he was not to use the slide for the rest of the day.

Rayshawn, age 2½, was stringing plastic spools onto a shoelace. Each time she filled the string, she would take all the spools off and start all over again. Mrs. H. noticed that Rayshawn had been doing this, alone, for the past 20 minutes. She approached Rayshawn and said "Come along. Let's put those away so we can play another game together. I have some fun puzzles for us to do." Rayshawn put away the beads and eagerly went to the table with Mrs. H.

Four children were dressing up in the role-playing corner. Spencer, age 3, had put on a lady's dress and a lady's hat and was dragging a big purse around as he clomped in high-heeled shoes. His 4-year-old cousin, Gail, told him "Get out of those clothes, silly. Those are mommy clothes." Mr. S. intervened: "Oh, it's all right, Spencer. In the pretend corner you can be anything you like."

Two parents were observing the classroom during free-play period. Their respective children, Matthew, age 3½, and Deborah, age 3, were playing together with little toy cars. They were driving the little cars on the floor under a table, making detours around the table legs to get to "top of mountain," as Deborah explained. Deborah's mother said to Matthew's mother "They came here to play? They can do that at home. When do they learn something?"

In a Head Start program for 4-year-old Black children, the participants were preparing a school skit. After discussing their skit with their teachers, the children had decided to put on a rock concert—dressed up like rock singers, they would pantomime records of their favorite TV stars. During a rehearsal of a number by The Supremes, several visitors came into the observation room. One of them, Mrs. D., was a Black administrator of the community's Aid to Dependent Children program. It was reported later that Mrs. D., while watching three little girls dancing and shaking in unison with the record, had made the following side comment to another visitor: "We don't need any more of that shaking the rear end. They should be learning something useful."

Mrs. S. had given each child a spoon and placed a hard-boiled egg in each spoon. After the children had practiced walking around, egg in spoon, without dropping the egg, Mrs. S. asked them to line up for a race. The first child to reach a line ten yards away would receive a blue ribbon on a badge that read "First." The next day the parent of the winning child called the teacher and complained about the use of competition in preschool.

Mr. F. had brought in a small paper bag for each of his 4-year-old children. They were scheduled to make puppets from the bags, using crayons and scissors. Mr. F. made a puppet while the children watched. Then he instructed the children to make puppets just like his.

At nap time the 3-year-olds of the Twelfth Street Day Care Center had learned to get their mats and lay them on the floor for napping. Several of the children seemed to like laying their mats quite close to one another, and this often resulted in a girl and a boy napping next to each other. The teachers decided to invest in light cots in order to discourage this habit.

As we hope to have made clear in our discussion, basic assumptions regarding human development involve more than basic principles of learning. They also involve value judgments regarding what should be learned. However—and this is an important point—our view of what should be learned in preschool is influenced by how we think children learn. For example, free play—the case of Matthew and Deborah—is more highly valued if one believes that learning is a process directed by the child. Competition in the classroom—the case of Mrs. S. and the spoon race—is more highly valued if one believes that learning is dependent on extrinsic reinforcement. The reader is encouraged to take each of the preceding examples and examine it in terms of the assumptions presented in Table 8-1. First identify the general assumption that underlies the particular example. Then identify the specific assumption regarding the learning process that applies to the case. And, finally, rewrite the example to illustrate how the alternative assumption would apply to that same situation.

In staff meetings a certain amount of time needs to be spent analyzing basic assumptions. Consciousness raising tends to throw light on and reduce those otherwise unexplainable "communication problems." One teacher says "You describe children as if they were little computers with no feelings." The other replies "Perhaps, but I don't *treat* them like little computers. I talk this way only to help myself understand how complex children are." In another exchange one teacher says "I don't understand why you let Bernie do that. I would never let him get away with it." "But why not?" the second teacher asks. "He didn't intend to do it." The first concludes with "It doesn't matter. Above all, they must learn respect for the teacher." The second thinks for a moment and ventures forth with "They must learn respect for everyone, not just teachers as a special group; but this takes time."

These confrontations contribute much to the growth of the individual teachers, to the overall atmosphere, and, most important of all, to the quality of the program. But these confrontations can also represent an emotional challenge that not everybody is willing to accept—at least right away. They stir up emotions that originate in one's own childhood and early education and that can be quite difficult to deal with. An atmosphere of acceptance is therefore a must. But what else, besides creating this atmosphere, can we do to reduce a teacher's resistance to listening and to change?

## Openness to Change

Changing the way in which we interact with young children is as difficult as changing the way in which we interact with our peers; in both cases strong personality traits may be involved. Change is easier when the teacher realizes, perhaps for the first time, that he is doing something that is against his own ideals. In this case change occurs after the teacher learns to monitor his behavior in the classroom and to check tendencies to behave in ways that are inconsistent with his ideals—keeping in mind, of course, that slips will occur now and then. We will discuss several techniques of self-monitoring in a later section.

Resistance to change is greater when there are fundamental differences between the philosophy of the program and the personal philosophy of the teacher. Guarding against such a conflict begins during staff recruitment. During the interview for a teaching position, the program director outlines the philosophy behind the classroom practices, the school's views on parent involvement, ability grouping, children with special needs, modes of discipline, need for order, degree to which structure is needed, and so on. Ideally the candidate is given an opportunity to see the class in action and sit in for a day or two to observe and teach. The compatibility between the candidate's philosophy and the program's philosophy, as stated *and* practiced, is a major criterion for hiring the candidate and for accepting the offer.

Many times the teaching staff is fairly permanent and may consist of teachers with basic differences in philosophy. As we said in the previous section, the first step toward improving the program is to identify the teachers' basic assumptions. Sometimes, in the course of this process, teachers realize that an assumption concerning one particular area actually conflicts with another assumption concerning a second area. For example, a teacher may take a strong stand on a child-directed approach to art and an equally strong but opposite stand on a teacher-directed approach to number skills. There may be good reasons for taking two different approaches. It could also be that the teacher has never considered that these two approaches are contradictory. The purpose of staff meetings is to clarify these apparent or real inconsistencies. The inconsistencies may be rational or irrational. If they are irrational, the staff discuss ways of resolving them.

Support from the rest of the staff reduces a teacher's resistance to change. Once an inconsistency has been identified and the teacher agrees that change is needed, the teacher and the other members of the staff make specific suggestions to implement the change. The purpose should always be the child's education, and the focus should always be on the problem, not on blame or individual responsibility. Education in preschool classrooms is a group responsibility. Once it has been decided that the approach needs improvement, there is no need to labor the point of why a teacher did what he did. By focusing on the teacher's motives, the discussion shifts from seeking explanations to asking the person to defend his or her personal

Inconsistencies in classroom policy are discussed during staff meetings.

worth. The program director or head teacher plays the most important role in keeping the discussions on the children's education and not on the personal worth of the teachers. When the staff members work well together, personal worth does not become an issue. To clarify this point, let's eavesdrop on a staff meeting that gets bogged down in a challenge to personal worth, and then let's see how the meeting might have gone with a more supportive head teacher.

*Mrs. R.:* Well, that was quite a scene today—all the children running around the room with paint on their feet. Carol, that was your area. What on earth happened?

*Carol:* It was going fine at first. The children put finger paint on their feet and walked across the butcher paper, making footprints. Then Karen's group wanted to join in, and, with ten children altogether, it was too much to handle. Karen should have kept her children involved at the small-games table.

*Karen:* With all that noise and fun nearby? No way! And you know how hard it is to keep Timmy's attention, anyway. Then Buzz came over with red feet. This created a big commotion.

*Carol:* It was pretty hard to wash off all the paint in that little pan of water. The other children grew impatient and ran around. Then the paper got so covered with paint that the children couldn't see their footprints. So they began to make running slides on the paper while I washed feet. They got more and more excited. It was a total flop.

*Susan:* And then those visitors came from the university. I wonder what they thought. They couldn't have come at a worse time.

*Mrs. R.:* Oh, the visitors were students of architecture. What they were interested in was the physical layout of the room.

*Carol:* That's good.

*Mrs. R.:* Carol, try to keep the number of children down to four or five, OK? I think it will work better next time, now that you know some of the problems. Less paint, more water, and more paper would also help. You did the best you could under the circumstances, Carol.

Several things are wrong with this meeting. Mrs. R. unwittingly sets the meeting off on a defensive note by using emotional words like "quite a scene" and "What on earth happened?" despite her intention to be empathic with Carol's dissatisfaction with the painting activity. The teachers then spend too much time talking about what should have been done rather than what can be done next time, which has a more positive tone. Carol passes the blame—at least in part—on to Karen. Karen passes the blame on to the children. Carol makes another defensive move, this time pointing to the inadequacy of the materials. Susan is embarrassed for Carol. Mrs. R. addresses Carol's embarrassment with a comforting comment and then prescribes objectives, without specifying in any detail how these objectives will be implemented.

Let's listen now to another, and much more constructive, version of the same staff meeting.

*Mrs. R.:* Let's talk about the foot-painting activity. As you know, it was the first time we tried it. Carol, let's review the objectives of that activity and then proceed in our usual manner to discuss the activity as it occurred today.

*Carol:* The objective related to the general area of body awareness through graphic representation. By seeing their own footprints, the children could learn a lot of things—for example, the size of their own feet, the span of their own step, and the path they had taken when walking in one direction or another. They were also supposed to try to match footprints with different children. But, wow, what a mess! (Laughter from the staff.)

*Mrs. R.:* Of course, it takes time to work the kinks out of a new activity. I think the objectives of this activity are exciting. Let's proceed to list those things that worked for the objectives and those that worked against them. Then, as we have done before, we will list ways to increase things that help and reduce those that don't. (Mrs. R. stands at the blackboard, chalk in hand, waiting for comments from the teachers.)

*Carol:* It was going all right at first. The children put paint on their feet and walked across the butcher paper, making footprints. Then Karen's group wanted to join in, and, with ten children altogether, it was too much to handle. Karen should have kept her children involved at the small-games table.

*Mrs. R.:* In the left column we can list "too many children" as an obstacle. What can we put in the right column?

*Carol:* Well, before the activity got so crowded, I was able to make comments on the footprints. I asked Buzz to point to his own footprints and to tell me in which direction he had walked. His were the red footprints; the others' were green. He pointed to them correctly and also indicated the direction in which he had walked.

*Mrs. R.:* So, in the right column we can put "teacher's questions" and "color-coded footprints" (staff laughs lightly) as two things that helped the objective. What else?

*Karen:* Buzz came over to my table, his feet all red. My children wanted to know why his feet were so funny-looking. Seeing red feet certainly increases "feet awareness," but it also creates a commotion. My children, too, wanted to paint their feet.

*Mrs. R.:* You have mentioned something that did help, as well as something that didn't. In the right column we will list "contrast between painted and unpainted feet" as an aid to body awareness. In the left column we will list "overflow into another group." Anything else?

*Susan:* Did you see those visitors from the university? I wonder what they thought! They couldn't have come at a worse time.

*Mrs. R.:* Those were students from the architecture department. They are doing a special project on space for young children. Which reminds me: is there anything about the layout of our room that helped or hampered the objectives?

*Susan:* I think the space was too big. It encouraged the children to run around too much. Before long there was so much paint on the paper that no child could see his own footprints. That's when they started sliding into the paint.

The staff meeting continues, and more items are added in the two columns. But the discussion doesn't stop here. It continues into a second, and most important, phase—*prescriptions and assignments,* or what needs to be done and who will do it. Such questions as those that follow speak to some of the important aspects of the activity discussed at the staff meeting. Who will get the large pan of water? Who will rearrange the space to discourage running? How will Karen help prevent this activity from interfering with her own activity? What activity may facilitate transfer of learning within the general objective of body awareness through graphic representation?

This analytic approach to solving problems reduces defensiveness, actually saves time, and increases the effectiveness of teaching. The teachers eventually adopt this neutral and objective approach so automatically that they begin to use it in the classroom, and that is the real payoff of good staff meetings.

## Going beyond the Particular Behavior

An effective teacher can think beyond the particular behavior he observes. He is fully aware of the richness and uniqueness of each single act that the child performs but can also see that act as an instance of general child development. Bouncing a ball is "experimenting with gravity." A brief battle with a peer is "establishing autonomy." Specific behaviors are instantly identified as instances of more general categories of development. This is not done out of a pedantic need for psychological jargon. It is done to give the teacher a number of good ideas for improving his performance in the classroom and to increase the child's generalization of learning from one situation to another. How does the teacher learn to recognize theoretical concepts in raw behavior?

Many programs for teacher development now have videotaping facilities. When used properly, videotapes can greatly contribute to teacher development. Videotapes can be used in at least two ways: (1) to film children interacting with materials and with each other and (2) to film teacher-child interactions. Both uses can help the teacher understand child development in general; the second is also of help in evaluating the effectiveness of teaching.

*Videotapes of Child Behavior*

Good teaching begins with a comprehensive understanding of child development. In the calm of a videotape viewing room, the teacher can relax and study, perhaps for the first time, what actually happens in the classroom. By watching concrete episodes, the teacher gradually assigns personal meaning to abstract concepts like decentration, displacement of aggression, attachment behavior, territorial behavior, and problem-solving strategies. Yet, these instances of specific kinds of behavior do not pop out in bold relief from the video screen. There are techniques of filming and methods of viewing that can make critical events more noticeable.

When filming the children, it is best to begin with a wide angle shot that sets the total context. This wide angle shot gives the viewer information about the number of children in the immediate proximity, the number of adults, the layout of the room or playground, and the range of materials and equipment available. After the setting shots and several pans across the total area, the camera operator should focus on a smaller area—a small group, perhaps, or two children in parallel play. Teachers may of course be included, but for the moment we are discussing videotapes to be used to understand child development rather than videotapes designed to critique teaching effectiveness. Once this smaller context is set by several minutes of tape, you can zoom in on a single child. The choice of the child may be determined in advance during a staff meeting, or it may be arbitrarily made when filming. If the latter, you should choose a child who is apparently engaged in some purposive behavior—for example, trying to tie her shoes, trying to wash a doll, or listening to and imitating rhythms.

Once you have selected an individual child, keep the camera focused on that child even during those times when he or she is passively watching an event. If the child is watching something, shift the camera only briefly enough to show the object of the child's attention. Don't lose the continuity of the child's behavior. This is one of the most common mistakes students make in filming children. Videotapes that jump around from child to child leave the viewer confused and with no sense of the individual child's style of solving problems, coping with distractions, and following through on objectives. When the camera maintains focus on one child, teachers begin to discover how one episode in the block corner is perhaps a generalization of another episode in the kitchen corner. While involved in the ongoing activities of the children, the teacher cannot follow the child from area to area; she doesn't know that the block that Byron is placing under the block bridge is in fact the pretend cake that the child was not permitted to place in the oven in the kitchen corner. Videotapes afford the teacher this opportunity.

If the child's intention seems to be the establishment of social contact, both the child and her peers are shown. If the child's attention seems to be directed toward the function of materials, the camera zooms in to capture the details of eye contact and manual manipulations. Microphones can be stationed in key areas—for example, over the sandbox, over tables, and over small play spaces. Microphones built into the camera are generally not effective in picking up conversations clearly.

A camera placed high on a tripod is useful for getting a good angle on manual actions and peer contact. Periodically the camera should be lowered to the same height as the child's head. This gives the viewer a better feeling of how objects and adults look to the child himself. Zoom in when the child's attention is focused on materials. Zoom back when the child's attention is directed to other children, adults, or events at some distance.

Sometimes the teachers can prepare a problem for the children to solve while being filmed. Before the children enter the room, the stage is set, with camera ready. In this case, the initial focusing of the camera is on the area where the problem is staged rather than on an individual child. This technique was effectively used one day at the laboratory school of the University of Massachusetts.[1] The children entered the playroom and discovered that all the sand had been removed from the free-standing sand table and placed in a huge cardboard box about five feet from the sand table. As the camera rolled, one child began to transfer the sand from the box to the table, using his hands. During the next 20 minutes this child progressed from using an inefficient means (his hands) to using more and more efficient means, like a large saucepan, and even enlisting and directing the aid of another classmate. That tape was one of the best of the year. It portrayed means-ends relationships, the discovery of the contrast between empty and full, the social interaction of two children working toward a common goal, and the development of certain physical concepts like the correlation between size and weight. Staging problems in advance can yield videotapes that will be useful for years to come.

Once the videotape has been made, there are methods for viewing the tape that make critical events more noticeable. Play the videotape segment with the audio turned off. This draws attention to the action on the screen and gives you more time to think about the implications of the action. (Off-camera noises won't distract you from your chain of thoughts.) Look closely at the child's eyes. Are they tracking what he is doing with his hands? Are they looking at some object or event irrelevant to the action of his hands? Or are they looking ahead at some part of the environment that will be shortly integrated into the child's ongoing behavior? What actions is the child repeating? And in what ways is he varying his behavior? Is there a general theme in these variations? What obstacles does the child encounter along the way? How does he accommodate to these obstacles? Does the child seek help from adults? All these questions are general enough to be applied to the viewing of most videotapes and help the viewer focus on critical moments.

Sit with the video monitor before you and a tablet of paper and a pencil in hand. As you watch the videotape, you can diagram a simple flowchart of the child's objectives and of the obstacles he encounters in meeting these objectives. Here is an example. The videotape shows Byron, a 2-year-old, sitting on a wooden truck, scooting around the floor. The teacher makes the following notes from the videotape.

[1]This clever project was designed, filmed, and managed by Elaine Batchelder. Many thanks to Ms. Batchelder for her creative efforts.

Byron drives his truck toward sunporch.
His passage blocked by sliding glass door.
Byron leaves truck to get teacher to open door.
While Byron is on other side of room, Janine opens sliding door.
Byron tugs at teacher's skirt and points toward sunporch door.
Teacher walks with Byron to door, now open.
Byron pushes his weight on door to *close* it.
Looks up at teacher in supplication.
Teacher closes door for Byron.
Byron gets on truck and drives away.
*Implication:* Difficulty with maintaining goal in mind. Couldn't relate move-
ment of door with movement of truck. During time it took him to get from
door to teacher and back, all he could remember was that he wanted the door
moved but couldn't remember why or in which direction.

Sometimes the child's goals are not as clear as in Byron's case. Imitating the
action shown by the videotape can bring in relief subtle details of child behavior.
You can reenact the play of a child very exactly. Take a ten-minute segment of one
child—for example, a child who, in the staff's opinion, needs special attention.
Leroy—a sullen child prone to play alone under any available table—is a good case
in point. The videotape segment first shows Leroy playing with play dough at the
table. Then it shows Leroy retreating under the table and several teachers trying to
coax him out of his hiding place and into joining a group game. Finally the videotape shows Leroy refusing to come out from under the table. The teachers decide to
reenact this whole segment as faithfully as possible. First, the comments that the
teachers make while watching the tape a couple of times are recorded. Here are
some of the teachers' comments.

Leroy was playing fine at first, then he withdrew.
He doesn't do anything under the table; just hides.
Leroy is such a serious child; he never smiles.
I think Leroy is afraid of all the noise in the room.
Carol may have made him withdraw even more by asking him several times to
join the circle game.

Then the teachers set up the table as it was when the children were there. (The
table is larger, of course, so that the teacher can role-play Leroy hiding under the
table.) The teaching staff play about a minute of the tape and then act it out, then
they play another minute of the tape and act it out, careful to be as true as they can to
the pace of behavior, the emotion, the language, and the body posture shown by the
tape. After three or four minutes of imitating Leroy, the teacher who is playing
Leroy's role begins to feel a little like Leroy. These are his comments after the reenactment is finished. The teacher, Mr. J., uses the first person to refer to Leroy.

I don't think I'm as afraid as I'm angry. I was sitting here rolling my play
dough when Stanley muscled in real close and began to roll his play dough. I
stopped rolling and watched him. He grabbed a big piece of play dough from the
bowl in the middle of the table. I knew I was next, so I pinched off a little piece of
my own dough and slid under the table. Then I dropped it and couldn't find it. I

was really mad then but didn't want to come out. It was sort of fun under there anyway. Some of the kids would peer under the table at me, and I would make a face like a snarl. I sat there sort of on all fours, watching people's legs. Then all the children left the table and I was alone there. They began to play "All fall down." I could see them stoop down at the end of the song. I stooped down myself under the table, remembering the game. Then Mrs. C. tried to coax me out. Her face took up almost the whole space between the table legs. I turned my back on her and hurt my hand. I held my hand and decided to stay under the table.

After Mr. J.'s reenactment of Leroy's behavior and his "retrospective" analysis of Leroy's thoughts, the teachers form new opinions about Leroy's problem. They decide that Leroy needs more private space than some of the other children. This opinion fits with the information they have about his home—a small apartment he shares with many siblings. The teachers also feel that Leroy was involved, albeit vicariously, in the circle game but that the teacher's looming face and his hurt hand frustrated him so much that he wouldn't leave his sanctuary. The teachers decide that, the next time Leroy adjourns under the table, they will let him play there and that one teacher will sing the circle songs near him but not directly to him. Perhaps this peripheral role of the teacher will be a sufficient bridge between Leroy and the other children, and Leroy will venture out to play. (Aside: the real Leroy did grow to enjoy the other children, and he did create sunshine in our hearts with one of the biggest smiles in the group.)

Sometimes the simple question "What did the child *not* do?" can produce insights regarding what the child did do. Look at the videotape as if you were seeing both the positive and the negative of a photograph.

> Stanley grabbed the clay. He did not ask for it.
> Laura held the doll upside down. She did not hold it right side up.
> Tim pounded the board with the hammer. He did not pound the hammer with the board.
> Maria pretended to crack the eggs and then stir them. She did not pretend to stir the eggs before she cracked them.
> Susie removed the blocks from the tower one at a time. She did not knock the tower over all at once.
> Michael dabbed his paintbrush into the paint cup and then made a stroke on the paper. He did not dab his brush into two different paint cups before making a stroke.

What a child doesn't do may be the result of a deliberate choice not to do that. This means that what a child doesn't do indicates what he knows how to do. If very young children have a tendency to dab their brushes into several cups of paint rather than into only one, then Michael, who doesn't do this, knows more about painting than we can observe on the videotape. He also knows what not to do.

Thinking about what the child didn't do forces us to place the given behavior on a dimension of child development. The fact that Laura doesn't hold the doll right side up indicates that she is at a lower stage of development than the child who is careful to hold the doll in the right position while cradling it; that is, Laura is at a lower stage on the developmental dimension "representation by pretense." If Maria knows the right sequence of cracking and stirring a pretend egg, she is placed higher on the dimension of "representation by pretense" than a classmate who inverts this order. Looking at a videotape as if it were both a positive and a negative image helps the teacher understand the significance of what does happen.

### Videotapes of Teacher-Child Interaction

Essentially the same guidelines that apply to filming individual child behavior apply to filming teacher-child interaction. A good soundtrack becomes somewhat more important, however, because of the greater verbal interaction that occurs when teacher and child are together. A teacher who is aware of the importance of good camera angles and good sound pickup can do much to improve both. The teacher can use her body to protect a child's work space and, at the same time, block distractions as the child works. The teacher can right a fallen microphone, repeat a less-than-audible comment made by the child, and do a hundred other things that improve the quality of the tape.

The teacher's self-awareness increases when she knows that she is being video-taped. The teacher gains a proficiency in monitoring both her own and the child's behavior and language that she may not demonstrate off camera. When members of the staff have good rapport and can accept the candor of videotapes, the very act of being taped helps the teacher gain greater self-awareness, which is essential to the task of becoming a better teacher. Self-awareness should not be confused with self-consciousness, which is often the result of insecurity about personal worth. Self-awareness is the ability to identify what exactly one does, the positive as well as the negative.

Young teachers are generally greatly surprised when they are shown how well they did in a learning encounter. When they are removed from the pressure of the classroom, they can see that their words were well chosen, that they allowed the child time to complete a task, that they effectively supported a child's efforts, or that they anticipated the child's objective enough to move in with an effective challenge. Young teachers seem to remember much better what went wrong than what went well. Their preoccupation with mistakes narrows their capacity to remember accurately. They fail to keep in mind that the child learns despite the teacher's mistake. What is remembered as a disjunctive half hour is seen on videotape as a series of scenes with a common story line. Seeing yourself on videotape is like seeing a film of a play in which you were a character. When you played your part you remembered only your own lines; when you see the play as a spectator, you are surprised to discover that the play has continuity and a message.

Staff meetings held to view videotapes of teaching techniques should be approached with positive feelings. Strengthen these positive feelings by listing all those things that you yourself liked about the session on tape. This technique is not a defensive ploy to ease the pain of negative comments from others. Identifying the positive is essential if the teacher is to resist the temptation to reject his or her approach in total. The teacher-child interaction is seldom, if ever, completely bad. The answer to the question "Was I effective?" cannot be given in a yes/no form, any more than can the answer to the question "Did Leroy have a good day today?" For example, an instruction or question may be well worded but poorly timed. A challenge may be well timed but poorly conceived. A game may be well conceived but poorly managed. Videotapes give us the data we need to resist discarding the message with the noise.

The teacher-child interaction is more than the individual behavior of the two people involved. The interaction is a set of exchanges, a series of reciprocal influences of child on teacher and teacher on child. Any diagram of the teacher-child interaction needs to capture both directions of influence. Teaching effectiveness can then be evaluated both in terms of the child accommodating to the influence of the teacher and in terms of the teacher accommodating to the influence of the child.

## Monitoring Teacher-Child Interaction

The difficulty of watching yourself while you teach (*in vivo,* as the naturalist says) rests in the double effort it takes to monitor what is going on while, at the same time, contributing to what is going on. The effective teacher develops an image of himself working with the children while the encounter is in progress. The effective teacher can dissociate enough from the pace of and emotional involvement in the immediate situation to weigh, evaluate, anticipate, and accommodate to the specific encounter. The effective teacher can reflect on the pattern of an encounter without losing empathy for the individual children involved. The teacher's thoughts alternate back and forth between the encounter as a system and the child as an individual. How can a teacher do all this? Some people feel that these are intuitive skills and that the art of teaching cannot be directly taught. These people believe that our training programs do more to select teachers who have these intuitive skills than to train teachers who don't have them. We feel that this is an overly negative view of teacher preparation. There are heuristics, analogies, models, and rules of thumb that the beginning teacher can use to improve his or her ability to think quickly on the classroom floor. The teacher uses all or some of these analogies as the encounter proceeds.

Before the teacher can engage herself in monitoring her own interaction with the children, she needs to put aside all other thoughts. The time when the teacher is in the classroom initiating and maintaining learning encounters is not the time to be worrying whether the school bus will be on schedule or whether the parent conferences will go OK. Since the teacher must simultaneously *be in* and *reflect on* the learning encounter, she doesn't have any "thinking space" left to ponder details currently irrelevant to the encounter. The first rule for effective self-monitoring is: forget everything else but the present encounter. An inexperienced teacher may resist this injunction because she is afraid that emergencies may be brewing and that, if she doesn't anticipate them, they will develop into real crises. But emergencies do not occur as often as a new teacher imagines, and they can usually be prevented by careful planning before the children arrive. And, anyway, teachers seem to develop a sixth sense for the signs of brewing emergencies, without having to be constantly on the alert about this or that. So, we repeat, relax and throw mind and body into the present.

Don't be overly concerned about one child being ignored while you work with another. You can shift your attention to that child later. But if you keep worrying about not giving one child your attention, you end up by giving both children only part of your attention. Be in the present; concentrate on the movements and intentions of one child at a time. Make an entry, follow through, reach closure as much as possible, and then shift to another child. If two children are working in a well-functioning dyad, relate to this ongoing interaction, and challenge, expand, summarize, and exit, trying to achieve as much closure as possible.

*Techniques for Monitoring Teacher-Child Interaction*

You and the child create an interaction that has a form, a pattern of its own. Self-monitoring of the interaction can be improved by describing that pattern through analogies while you are teaching. Teachers do use analogies this way even in everyday conversations: "Working with Andrea was like a tug-of-war" or "Today in the science area Leslie and I had our ups and downs, but then it smoothed out." These analogies usually refer to our emotional highs and lows, as we meet with cooperation or resistance from the child. But most of the time the analogies we use are not precise enough to be of much help. How can we use analogies more precisely and, consequently, to greater purpose?

Let's try three different analogies to describe the teacher's entry. The key analogy for all three is the vector—a line of force with a particular direction. Look at Figure 8-1. The solid vector represents the child's goal-directed behavior. The

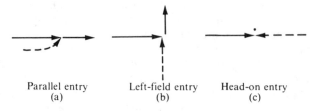

Parallel entry          Left-field entry          Head-on entry
(a)                           (b)                             (c)

*Figure 8-1.*

dashed vector represents the teacher's approach to the child at work. The teacher makes contact with the child at the point where the arrowheads meet. As the teacher observes the child, he plans an entry into the child's world. He also monitors the form of that entry while he is making it. Is he making a parallel entry (Figure 8-1a)— that is, does he assume the child's objective for a while and then present a challenge (where the arrowheads meet)? Or does he come in from left field, make contact, and knock the child off his own objective (Figure 8-1b)? Or does he enter head on, thereby stopping the child's goal-directed behavior altogether (indicated in Figure 8-1c by the period)? A teacher who can use analogies, such as vectors, finds that he has more time to think about both the pattern of the encounter and the richness of its specific content. This economy of thinking is a result of being able to use analogies to monitor oneself in vivo.

Analogies, models, catchphrases, rules of thumb—all help the teacher meet the individual needs of the children, restructure an area, make a task more interesting, change the focus, and capitalize on the spontaneous. By carefully monitoring the environment-teacher-child interaction, the teacher becomes an active developer and rearranger of the educational experience. Compare the three different ways of thinking about this interaction diagrammed in Figure 8-2.

In Figure 8-2a the child is represented as a "subset" of the teacher and the teacher-child as a subset of the environment. This model fails to represent that the child's perspective of the environment is different from that of the adult. Figure 8-2a also suggests that the child's access to the outside world is completely dominated by the influence of the teacher. Figure 8-2b represents a better way of seeing the environment-teacher-child interaction, because it shows that the child and the teacher have independent access to the outside world; however, this world is still represented as the same for both teacher and child. Figure 8-2c illustrates the best view, because it captures both essential relations—the independent access to the outside world and the fact that this world is different for teacher and child. The area of overlap represents shared interpretations and efficient communications. Keeping Figure 8-2c in mind while working in the classroom helps the teacher remember that effective communication with a child is always a matter of "negotiating" for a common interpretation of experiences.

The teacher can profit from the use of an economical way of thinking about the motivations of individual children. The ease with which children can assimilate

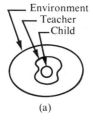
(a)

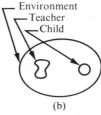
(b)

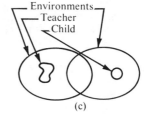
(c)

*Figure 8-2.*

new experiences is determined, in part, by momentary states of interest, fear, defensiveness, and openness. In teaching teachers to think about these momentary states, we found that diagrams like those in Figures 8-3, 8-4, 8-5, and 8-6 are quite useful. These diagrams represent the possible problems of the moment and the changes that would once again make the learning encounter proceed smoothly.

In Figure 8-3a the child is not sensitive to significant experiences. His fears cause him to build an impervious barrier of passivity to new experiences (the barrier is represented by the bold circle). The teacher senses this, lays the current task aside for the moment, and soothes and comforts the child until his defensiveness decreases (the decrease is represented by the lighter circle in Figure 8-3b). Once this is done, the outside experiences are assimilated, rethought, manipulated, and transformed into some new knowledge (arrow leaving circle in Figure 8-3b).

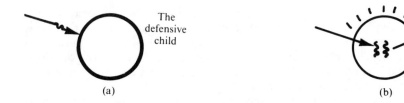

*Figure 8-3.*

In Figure 8-4 the child is actively rejecting the entry of a new experience. This is not a matter of passive resistance, as in Figure 8-3, but a rebellious rejection of new experiences. In order to restore the value of the learning encounter, the teacher once again directs her attention to the motivational state. If information is being actively deflected (bent arrow in Figure 8-4a), at least the child is thinking, since he must think in order to deflect the experience. If the teacher can follow the "direction" of this deflected experience and move more in the direction of the child, the child's resistance may diminish. For example, if the teacher hands a shape to the child, so he can compare it with another one, and the child throws it to the floor, the teacher follows the direction of that "deflected" experience by shifting to a comparison of how different shapes roll and toss.

*Figure 8-4.*

In Figure 8-5 the child is neither passively resistant nor actively rejecting. For some reason the experience is being distorted once it enters the child's consciousness (the shift from the solid arrow to the dashed arrow in Figure 8-5a). Once the teacher senses that this is the nature of the child's problem, she can begin to accommodate to

*Figure 8-5.*

the child's way of thinking. For example, say that Cindy sees her friend Audrey in a white housecoat merrily playing in the dress-up corner. To Cindy the white house-coat is a doctor's smock, and she is afraid to get close to Audrey. Once the teacher senses this distortion, Cindy and the teacher touch the housecoat, talk about it, until Cindy is no longer afraid that her friend Audrey is going to "doctor" her.

Figure 8-6 illustrates a common occurrence in the classroom. The child, probably because of fatigue or frustration, seems to be watching and listening to what goes on around him, but he isn't doing anything with those experiences. This is the in-one-ear-and-out-the-other situation; not much thinking is going on.

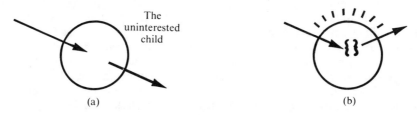

*Figure 8-6.*

Throughout this book, we have suggested things that the teacher can do to motivate thinking when this situation occurs, and in Chapter Five we discussed how the teacher can generate mild levels of conflict to increase the child's interest. Rests, retreats to private spaces, and a change of activity are also means to accommodate to this situation. The preceding diagrams can help the teacher think quickly while working with a child or a group of children in the hum and buzz of the classroom.

## Preparing the Educational Environment

The staff can improve the quality of the program by designing an educational environment that will support the program's objectives. The physical space within which the child works, as well as the curriculum materials, certainly influences what the child learns (see Figure 7-2, Chapter Seven). The teacher takes an active role in preparing the educational environment.

### Improving the Physical Space

We will refer to the world of the classroom—its layout, colors, furniture arrangement, and so forth—as physical space or physical environment. This is the space within which the child lives. The teaching staff soon discover that much of the children's physical space is shaped by the decisions that the adults make from day to day. Despite the fact that the classroom has a fixed floorplan, fixed windows, and other fixed elements, much can be done to improve the physical environment to support educational objectives.

After observing the classroom for a week or two, the teaching staff can decide on a priority of needs. Here are some common findings and some common solutions to problems in preschool programs. To reduce noise level, acoustical insulation can be achieved by draping bellows of fire-resistant fabric between horizontal guy wires across the ceiling. Traffic patterns can be controlled and channeled by low shelves and platforms placed in the center of the room. This also reduces running in the classroom. Large-motor climbing equipment, like a floor-to-ceiling structure with balcony, tunnel, stairs, overlook, and niches, does wonders to focus children on more social and less expansive play (Sommer, 1969). Carpeted areas encourage children to sit on the floor, thus also increasing focused activity and/or social interaction. Windows serve no purpose if the children cannot see out of them. Carpeted risers under windows and elsewhere in the room solve the problem of a room built for adults. The risers, like other carpeted areas, increase focused activity because they have a soft texture and because they provide a convenient space for sitting. A dead corner of the room can be brought to life by adding cushions and some plywood partitions for privacy. Young children need spaces, large enough just for them, to retreat to when the frustrations of a bad day begin to build.

These dimensions of the physical space—scale, privacy, traffic patterns, and functionality—are the common-sense features of good classroom design. We know that a chair seat that is 20 inches from the floor undermines a 2-year-old's feeling of security. We know that a wall cluttered with three dozen paintings by an equal number of children will create distracting visual "noise." There are many useful publications on how to improve the classroom's physical space (for example, Aaron & Winawer, 1965; Kritchevsky, Prescott, & Walling, 1969). Here we wish to make a few comments on physical space from the particular angle of how physical space relates to the theory underlying this text. It is unlikely that other publications emphasize specifically these points, even though a similar theoretical perspective may be implicit in them.

Throughout this book we have stressed the role of transformations in the child's construction of knowledge. The physical space in which the child plays can be responsive or not responsive to the child's need to transform space. The teaching staff should decide how to make the physical environment responsive. Tables that are too heavy to be moved, slides whose angle of incline cannot be adjusted, and steps that are attached to only one corner of a riser deny the child the opportunity to learn by transforming space. Many of the fixtures can be made less fixed and still remain quite safe. What better way to learn the functional relation between pitch and velocity than to have a slide that can be adjusted to several different angles of incline?

A room with no spaces raised above floor level denies the children the opportunity to look down on things and to look up at things. Climbing to a balcony and looking down on the room can transform the child's view completely. The general pattern of the room becomes more apparent. Spaces that the child could never see simultaneously while he was on the floor become apparent all at once from above. Towers, partitions, crawl spaces, and platforms help the child structure detours as variations on the same space (see Figure 4-1 in Chapter Four).

With a little carpentry, teachers can build work spaces that can change in elevation, rotation, and inclination. In Chapter Seven we mentioned one work space that rotates—a table with a lazy-Susan top. By transforming the work space, children can construct a network of spatial relations that includes the other person's point of view. By changing the elevation of a work space, the children can integrate the on-line view with the bird's-eye view. By changing the inclination of a work space, children can encounter new and challenging problems—for example, a vertical block tower that keeps collapsing even though the blocks are perfectly stacked. All of these transformations should increase the child's awareness of the relativity of spatial orientation—that is, of the fact that orientation depends on some arbitrary frame of reference.

Physical spaces that are usually bounded by opaque walls can be bounded instead by transparent or reflecting walls. A wall or floor of nonbreakable mirror tiles or an easel with a Plexiglas board creates exciting possibilities to increase body awareness and provide contrasting experiences. However, these unusual surfaces should be introduced gradually, one at a time, and then removed. Too much contrast can confuse and overwhelm the young child. Furthermore, these surfaces should be under the child's control. Mirrors on casters, Plexiglas mounted in wooden frames that can be angled like an easel or a tracing table or even set up like a vertical partition give the child control over the surface. The child can make marks on the Plexiglas with a grease pencil and then change the marks or change the inclination of the surface.

With some more sophisticated carpentry, outdoor equipment can be made convertible. The seesaw can be notched so that the child, with the teacher's help, can move the pivot forward or backward and note how the seesaw's motion changes. Climbing gyms can be anchored and joined in such a way that the teacher, under the child's direction, can reposition crossbars and vertical supports. The child learns that the climbing gym is one set of parts that can be arranged in many different ways, that the climbing gym was not "born" the way it looks now, and that some structural alternatives are neither aesthetically nor physically sound. The crossbar on the swings can be raised or lowered so that the child can notice how shortening or lengthening the swing chain affects the arc of his swing. Convertible equipment can increase the chances that children between the ages of 2 and 5 will construct functional relations, which in Piaget's view is the primary achievement of this stage of development (see Chapter Four).

### Choosing Curriculum Materials

Teachers need to test the curriculum material themselves. We can't rely on the clever titles of commercial materials as an indication of their value. Materials that are labeled "number games" often have nothing to do with number concepts. Many products advertised as materials that build classification skills do no more than develop elementary forms of discrimination skills. Some expensive products offer no more than do the recycled materials teachers can make themselves. Here are some guides for selecting and designing curriculum materials.

Use materials that can offer a range of difficulty. Material that requires just one level of ability will be used while novel and then never used again. Look for material that specifies the range of difficulty and tells you why some activities are more difficult than others. Jigsaw puzzles are a good example. Too often the degree of difficulty of a jigsaw puzzle is determined by the number of pieces; the more pieces there are, the more difficult the puzzle. This quantitative difference misses the point of what we mean by difficulty as an aid to developmental growth. Difficulty can lead the child along a dimension of development—for example, from empirical to logical. This is more than a quantitative difference. The *Young Learners Puzzles,* produced by Teaching Resources in Boston, are a good example of a curriculum material with a developmental sequence.

The *Young Learners Puzzles* begin at the empirical level and progress to the logical level. At the first (simplest) level each puzzle piece has a different shape. Therefore the placing of pieces is self-correcting; a piece fits or doesn't fit. At the second level all pieces are squares. The child cannot rely on the shapes of the pieces in order to reconstruct the scene. He must go beyond the physical element of the fit and progress to the visual element of the picture he is trying to put together. And at the third level of difficulty the child must think about the meaning of the picture; the fact that the scene looks scrambled or not is no longer enough to solve the puzzle. At this level there are four pieces that can fit in the one space adjacent to a picture of a child's hand. In order to solve the puzzle, the child must decide if the space should contain a sand shovel, a watering pitcher, a block, or a paintbrush, depending on the context of the puzzle at large. All four pieces fit physically, but only one piece makes sense logically. The levels of these puzzles move the child from the empirical world of physical fit to the logical world of meaningful fit. Teachers should look for other such curriculum materials.

Use material that causes the child to think. Many curriculum materials involve problems that can be solved too easily. One example is a game that supposedly develops number concepts but that the child can solve without even counting. A set of rubber squares with holes are placed over a set of pegs. The pegs on the board ascend from one peg to two pegs to three pegs in a cluster, up to five pegs. Each rubber square can fit only on the peg cluster that has as many pegs as the square has holes. The children soon learn to place the squares over the peg clusters without making mistakes. They can do this by simply looking at the *pattern* of the holes. This game has no more to do with numbers than does a common jigsaw puzzle. Teachers should look at the material, decide what the easiest way to solve the problem is, and then assume that that's how the children will solve it.

Increase the "degrees of freedom." Self-corrective material offers very few degrees of freedom, since the chance of error has been reduced by physically constraining many alternative responses. A jigsaw puzzle whose pieces are all different in shape (that is, only one piece fits a particular space) offers fewer degrees of freedom than a jigsaw puzzle whose pieces are all the same shape. The Montessori cylinder blocks offer fewer degrees of freedom than the Montessori pink tower. The cylinder blocks are a self-corrective seriation task, and the pink tower is a free-form version of the seriation task. Number games that have few degrees of freedom, like the rubber-square set just mentioned, don't deal with number concepts, because number concepts involve free-form one-to-one correspondence rather than self-corrective one-to-one correspondence. Montessori's notion that we can train the senses to be responsive to number and seriation misses the point that these concepts deal with transformations and not with the world of physical appearances (see Chapter Three).

Use material that can be transformed. There are commercially available good examples of transformable toys and materials. Even if the material is not meant to be transformable, you can make it so. Let's say that you buy a pull toy with fixed wheels and axles. You can slightly modify the toy to allow the child to change a centered axle hole to an off-centered axle hole. By changing the position of the axle, the child can create different effects—a smooth-rolling toy, a lopping toy, or a wobbling toy. Each is a variation of the same toy, and each moves in a different way. A Styrofoam oval can be the head of a child and, by adding a felt moustache, the head of an adult. Tinker toys, blocks, clay, pipe cleaners, Lego blocks, and felt boards—all allow the child to construct relations, transform them, and think about the operations involved in the change. Chapter Nine presents a set of curriculum activities that support the objectives that derive from our constructivist theory of development.

## Summary

The improvement of teaching at any level of education has four basic requirements. First, clear teaching objectives must be specified. This requires discussions among staff members on their respective values and assumptions about the nature of learning and knowledge. Second, good techniques for monitoring teaching, both by observers and by the teachers themselves, need to be adopted. Third, teachers must be open to constructive criticism and to the very process of change. This will require sensitive leadership and guidance on the part of the directors and head teachers of the particular program. The last requirement is a result of the other three: the elaboration of explicit plans for change.

It is important that, at the very beginning of the program year, teachers spend some time discovering and discussing the basic assumptions they hold concerning children, teaching, learning, and knowledge. This is not to say that everyone should be of one mind. Discussions of this sort ensure that staff members will not work at cross-purposes and can greatly help the teachers become more conscious of their own assumptions and beliefs and determine if their actual teaching reflects these assumptions and beliefs.

Once the program year has started, teachers can use a variety of techniques to promote the development of their teaching skills. Frequent use of videotapes, both of children interacting with materials and other children and of teachers interacting with children, can provide excellent opportunities to reflect on teaching behaviors, both negative and positive. These tapes should not be used to judge or to score but, rather, to promote open discussion about ways of successfully interacting with children.

Teachers need to have many opportunities to explore how they can become more aware of the general dimensions of development and general categories of knowledge that are intrinsic in each particular action by a child. Videotapes, by preserving the actions of children, provide the teacher with some of these opportunities. Analogies and metaphors can be very helpful to conceptualize the advantages and disadvantages of different approaches. Teachers should be encouraged to use analogies and metaphors at staff meetings as a way of clarifying important issues.

A discussion of teaching improvement would not be complete without acknowledging the crucial role that the environment plays in the teaching/learning process. Teachers should spend considerable time discussing how physical space can be arranged to maximize the child's experiences. It is also important that the teacher devote some time to analyzing the curriculum materials to make sure that they do indeed facilitate the construction of knowledge.

## Suggestions for Further Reading

Rowen, B. *The children we see: An observational approach to child study.* New York: Holt, Rinehart & Winston, 1973. An excellent aid for teachers who are engaged in the exploration of their own values and assumptions about children and learning.
Schwebel, M., & Raph, J. The developing teacher. In M. Schwebel & J. Raph (Eds.), *Piaget in the classroom.* New York: Basic Books, 1973. This article raises some interesting points from the Piagetian perspective about the development of teachers.
Stevens, J. H., Jr., & King, E. W. *Administering early childhood education programs.* Boston: Little, Brown, 1976. Two chapters of this book are especially recommended: "Teacher selection, training, and supervision" and "Selection of appropriate curriculum materials."

# Section 5
# Practical Suggestions

# Chapter Nine

# Suggested Learning Encounters

The following is a set of six learning encounters that the authors have found useful in working with children 2 through 5 years old. Each encounter is presented in three forms. The first form describes the basic objective and the behavioral setting. The other two forms represent a simpler and a more difficult version of the same encounter. Most of these encounters begin with the children already engaged with some material of their choice. Of course, the teacher may have prepared the environment by setting out materials, or he may begin an activity alone and wait for the children to take note of what he is doing. The teacher may make general comments to orient the children toward the materials, but seldom are these comments so specific that they rob the child of a discovery or an invention. Also, the teacher most often works with a single child, even though other children may be nearby. Working with a single child ensures continuity of the sequence and allows the child to think at his own pace—a point made most emphatically by Blank (1973).

## Definition of Terms

These encounters have been organized in a somewhat unorthodox system. Instead of using category headings such as math, art, and language, we have chosen a more general system that highlights what we consider to be the major aim of education: improving the child's awareness of the knower-known relation. When in Chapter Two we discussed the knower-known relation, we explained that, when there is no continuity between two pieces of information, we tend to forget the role that the self plays in our construction of knowledge. Through representation (mental imagery and language), the child learns to bring discontinuous information together and, in the process, becomes aware that certain discontinuities can be treated as variations of one another. The change from $A$ to $A'$ has been a repeated theme of this text. The purpose of education can also be stated as helping the child reflect on the procedures that he (the knower) uses to convert discontinuities into continuities (the known). We explained this process in Chapters Three and Five. Through conflict inducement and/or mental representation the child is led to consider the transformation of $A$ into $A'$.

Thinking about the transformation of $A$ into $A'$ is the same as thinking about the relation between the knower and the known. Transformations are the knower's contribution to the "facts" of external reality. And, since there are no facts without transformations, the knower-known relation must become part of awareness before the child—or, for that matter, the teacher, the scientist, or the philosopher—can understand anything with clarity. If knowledge is the ability to relate the knower (the transformations) to the known (the "factual objects"), then educational practices should center around the concept of transformation. The word *transformation* as used in the encounters to follow refers either to (1) what the teacher changes to establish a problem or to (2) what the child must change in order to solve the problem. The second use of the term can refer to some physical change in an object in the real world or to a mental manipulation of objects or relations.

The teacher can create interesting problems for the child through continuous or discontinuous transformations. An example of *continuous transformation* is the teacher's moving two pillars of a block bridge farther apart to see if the child can either move them back as they were or get a longer board to span the new distance. The transformation is called continuous because the child witnesses the whole change—the complete act of moving the pillars to increase the distance between them. An example of *discontinuous transformation* is the teacher's presenting the bridge builder with a new pair of supporting pillars already spaced apart, in the hope that the child will generalize what he knows about one pair of pillars to the new, more widely spaced, pair. The change is discontinuous because the child did not see the two pillars being moved farther apart; he was presented instead with the pillars already spaced. Similarly, flattening a circle into an ellipse while the child watches is an example of continuous transformation; presenting the child with a picture of a circle and then with a picture of an ellipse is an example of discontinuous transformation. This distinction will help the teacher understand what sorts of cognitive demands are being placed on a child faced with problems she wants to solve.

The type of materials that the child plays with affects the types of transformations that are possible. The teacher and the child can change the position of *fluid material,* like water and dry sand, but they cannot change their shapes, simply because these materials have no shape of their own but assume instead the shape of the container in which they lie. *Moldable material,* on the other hand, can be both reshaped and repositioned. Clay, moist sand, and silly putty can be changed from round to square and moved in space from here to there. *Discrete material* cannot be changed in shape but can be changed in position and orientation. Jigsaw pieces can be fitted into holes; wooden blocks can be stacked vertically or aligned horizontally; and so on. Most of the types of media that preschoolers use fall into one of these three categories or into a combination of them. For example, three balls of clay are a combination of moldable and discrete materials. The three balls of clay are discrete because each is separate from the others, and they are moldable because their shape can be changed. Changing nine buttons arranged in a square into nine buttons arranged in a circle while the child is watching is a continuous transformation of discrete materials. If the child does not witness the change from the square to the circular arrangement, the encounter is an example of discontinuous transformation of discrete materials. Changing the pitch of an incline before rolling a toy car down the slope is a continuous transformation of discrete material if the child witnesses the act of changing the pitch of the incline.

As we said earlier, each of the following encounters is described first in a basic form and then in both a more difficult and an easier form. In most cases the encounter is made more difficult by using a discontinuous transformation. For example, if the child wants to turn a train to the right, the teacher may switch the track to the left while the child is looking at something else. This variation poses a more difficult problem than switching the track while the child observes the teacher do it. In the more difficult variation the child must mentally reconstruct the change, using only the effects as a clue. In the easier form the child must reconstruct the actions that she actually saw. It should be noted, however, that reconstructing witnessed actions is by no means an automatic activity (Uzgiris, 1972) and that the task may need to be simplified. One way of simplifying a task is to change the material from a discrete medium to a continuous medium. In the above example, if the track was made of plastic sections (discrete material), a simpler version of the problem would be to use a bendable track, such as a rope track (moldable material). This would permit the child to practice the general objective (relating a path to a terminal point) with material that does not also require relating a series of parts (see Laurendeau & Pinard, 1970, about the difficulty children have in making directed lines with discrete materials).

In addition to the type of transformation performed by the teacher, the following encounters discuss the types of countertransformations the child must make in order to solve the problem at hand. In the example of the switched track, the child may simply reverse the teacher's action—that is, switch back the section of track to the right. In this instance the countertransformation is a simple *negation* of the teacher's change. As you may remember, negation reverses the effect of a transformation by undoing exactly what was done. However, there are other ways of reversing the effect of a transformation. If the objective in the above example was to get the train to the station and the station was on the right, instead of switching the track toward the station, the child could have moved the station to the left, so that the newly directed track would lead to the station. (What we are saying here is that not only are roads built to meet buildings but also buildings are erected where roads lie.) If the original transformation had moved the track away from the building, moving the building would be the *reciprocal action* of moving the track.

Of course, if the teacher had moved the building away from the track, then moving the building back to the track would be an example of negation. *Reciprocity,* like negation, places the two elements (track and station) back in their original relation, but reciprocity does so by moving an element other than the one moved by the teacher. Negation, instead, places the elements back in their original relation by a movement of the same element that the teacher had moved. To cite another example, if the teacher adds a few toy animals to a pasture, thereby reducing the grazing space for the original number of animals, the child can negate the transformation by taking away some of the animals. Alternatively, she can reverse the transformation by using the reciprocal operation of expanding the total area of the pasture. Not surprisingly, reciprocity is often more difficult to think of than negation, since reciprocity is a less direct method of reversing effects (Piaget & Inhelder, 1969b).

Yet, the reciprocal action is often the only solution available, because, when the negation of an action is impossible, the reciprocal may still be possible. For example, the act of adding too much sugar to Kool-Aid cannot be negated, since it is impossible (practically speaking) to "remove" the sugar from the water. But the effect of oversweetening can be reversed by using the reciprocal action—adding more water. Adding water is the reciprocal of adding sugar. Children of all ages are quite inventive in their methods of reversing effects.

Before the child makes the counterchange, it is important to discover if he sees the consequences of the transformation. The child may negate the teacher's change out of simple habit or displeasure at being interrupted. The teacher should discover methods that will lead the child to predict the effect of the original transformation. For example, after the teacher switches the track to the left, away from the train station, the child may say "But now the train won't work!" The teacher probes "You mean the wheels won't turn?" The child replies "No, the train won't make it to the station." To *predict* is to express the anticipation of new effects—an extrapolation of a change into the future. "Will each doll have as much room to sleep if I push the two beds together?" Here the child must represent the effect of a transformation before it occurs. As we stated in Chapter Two, representation is essential to the process of creating continuity between discontinuous events. Predicting verbally is a more difficult task than comprehending an effect after seeing it occur. Therefore, asking the child to predict is another way of making a simple task more advanced.

Prediction may also be used to generate conflict in a situation. The teacher, in the natural flow of spontaneous play, asks the child to reflect on what will happen if $A$ is changed to $A'$. Suppose the child reasons incorrectly but not haphazardly. Once the child has made a prediction, which expresses his expectation of the effect of the transformation, the teacher makes the transformation and the child tests the effect. The effect was not what he had predicted. At that point the child, hopefully, will be confused. If the child cannot make a prediction that has some rationale or if the actual effect does not perplex the child, chances are that the child is not ready to cope with that particular problem. He has other relations to learn first. Several suggestions will be offered in the following encounters on how to recognize when a particular transformation is likely to lead to new knowledge. The teacher is cautioned to use prediction judiciously. If you overuse or misuse prediction, the child will begin to avoid you.

The encounters have also been categorized according to objectives. By *objectives* we mean those experiences that the particular encounter promotes. A source of these objectives are the four areas of knowledge—physical, social, self-, and logico-mathematical. Please note that we are not advocating the direct teaching of any of these areas of knowledge. What we are suggesting is that children can be engaged in experiences that provide the "foodstuff" for their construction of that knowledge.

## Six Learning Encounters and Their Rationales

### Funnels

> *Fluid material:* Water.
> *Behavioral setting:* Two children are standing at the water table, pouring water into assorted containers.

*Discontinuous transformation:* Teacher adds funnels to the water table. The bottoms of the funnels have been cut out at various heights along the taper to produce holes of different sizes.

*Objective:* Relationship between speed, space, and time.

*Entry.* The teacher has already observed that the children enjoy pouring water into containers. It will be a simple matter to have them pour water into the funnels. The child picks up a funnel with a medium-sized hole at the bottom and pours water through the top. The water comes out at medium speed. The child repeats this action many times. The teacher plays in parallel with the child and pours water through a funnel with a small hole. The water comes out more slowly and in a finer stream than with the other funnel. The teacher may say "Let's have a race. Who do you think will win?" This is an example of *prediction.* The teacher plays this game a few times, until the child understands that the objective is to see whose funnel will empty first.

*Negation.* The child has been transporting water from container *A* (a cup) to container *B* (also a cup). The teacher introduces a transformation in the nature of container *A;* she changes container *A* from a cup to a funnel. Now the child can no longer move container *A* to container *B,* because container *A* doesn't hold water or, at least, leaks water on the way to *B.* The child is faced with a problem that he cannot, in this case, solve by negation. He cannot replace the bottom of the precut funnel.

*Reciprocity.* If the objective is to get water from funnel *A* to cup *B,* the best solution to the problem is to change something about *B.* The child can move *B* directly under *A* rather than try to move *A* over to *B.* The game can be played with *B* resting on a bed of dry sand. The teacher pretends that the sand shouldn't get wet. Any water drops would instantly show a noticeable trace in the sand. If *A* now is a funnel (and, therefore, cannot hold water), the child is placed in a situation in which he must anticipate that cup *B* must be moved under funnel *A* before any water is poured into funnel *A.* This game will work only if the child is old enough to accept "just pretend" rules like "Pretend that the sand is sugar and will melt if you get it wet." Children younger than 3 have difficulty with these "just pretend" rules.

*Variations.* The game as described in its basic form can be made more difficult by asking the child to make a prediction about a funnel he has not played with before. Once the child has made his prediction, teacher and child scoop their water and the child can check if his prediction was accurate. If it was not—that is, if the consequences did not match the child's expectations—the conflict might cause him to search for an answer. This might lead him to notice the relationship between the size of the hole and the speed of the emptying.

The game can be made easier by using a *continuous transformation.* Instead of introducing precut funnels, you can present a funnel with a piece of flexible rubber tubing at the end. Then you demonstrate how the flow of water can be changed by slowly squeezing the end of the rubber tubing. Or you may give the funnel with the attached tubing to the child and let him explore and discover himself how he can stop the flow of water altogether. From that point on, the discovery of how to vary the speed of flow by varying the size of the hole should proceed with relative ease, perhaps after some modeling on your part.

Several other variations are possible, all of which reinforce the relationship between the size of the hole and the speed and quantity of water flow. The teacher can model once and then let the child explore on his own. Here are some examples.

1. Use a conical cup with a very small hole and make water traces in dry sand by moving the cup slowly above the sand. The child experiments with cups that have holes of different sizes and, in the process, discovers which cups produce the type of flow he desires.

2. Use two conical cups with different-sized holes to fill the little cubicles of an empty ice tray. The child may pick up on your action and attempt to do the same. What he will discover is that, with a large-holed cup, he will have to advance his hand faster from cubicle to cubicle as each compartment becomes filled with water. With a small-holed cup, he will have to advance his hand more slowly. This game is

The bigger the hole, the faster the drip.

particularly instructive because it reinforces the notion that speed can be marked off into equal units—that is, into the time intervals between each two consecutive advances of the hand (from filling one cubicle to filling the next, to filling the next, and so on).

3. Another interesting variation is to suggest to the child (perhaps through a brief modeling) that he empty one funnel into another funnel. The child will discover after some exploration that it makes a difference which funnel he empties into which. A funnel with a large hole drained into a funnel with a small hole will cause the funnel below to overflow, since the rate of emptying is faster for the one above than for the one below. Conversely, if the small-holed funnel is drained into the large-holed funnel, the water in the funnel below will not overflow. This variation allows the child to compare, through his own spontaneous activity, the effects of two different temporal rates. After the child has indicated that he understands the relationship between the two funnels, you can feel free to suggest that the words *fast* and *slow* be used to describe these events that the child understands at the empirical level. You should not apply labels to these events until it is apparent from the child's actions that he understands which funnel causes overflow.

Presenting a third funnel with a hole of yet another size would make the variation even more difficult. A 4-year-old might be led to the discovery that, while funnel $B$ makes funnel $A$ overflow, funnel $C$ makes funnel $B$ overflow. Although it is not likely that a 4-year-old will ever use the logical rule of *transitivity* (if $B$ overflows $A$ and $C$ overflows $B$, then $C$ necessarily overflows $A$), these early explorations of physical objects serve to develop the transitive operation (Piaget & Garcia, 1974).

### Tunnels

*Discrete materials:* Toy train and riders.

*Behavioral setting:* A child is pushing a toy train around an elliptical track. The train has open boxcars. The child has placed little wooden people in the boxcars. The little wooden people are painted in different colors and are graduated in size.

*Discontinuous transformation:* The teacher puts a papier-mâché tunnel over the tracks. When train and riders pass under the tunnel, the child can no longer see which rider is in the front, middle, and rear of the train. When the teacher changes the train's direction in the tunnel, the child does not witness the change.

*Objective:* Ordered relations.

*Entry.* The teacher has already noticed that the child watches the train carefully as she pushes it. The child tilts her head down to look at the train at eye level, pushes it, and makes noises like a train. She also enjoys giving the little wooden people a ride from one point on the track to another.

The teacher begins by trying to engage the child in a conversation about the people on the train. In the course of the conversation teacher and child decide on a name for each of the three people on the train—for example, Mommy, Daddy, and Baby. Once names have been given to the little people, the teacher can begin the encounter with ordered relations.

As the child pushes the train through the tunnel, the teacher blocks the forward end of the tunnel with his hand. "Can you tell me who will come out of the tunnel first?" he asks. This is an example of *prediction*. Up to this point there has been no transformation in the order of the little people. The child needs to recall only the original order from the front to the back of the train. The teacher then removes his hand to let the child check her prediction. After allowing the child some time for free play, during which time the teacher reinforces the labels the child uses to distinguish the little people, the teacher cries "Rock slide ahead!" just as the rear car of the train disappears into the tunnel. This means that the train will have to come out backwards. Now the teacher asks the child to predict which of the little people will be the first one to emerge from the tunnel. This is a *discontinuous transformation of discrete elements* (the little people).

There are several ways of making this encounter easier. The concept of order can be developed without using the tunnel. Place a red house and a white house at opposite curves of the elliptical track. As the train passes the red house, ask the child which of the little people will get to the white house first. See if the child can anticipate that the first person on the train will always get to a point first, as long as the train does not travel backwards. Sometimes a child will predict that the lead person will get to the white house first but that the rearward person will get to the red house first. This is because the child has not made the right mental transformation—the train rounding a curve rather than moving backward. At times the teacher will cry "Rock slide!" and the train will have to travel backwards. Then the child will need to distinguish the effects of rounding a curve from those of traveling backward. If the child attends only to the question of which house the train is traveling toward, she will make errors regarding which person will arrive first. The train may move to the red house after rounding the curve, or it may move to the red house by backing up. In the first instance the original order of who is in the lead is conserved; in the second instance the order is reversed.

The encounter can be made more difficult by rotating the train while it is in the tunnel. Place the tunnel on a section of track that can swivel on a pivot, like a turntable. You can give the tunnel a single 180-degree turn or a complete 360-degree turn or two 180-degree turns in opposite directions. The complexity of this variation is limited only by the child's willingness to keep "track" of the transformations.

*Negation.* If the child has some reason for thinking that a particular person on the train will arrive at a location first, then the teacher's transformations represent something that must be reversed. If the train is rotated on the open (not covered) turntable, the child can reestablish the original order by rotating the turntable in reverse.

*Reciprocity.* If the turntable "locks" after it is rotated 180 degrees, the child can reestablish the original order by picking up the train and turning *it* 180 degrees in reverse. Turning the train is the reciprocal of turning the track.

*Variations.* Several variations are possible, all of which reinforce the child's understanding of the order of discrete elements that is inherent in circular and linear movements (see Piaget, 1970). While the child is busy pushing the train along the track, the teacher places a telephone pole very near the track on the inside of the track loop. He also places a little person on the train. One of the little person's arms is outstretched toward the inside of the loop. As the child pushes the train farther, the little person's arm knocks over the telephone pole. The teacher cries "Wow! He knocked over the telephone pole." Once the child takes note of what has happened and seems to be interested, the teacher can develop an encounter of some duration. In order to avoid the collision, the teacher can vary the position of the little person's arm and have the child position the telephone pole accordingly, or the roles can be reversed: the child changes the position of the doll's arm and tells the teacher where to place the telephone pole.

Quite often children will predict that, if the little person's arm faces inward while the train is on the near side of the loop, the arm will be facing outward on the far side of the loop (Duckworth, 1974). The problem lies in the difficulty of imagining the spatial relations after the train rounds the curve. The arm is facing away from the child on the near side of the loop; she thinks it will still be facing away from her on the far side of the loop. This is another example of how young children use their own body as the primary point of reference (Pufall, 1973).

Once the child has had some experience with an elliptical track, the encounter can be made more challenging by changing the shape of the track loop. A kidney-shaped loop is particularly challenging because it gives the illusion of reversing the direction of travel while the train is still on one side of the loop (see Figure 9-1).

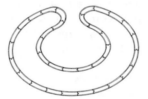

*Figure 9-1.*

## Mirrors

> *Discrete materials:* Full-length metal mirror and full-length plain glass. (With young children it would be safer to use Plexiglas or clear acetate.)
>
> *Behavioral setting:* Two children are looking at their images in a full-length mirror mounted in a free-standing frame. Adjacent to the mirror is an identical plate of clear glass in a free-standing frame (for example, an old mirror with all the silvering removed from the back). The frames are mounted on casters so that they can be easily moved back and forth.
>
> *Continuous transformation:* The teacher rolls the glass in front of the child, or the child moves from one frame (mirror) to the other (glass).
>
> *Objective:* My-image versus not-my-image.

*Entry.* Mia and Janine are looking at themselves in the mirror. David, the teacher, is watching nearby. Mia stoops, squats, and sways, watching her mirror reflection do the same. Janine watches Mia and imitates her, inattentive to her own reflection in the mirror. David moves behind the mirror and peeks out from there, trying to coax either child into a peekaboo game. Mia picks up on the game.

When Mia is in front of the mirror, she sees her own image. When she bends her torso to the side in a peekaboo motion, she sees David, who is likewise bending over. She can transform the sight of David *(A')* back into the sight of herself *(A)* by returning her torso to its original upright position, as long as the mirror is interposed between her and David. Now David deftly exchanges the plain glass for the mirror and attempts to maintain the peekaboo relationship with Mia. This time, as Mia moves her torso, there is no change in what she sees. When she is in an upright position and looks through the plain glass, she sees David *(A')*, and, when she bends to the side far enough so that the plain glass is not interposed between her and David, she still sees David *(A')*. David attempts to maintain the peekaboo game, sometimes using the mirror and sometimes using the plain glass.

This learning encounter should impress upon Mia that changing $A$ to $A'$ and $A'$ back to $A$ is not determined exclusively by her own movements. Her own movements (the transformational operation) change $A$ to $A'$ only in a certain environment (when the mirror is present). The difference that a mirror and a plain glass make may confuse the child, who egocentrically believes that it is her action alone that creates the change from $A'$ to $A$—from sight of David to sight of self. The contrast between mirror and plain glass should help the child to understand something about the nature of objects external to self and to see how the same behavior in one case transforms $A$ into $A'$ and in another case does not transform $A$ into $A'$. This eventually leads the child to understand that a given behavior is not inherently transformational; that is, the behavior is not transformational regardless of environment. Knowing when a behavior is transformational and when it is not is, in essence, a step toward greater awareness of the knower-known relation.

*Negation.* The direct inverse (negation) of changing $A$ to $A'$ (seeing self to seeing David) by bending at the torso is simply to straighten up again, thus reestablishing the sight of self *(A)*.

*Reciprocity.* Mia sees herself in the mirror (state $A$); then she steps to one side and sees David *(A')*. She activates the reciprocal operation by moving the sliding mirror between herself and David, reinstating the sight of self *(A)*. The indirect inverse (reciprocal operation) of changing $A$ to $A'$ (seeing self to seeing David) by stepping to one side is to move the mirror rather than the body.

If the child learns that the mirror can itself be moved, chances are that the child will experiment with the two ways to reinstate sight of self. This type of experimentation is accepted as valuable on theoretical grounds. The contrast between negation and reciprocity in the younger years leads to a coordination of negation and reciprocity in the older years. The coordination of these two operations is fundamental to the conservation of relations that remain invariant across transformations from $A$ to $A'$ (see Chapter Four). The contrast between negation and reciprocity in the case discussed above leads to a greater awareness of the distinction between self and reflected self. What remains invariant across the preceding transformations is the permanent presence of self.

*Variations.* Younger children—younger than Mia, who is 2½—can play a variation of this game with a hand mirror. Sometimes the child moves his head to and fro; sometimes he moves the mirror. While this game does not include a distinction between self and other, it does provide movements that are essential to the construction of the awareness that the reflected face is under the control of the self, while the real faces of other children are not. However, the very young child may still treat his own face reflected in the mirror as he would treat another child's photograph glued to the mirror. At what age does the child begin to use his reflection in the mirror as a source of information about his own face—for example, to check a smudge on his forehead (Gallup, 1970)? What types of transformations are important to the construction of the awareness that the face he sees in the mirror is his own face and not a picture of some other child? This knowledge probably comes from a grouping of the relations among head movements, hand movements, and the changes in facial expressions that are both felt and seen.

The following variation can be used to provoke the construction of self-awareness in older children. Let's assume that a group of 4-year-olds have been watching an educational television program every morning at 9:30. The program opens with a theme song. One morning the teaching staff make a change in the children's routine. Having prerecorded the program's theme song, they begin to play it to prepare the children for their usual program; but the scene that the children now watch is not a scene from that program but their own actions being picked up by a live video camera in the next room! The teacher that appears on the monitor—say an unfamiliar face imported for this production—can talk to the children watching the program. She does this by looking and listening to the children through a one-way vision screen that separates her from them.

The video recorder is set on record, and the video monitor shows the teacher. The video monitor has a long cord that connects the video recorder in one room to the video monitor in the next room. To the child the video monitor looks like any other television set. But the difference soon becomes apparent. As the teacher starts her lesson—perhaps a game about "Which one is just like the other one?"—the children settle in their usual fashion, ready to play the game. Then the voice from the monitor says to Byron, sitting in the back of the group, "Byron, can you move closer?" Does this direct reference to his position surprise Byron? (Of course, a teacher on a network broadcast couldn't make such a personal observation.) The surprises continue. "Shelanda, can you find another one of these [a shoe] in the room?" Shelanda points to her own shoe. "That's good!" says the TV image. "You pointed to your own shoe."

How do children respond to a television set that can see? Does this surprise them? Do they search for the hidden camera? Are they aware at all that being seen by a machine is unusual? We know that children go through a stage, called *picture realism* (Werner, 1948), in which they confuse a photograph with the real object pictured in the photograph. (One of the authors once saw a 3-year-old boy stomp in earnest the picture of a honeybee!) Do children make similar errors of realism with regard to a television picture? If they do, they wouldn't be particularly surprised at a television image that makes comments implying that the image can see the child.

The spatial discontinuity between the real teacher in one room and her image in the next room makes it difficult for the children to understand how that image can engage in a dialogue with them. After all, not many adults, either, understand the operation behind the transformation from $A$ (the real teacher) to $A'$ (the teacher's image). The change from $A$ to $A'$ is virtually instantaneous. The transformation from real teacher $(A)$ to teacher's image $(A')$ is not at all like the transformation from teacher here *(A)* to teacher there *(A')*—that is, seeing the teacher walk from one place to another. Rather, it is like seeing her here *(A)* and there *(A') at the same time*. But this violates the world of real, physical objects. Furthermore, the child does not even see state *A* (the teacher in the next room). The child who catches on to what is happening *infers* the existence of *A*. The child who says "Where is the teacher?" gives us at least suggestive evidence that he has inferred the existence of *A* (the real teacher). This is how that child would have come to his inference: state *A'* (the image) is not a real person; state *A'* makes remarks that only a real person can make; therefore there must be some relation between a real person who sees me and this image on the screen. These component thoughts then lead the child to search out the means by which *A* (the real teacher) is transformed into *A'* (the television image). "How does she know I did that?" the child asks.

At this point we wish to make a parenthetical, yet emphatic, comment about our 20th-century technology. In a world of photographs, films, and television shows, the mind of the young child is bombarded by thousands of inputs that violate the continuity that exists in the movements of physical objects in the child's everyday world. On film the difference between one object twice and two identical objects appearing in succession is blurred, warped, and transformed beyond distinction. On television the same actor can be himself and his twin brother. In the cartoons a falling object can pass the same window three times before it hits the street below. Whereas this might be a source of surprise and amusement for the 7-year-old, what does a steady diet of these distortions do to the mind of the 4-year-old? This passive viewing of transformations that violate physical laws could effectively compete with the child's ability to accurately reflect on real transformations. We are not saying that the child who watches TV will have difficulty learning temporal and spatial relations—for example, anticipating the fall of a real object. However, watching these graphic representations that violate physical laws may compete with the child's ability to construct mental representations of real physical relations.

To conclude this digression, it is important to have the child himself perform transformations, so that he can learn to represent and thereby reflect on such differences as those between one object twice and two objects once. In the case above, let the child walk back and forth between *A* (the real teacher) and *A'* (the television image)!

*Cones-through-the-Hole*

> *Discrete materials:* Cardboard cones, Masonite screen with a hole in the center large enough for one cone to pass through it.
> *Behavioral setting:* The Masonite screen is secured so that it is in a vertical position. Two cones are sitting on the floor on one side of the screen. Attached to each cone's tip is a line of string. The two lines of string run through the hole in the screen, with their ends lying on the floor on the other side of the screen. Two children, Judy and Barry, are each given one line of string; Judy's string is attached to the red cone, and Barry's to the green cone. The teacher explains that each cone has a bunch of candy inside but the candy melts easily; so, if they hurry, both children can get the candy out before it melts. The teacher doesn't mention the fact that only one cone at a time can pass through the hole in the screen. As the two children simultaneously pull their respective strings,

the "bottleneck" occurs. Keep in mind that the children have not seen the teacher pass the cones through the hole in the screen.

*Discontinuous transformation:* The task in this encounter is to reverse the position of the two cones from being on one side of the screen to the other side. Since the children did not see the original transformation of $A$ to $A'$ (the cones passing through the hole), this game involves a discontinuous transformation that the children must reconstruct in reverse.

*Objectives:* Taking turns; cooperative behavior.

*Entry.* Once the teacher has set the problem, the rest is left to the children. In a case like this one, quite often one child is simply faster than the other one and pulls his/her cone out before the other child even begins to negotiate the pulling. If this happens, the teacher can give the faster or more dominant child a longer string, the extra length of which is curled up on the floor where the cones lie. As the faster child begins to draw his/her string through the hole, the other child starts to do the same, and the chances of a bottleneck increase. The point is that, if the two children get the cones out as a fortuitous consequence of one child being faster or more dominant than the other, the game fails to encourage the solution of taking turns. Note that it is important to have stout twine and the Masonite screen firmly secured.

*Negation.* The original transformation (the unseen passing of the cones through the hole from one side of the screen to the other) must be negated. This is done by drawing the cone through the hole in the screen. It is most unlikely that the child imagines that the screen was moved so that the hole was passed over the cones. If he did, however, passing the cones through the hole would be the reciprocal action of passing the hole over the cones.

*Reciprocity.* Passing the screen over the cones is the reciprocal action of drawing the cones through the hole. Given the structure of this game, the reciprocal action is quite difficult.

There is, however, another and more important set of reciprocal relations: the two children themselves must relate to each other! The child knows that relaxing his/her own string negates his/her attempt to move the cone from $A'$ to $A$. What neither child has learned so far is that pulling his/her string—which is an attempt to accomplish one's own personal objective—can negate the objective of the other child. In other words, the realization of one's own goal is inversely related to the other person's goal.

Once Judy understands that pulling the red cone negates the passage of Barry's green cone, she is in a position to understand a more subtle relation; that is, the momentary negation of her goal is actually the reciprocal of the realization of her goal several moments later! She learns to relax her string long enough for Barry to draw his cone through, which makes it possible for Judy to draw her cone through with ease. No wonder it is so difficult for children to learn to wait. They must understand that turning away from their goal can be another way of reaching that goal. The paradox is too much for the young child to handle. Judy must think: depending on the timing of my moves and Barry's moves, I can get to $A$ by pulling my string and I can get to $A$ by relaxing my string. While it is true that Judy can negate Barry's goal, by doing so she would negate her own goal. Here is another reciprocal relation: negating Barry's goal has the reciprocal effect of negating my own goal. Therefore, realizing Barry's objective may have the reciprocal effect; that is, it may be an indirect way of accomplishing my own objective.

We might take a moment here to clarify the distinction between reciprocal relations and inverse relations—a distinction that often presents problems for Piaget's readers. A *reciprocal* relation pertains to an indirect means of accomplishing the change from $A'$ back to $A$ (provided one knows how $A$ was originally changed into $A'$). The reciprocal operation is a method of reinstating $A$ other than negating the original method by which $A'$ was created. For example, removing the weight from the right side of a balance beam reinstates the original state of balance by negating the imbalance originally created by adding that weight on the right side. Adding a weight on the left side of the balance beam is another way of reestablishing the original state of balance, this time by an action that is reciprocal to that of adding a weight on the right side.

While the reciprocal relation pertains to equal effects, the *inverse* relation pertains to opposite effects. Placing a weight on the right side of the balance beam makes that side go down and the left side go up. The right and left sides are inversely related; they are not reciprocally related in the sense in which we are using the term *reciprocal.* Judy's tugging at her cone during the bottleneck is inversely related to Barry's success in drawing his cone through. However, Judy's relaxing the string of her cone is reciprocally related to her own success, because it is another way of doing the same thing—drawing her cone through the hole. When negation (changing $A'$ to

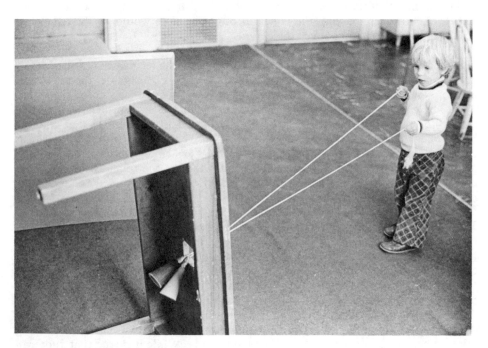

Cones-through-the-hole. Both cones will not go through at once.

*A* in a direct manner) is not possible, the children must learn the reciprocal operation (changing *A'* to *A* in an indirect manner—for example, by waiting).

*Variations.* The cones-through-the-hole game is difficult because it requires the child to think about someone else's actions besides his own. One way of simplifying this game for younger children is to give control over both actions to the same child. Learning the reciprocal relation between two different self-directed actions may set a base of generalization for constructing the relations involved in the cones-through-the-hole game. Give one child both strings, one attached to the red cone and the other attached to the green cone. As the child explores the respective results of pulling two strings at once versus pulling one and then the other, he learns that letting the green cone wait is one way of assuring that the green cone will eventually be removed without obstruction.

Two more variations, one of which is a more difficult version of the cones-through-the-hole game, follow.

1. This variation was suggested by Kamii (1974). A child is given the two ends of a rope that is looped around a table leg. A wooden pull truck is attached to the right span, between the child and the table leg. To make the truck move toward her, the child pulls the right span of rope. To make the truck move away from her, the

A clothesline pulley presents the problems of an inverse relation.

child pulls the left span of rope, which communicates force around the table leg and draws the truck toward the table. Kamii noticed that 4-year-olds had little difficulty making the truck come to them. They simply pulled their right hand toward themselves, and the truck moved in the same direction as the child's hand. Making the truck move away from themselves was quite another story, however, because it required the children to decenter from their egocentric perspective: in order to make an object move *away* from the body, they needed to pull their left hand *toward* the body. The action of the object was inversely related to the action of the body. Some children simply couldn't construct these relations. They would move their right hand forward in an attempt to make the truck roll forward! The result was, of course, zero for the truck and a lot of frustration for the child.

An inverse relation can underlie a reciprocal relation if the child's intention is to ultimately end up with the truck near herself. Let's assume that the left span loops around the table leg and is tied to the truck but that there is no span that runs from the truck directly to the child. In order to get the truck, the child must pull on the left span, which momentarily draws the truck *away* from the child. The child must understand that the truck's departure from herself is an indirect (reciprocal) way of getting the truck to eventually come toward her, assuming of course that the truck doesn't get stuck as it rounds the table leg.

2. This second variation, which makes the encounter more difficult rather than easier, restores the basic social nature of the game. The idea was first developed by a now classic study on the formation of social groups among young boys (Sherif & Sherif, 1953). The study traced the transition from competition to cooperation between two groups of boys when, in order to achieve a goal both groups wanted, they were compelled to work together to overcome a common problem. A span of rope was instrumental to this transition.

For some weeks the two groups, which were attending a summer camp, had been competing in a tug-of-war contest (two teams pulling against each other at opposite ends of a rope). The boys knew very well that one team's advance meant the other team's loss (an inverse relation). This situation changed dramatically when, at the contrivance of the camp director, the truck that was carrying the food for a picnic broke down. After some discussion the two groups decided to loop their tug-of-war rope around the front bumper of the truck and *pull together*. At first the two teams stuck to their original formation, each team pulling at one span of the rope. However, when the boys' efforts did not succeed, the group as a whole quickly went into action, all the boys pulling together, ignoring the usual team divisions. Instead of each team seeing the other as the opposing team, both teams now saw themselves as one group against a common enemy—the stuck truck. In these circumstances the greatest good for all was ensured by pulling with *equal* strength on both spans of the rope. This required some redistribution of boys until the two sides were nearly equal in strength—a cooperative act rather than a competitive act.

A similar situation can be staged in the classroom. Ask two children to help you move a piece of equipment, such as the mock-up model of an automobile. Loop a piece of rope through the front bumper of the car, and have the two children hold one end each and pull. The children will soon discover that, in order to make the car move, they need to pull with *equal* strength and in synchrony.

## Specific Language

*Discrete materials:* Any object of interest to the child.

*Behavioral setting:* The child and the teacher are sitting together at the table. The table contains a variety of objects—a puzzle, a set of quoits on a stick, a sorting box, and a shoebox filled with Lego blocks. The child turns to the teacher and asks "Gimme dat," looking at the Lego blocks. The teacher feigns ignorance: "What is it that you want, Melissa?"

*Discontinuous transformation:* The child wants to change the position of the Lego blocks from far to near. We assume that the teacher didn't push the Lego blocks away from the child while the child watched. Therefore the task involves the undoing of a transformation that was not witnessed. The more significant aspect of this encounter is the child's choice of means to reverse the change from $A$ (near) to $A'$ (far)—verbal means rather than direct action on the object. Yet the child's language indicates that she has not quite internalized the need for language to be specific. By asking the child to be more specific, the teacher in effect is asking the child to reflect on the operations by which the child's words are transformed (translated) by the teacher into action. The transformation from the child's words to the teacher's action is discontinuous in that the mental activity of the child is not continuous with regard to the mental activity of the teacher, despite the young child's assumptions to the contrary. Effective communication involves the understanding of the inherent discontinuity between one's own mind and the mind of another person. Good communication reduces this discontinuity between self and other by the use of words familiar to both speaker and listener. Through language the discontinuity between self and other can be bridged, but only if the speaker considers the difference between the self-to-topic relation and the other-to-topic relation. The child's saying "Gimme dat" implies that the child has considered only the self-to-topic relation. Effective communication is another form of a better understanding of the knower-known relation.

*Objectives:* Specific language; appreciation of listener's perspective.

*Entry.* The child who makes a request has already engaged the teacher in the child's world. Therefore the teacher has many options. If the child is not under strain, the teacher may choose to create a mild amount of dissonance in order to improve the child's use of language. Melissa's "Gimme dat" is underspecified (as are many sentences constructed by lazy adults who use vague demonstrative pronouns strung together like rows of unaddressed parcels). The teacher increases the demand for specificity by refusing to go beyond the exact words used by the child.

"What is it that you want, Melissa?" Melissa points to the box of Lego blocks. "I can't understand. Can you tell me what you want?" the teacher continues. "That" Melissa enounces clearly. The teacher passes Melissa the sorting box instead of the Lego blocks. (The sorting box was slightly closer to the child than the blocks.) "No, dat box!" Although "box" can refer to several of the objects on the table, the teacher decides that one step toward specificity is enough, considering the fact that these games are likely to frustrate the child rather quickly. There are variations, as we shall see, that obviate somewhat the problem of an adult appearing obstinately ignorant.

*Negation.* The child seeks to transform her own desire *(A)* into another person's action *(A′)* instrumental to that desire. The child makes a first attempt to change $A$ to $A′$ by saying "Gimme dat." The action of the teacher, however, leaves the child where she started—that is, with her desire for the Lego blocks. In other words, the attempt to change $A$ to $A′$ was followed by a variety of $A′$ that led back to $A$. We can call this lack of progress "the negation of the *anticipated* change from $A$ to $A′$." The child realizes that her attempts to effect $A′$ have been negated, so she adopts new tactics.

*Reciprocity.* The reciprocal nature of communication probably enters the child's consciousness when she begins to understand that her desires are not always clearly understood when she first attempts to express them to someone else. The child learns to accommodate her speech to the needs of the listener. At first the listener usually accommodates to the speech of the young child. To facilitate the transformation of $A$ into $A′$, the listener looks at the child's eyes and infers that the under-specified request refers to the Lego blocks. The gap between $A$ and $A′$ is reduced by some additional interpretation on the part of the listener. Sometimes, however, the listener does not do the additional interpretation, as in the case under discussion. The child must then do the additional thinking. Continuous repetition of the sentence "Gimme dat" will not bring about the transformation of $A$ (the expressed desire) into $A′$ (the action of the listener). There must be another way of transforming $A$ into $A′$.

If the direct mode of transformation (the teacher interpreting the child's desire) is blocked, the reciprocal operation must be activated (the child interpreting the teacher's action). At first the child thinks about the $A$-to-$A′$ relation from her point of view. Then she thinks of the $A$-to-$A′$ relation from the teacher's point of view. Finally the child reasons that changing her own words is the reciprocal action of waiting for $A′$ to move closer to $A$ (the original verbal expression) and represents another way of reducing the gap between $A$ and $A′$. Figure 9-2 illustrates this point.

| First attempt:    $A$       $A′$<br>Second attempt: $A$   $A′$ | First attempt:    $A$    $A′$<br>Second attempt:    $A$    $A′$ |
|---|---|
| Child repeats. Listener accommodates to child. | Listener does not understand. Child accommodates to listener. |
| The accommodation of the listener to the speaker is reciprocal to the accommodation of the speaker to the listener; that is, both operations improve communication. ||

*Figure 9-2.* The reciprocal nature of communication between the expression of the speaker *(A)* and the interpretation by the listener *(A′)*.

*Variations.* A representation of an object is always more difficult than a direct action on the object. Producing a string of words that unambiguously identify one object among many is more difficult than identifying that object by pointing at it or by picking it up. But even the nonrepresentational identification of an object can be more or less precise, and the child can be provoked to be more specific when she points at something. If two objects are in a line between the child and the teacher, the child's pointing can be quite ambiguous. To improve the child's ability to make specific requests, the teacher can respond to the child's pointing with as much "literalness" as the teacher used in responding to Melissa's words.

The same goal can be achieved by playing the "literal game" in reverse. It is easier than the original version, because it is easier for the child to understand verbal instructions than to formulate them herself. Suppose that child and teacher are together at a table, working on a common project. The teacher says "Melissa, please pass that thing over there to me." As he speaks, the teacher doesn't look up from the work at hand. Therefore, Melissa has no visual cues to help her identify the "thing" the teacher wants. "What thing?" Melissa asks. "That thing over there" the preoccupied teacher glibly answers. "This thing?" Melissa holds up a pair of scissors. "No, what I want is bigger than a pair of scissors" the teacher responds, and they continue the exercise in communication skills. Ultimately these types of games could lead the child to shift from attempting to find *the* object that the teacher is thinking about to attempting to set restrictions on the *class* of objects that the teacher is thinking about—for example, "Is it a green object?" rather than "Is it this green clay?"

The more the objects that share certain characteristics with the desired object, the greater the difficulty of specifying the desired object. The difficulty of the original version of this encounter can be increased by prearranging the table. If on the first day there is only one red object on the table, asking for "the red one" will unambiguously identify the desired object. But if on another day there are two or three red objects, the child must dip further into the attribute pool in order to identify the desired object—for example, "the tiny red one" or "the one near the edge of the table."

The child's willingness to play these word games can be increased by making the behavioral setting more natural. Toy telephones and playhouses serve this purpose well. A minimum of modeling on the part of the teaching staff can do wonders to stimulate the children's interest in the game. For example, two teachers briefly modeling a conversation between a grocer and a customer will elicit a windfall of conversation between children. One child (the "customer") on one side of the playhouse wall calls the "grocer" on the other side of the wall. The customer tries to describe as clearly as possible the items he wants from the grocer. These items are represented in pictures that the teacher has given to the children. "These," the teacher said, "are pictures of delicious foods that come from another part of the world. We have no names for them." Since the children have no names for these new foods, the customer must describe them so that the grocer understands what he is referring to. The test of the effectiveness of the speaker's communication comes when the grocer delivers only those items that the customer had successfully identified. Effective communication depends on the young child's ability to use conventional words rather than idiosyncratic words (see Glucksberg, Krauss, & Higgins, 1975).

*Who Am I Now?*

> *Discrete materials:* Chairs, ride bus, ride firetruck.
> *Behavioral setting:* Several children are in the role-playing corner, putting on
> hats and costumes. Damon puts on the bus driver's cap, sits on the ride bus,

and pretends to collect fares. Kathy puts on the satin cape and dashes off to her Batmobile.

*Discontinuous transformation:* The change from one's real identity to a pretend identity occurs as abruptly as the change of clothes. Once the pretend transformation of identity occurs, young children tend to act out rather stereotyped versions of the role they have assumed. The role, once adopted, seems to rest on the presence of a single prop (see Smilansky, 1968), such as a hat or a cape.

*Objectives:* Role taking; defining roles.

*Entry.* The children are relating the clothes and headgear in the role-playing area to models that they have seen at home, on television, or elsewhere. Damon is sitting on the bus, wearing a bus driver's cap and pretending to collect fares from imaginary passengers. The teacher drives up in a ride toy built like a firetruck, wearing a fireman's hat. The teacher imitates Damon in his pretense of collecting fares. "Good morning, what street do you want me to stop at?" the teacher asks her first imaginary passenger. Damon attends for a few minutes to this contradiction between actions and visual props and then says "You can't do that. You're a fireman." "What makes you think I am a fireman?" asks the teacher. "You're wearing his hat, silly!" Damon exclaims. "But I'm picking up people, just as you are" the teacher retorts. "You shouldn't do that. It's not right" Damon replies categorically. "I want to be a bus driver, too," the teacher pleads. "There is only one" Damon explains, probably referring to the fact that there is only one bus driver's hat.

At this point the teacher, who had anticipated this exchange, produces from her oversized pocket a bus driver's cap. She puts the cap on and confronts the child "Now can I be a bus driver?" Damon thinks and then says "I suppose. But you can pick up only firemen."

This encounter deals with the criteria behind social roles, with changes in these roles, and with what determines the transformation from one role to another. We can see in Damon's comments that the identity of a role is determined by the tangible trappings of the role—the bus driver's cap and the fireman's hat. The teacher tries to produce conflict between the actions of a bus driver and the trappings of a fireman. A more mature criterion for role identity is behavior, not apparel. Damon refuses to allow this contradiction between overt insignia of identity and overt behavior. He does make some small progress when he assimilates the firetruck into his preconceptions about the bus driver's cap ("I suppose. But you can pick up only firemen"). Damon's is a hybrid combination of fireman and bus driver, but at least it represents an attempt to define social role on the basis of behavior—that is, picking up passengers.

*Negation.* The basic transformation here is the change from bus driver *(A)* to fireman *(A')*. The child is *A,* and the teacher is *A'* but wants to be *A.* "I want to be a bus driver, too," the teacher pleads. The child is faced with the task of negating *A'* in order to maintain *A.* His comment ("There is only one") suggests that the change in the teacher's role may in some sense entail a change in his own role, and he is enjoying his role as a bus driver. Older children, not so bound to the regalia of a role, understand that one person's changing from *A'* to *A* does not jeopardize their own role as *A*—the bus driver, in this case. For the younger child a social role is something one possesses in almost the same way one possesses an object. This can pose the apparent problem that one person's possession of that role is the other person's dispossession. What the teacher has asked Damon to consider is a transformation from $A'$ to $A$, which pertains to herself and does *not* change Damon's role as $A$. Damon's role is conserved in spite of the teacher's change from $A'$ to $A$. Perhaps the teacher's presenting another bus driver's cap had the unfortunate consequence of reinforcing the wrong approach to roles and role transformation—changing hats instead of changing behavior.

*Reciprocity.* As you know, a reciprocal operation is an indirect means of accomplishing the same transformation effected by the negative operation. In this example, since the role of fireman was created by donning a fireman's hat, the direct way of reversing the transformation is to remove the fireman's hat—that is, a negative operation. (We should note that this encounter presents the child with some complex problems, because the child is asked to consider not only the undoing of the fireman's role but also the creation of the bus driver's role.) If, for one reason or another, the negation of $A'$ (fireman) cannot be carried out, is there another way to accomplish the same thing? Think about it. If the teacher wearing a fireman's hat begins to act like a bus driver, does her behavior "undo" the fireman's role? The teacher is trying to provoke the child to consider just this very question, but the child is not sensitive to the reciprocal relation between role behavior and role insignia. Instead of changing her hat, the teacher could have persisted in her bus driver's behavior—the reciprocal means of undoing the fireman's role. The incongruity between a fireman's hat and a bus driver's behavior may have done no more than make the child laugh, but out of laughter may emerge the thought that role identity can be defined by action (see Flavell, Botkin, Fry, Wright, & Jarvis, 1968).

*Variations.* Is a pet dog still the familiar dog if someone momentarily covers its muzzle with the mask of a cat (see DeVries, 1969)? Is the teacher in a Halloween mask still the teacher? Situations can be created that pose mild conflicts of identity for young children. Does the operation of putting on a mask change $A$ to $A'$ in any way other than visually? If the young child sees the operation of putting on a mask (a continuous transformation) and the quick reversal from $A'$ back to $A$, the child is less likely to be frightened. The basic psychological identity of the teacher is conserved throughout the transformation from $A$ (own face) to $A'$ (mask) back to $A$ (own face). However, a teacher walking into the room wearing the mask of Broom Hilda may cause a temporary panic in the preschool. Abruptly walking into the room as Broom Hilda is a discontinuous transformation, which is more difficult for young children to understand, since the original state $A$ (own face) has to be inferred rather than remembered. The teacher can begin these variations using continuous transformations between $A$ and $A'$ and progress gradually to more discontinuous transformations. This progression should help the child invent means to distinguish an apparent change from a real change in identity. Can the child correctly judge the difference between masked teacher $X$ emerging from behind a screen and masked teacher $Y$ emerging from behind a screen? What if unmasked teacher $X$ disappears behind a screen and masked teacher $Y$ emerges? Does the 3-year-old have

Who am I now?

the means to guess who is behind the mask? Can the child *predict* whose face will appear when the mask is removed?

More advanced variations can involve dual identities. Can one's teacher be also someone else's mother? As we explained in Chapter Two, thinking about dual identities is difficult for young children, who think of roles as if they were tangible objects. Given that an object can be in only one position at one time and given that social roles are conceived by young children in these concrete terms, for the young child it is absurd to call the teacher a mother. How can the teacher be both? How can the teacher be in two positions at the same time? It is not that young children have that much difficulty with a teacher pretending to be a mother—or with a teacher pretending to be a duck or a raindrop, for that matter. But the 3- and 4-year-old has difficulty with the concept that the teacher is in reality also a mother, an aunt, and a neighbor, all at the same time. For the young child these words refer to particular people—like Aunt Hennie, Mommy, and Mr. Kimball next door. Mr. Kimball is a neighbor, but in the egocentric mode of thinking of the young child "a neighbor" is understood only in terms of that person's relationship with the child himself. Mr. Kimball is not understood as "a father," because this would require the young child to relate Mr. Kimball to someone else, someone other than self.

"If I am Janine's mother and you are Janine's child, then what am I to you?" the teacher asks Mia. "My mommy too" Mia replies with some concern. Mia seems more concerned about being left out of the mother-child relationship with the teacher than interested in inferring that the teacher must be her pretend grandmother. The teacher is sensitive to Mia's needs. "If you were my mother and Janine were my child, what would you be to Janine?" Mia laughs. "You ain't Janine's mommy. I know Janine's mommy!" Mia insists. These exchanges don't work often, because they require the child to assume a hypothetical relationship that so flagrantly deviates from known facts.

Later in the day Mia is playing with a family of dolls. "Here comes the mommy, the daddy, and the baby." The teacher enters Mia's world with "What does the baby call him [pointing to the daddy]?" "Daddy" Mia answers. "What does she [mommy] call him [daddy]?" Mia answers in the same way "Daddy." The teacher probes a little further with "You mean that he [daddy] is her [mommy] daddy?" The teacher hopes that Mia will understand that this one doll has two roles. He is daddy to the baby and husband to the mommy, his wife. Mia pauses. "No, he ain't her daddy. He's just daddy daddy." Perhaps Mia's "daddy daddy" indicates that she is at least beginning to distinguish between a person's name and a person's relation to others. More encounters of this variety could assist the child in differentiating between objects (persons) and relations between objects (persons), a fundamental advance in the understanding of the knower-known relation. And, as we have repeatedly emphasized, language is an essential mode of representation. Language provides children with a means to think about relations and helps them transcend their bondage of thinking only about the static world of objects.

## Additional Ideas for Learning Encounters

The previous six learning encounters were spelled out in detail not to give you a recipe for cooking up an encounter but to give you a deeper understanding of Piaget's theory as it applies to the practice of early childhood education and to help you crystallize your thoughts about providing experiences for young children. We hope that, as you read the following suggestions, you will continue to think about the basic psychological principles of negation, reciprocity, and transformation, which this time are not discussed along with the encounter. In the pages to follow we offer a kernel idea, with one or two variations, which you can modify, expand, or transform to fit your particular needs and situations.[1]

### Negative and Positive Space

Teacher and children are sitting at a table with construction paper and paint. The teacher has cut a hole in an $8\frac{1}{2} \times 11$ piece of paper. She uses this as a stencil to paint a yellow moon on a piece of blue paper. Teacher and children explore various

[1]Many of these encounters are being used at The School for Constructive Play, which is part of the Early Childhood Education Program, University of Massachusetts, Amherst (Forman & Hill, 1977).

ways of getting a yellow moon on a blue background. They find four different ways: (1) yellow construction paper as background, with everything painted blue except for the portion covered by a circle of paper; (2) blue construction paper as background, with a yellow circle painted through a hole in another piece of paper; (3) yellow construction paper as background, completely covered by a piece of blue paper in which a hole has been cut out to show the yellow; and (4) blue construction paper as background, with a yellow circle of paper pasted on it. In this fashion the child can learn that the hole (negative space) and the circle that results from cutting the hole (positive space) can stand in reciprocal relation to each other.

*Variation.* The teacher can draw the child's hand on a thin mat board, cut out the outline, and have the child alternately put his hand in the hand-shaped hole and handle the cut-out outline of his hand.

## Constructing a Straight Line

The teacher and several children are standing around a table, observing a miniature village that lies on the table. The teacher informs the children that there has been a hurricane and all the telephone poles in the village have been blown down. The children are asked to arrange the telephone poles in a straight line from the power plant to the schoolhouse—a distance of about ten inches. Children typically have some difficulty making the sequence of poles head in the correct direction, even though they may start with the basic idea of putting the poles down one after the other.

*Variations.* The poles can be linked with pieces of string (telephone wires) to help the children make straight-line judgments. Stiff wire instead of string will make the task even easier, because it will create one ten-inch-long stiff track, and, as we mentioned in Chapter Eight, reducing the degrees of freedom makes the task easier. When the poles are not attached to one another, the degrees of freedom are greater and the problem is therefore more difficult to solve.

## Invisible Displacement

The teacher takes a familiar object that has an elongated shape—for example, a doll. She places the doll in a tunnel-like box that has three openings in a row (one toward each end and one in the middle) covered by hinged lids. The child is asked to find the doll's eyes, because the doll wants to see out. The child has to guess which lid he should open in order to expose the doll's eyes. The same is then done with the doll's tummy and feet. The activity can be expanded by using other objects. It can also be expanded by using the same object and then rotating the tunnel or by putting the object in the tunnel upside down.

*Variation.* Put an object on the end of a stick, and insert the object into the tunnel. The child has to guess how far down the tunnel the object has been pushed and lift the lid that will expose the object.

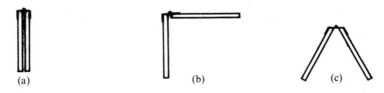

(a)     (b)     (c)

*Figure 9-3.*

## Changing Perspective

Acquire two pieces of Plexiglas, each about three feet by four feet in size. Mount the two pieces in wooden frames and hinge the two pieces together along the sides measuring three feet. The hinged Plexiglas can now be used as an easel in a variety of positions: the pieces folded flat against each other (Figure 9-3a), one piece perpendicular to the other (Figure 9-3b), or the pieces of Plexiglas at less than a 90-degree angle (Figure 9-3c).[2]

When used for drawing, the two pieces of Plexiglas provide the child with a number of different drawing surfaces. A child, for example, can be underneath a

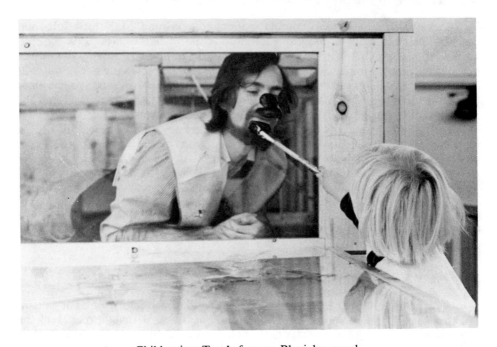

Child paints Tom's face on Plexiglas panel.

[2]We thank David Fernie, Early Childhood Education Program, School of Education, University of Massachusetts, Amherst, for this idea.

drawing surface (Figure 9-3b) perhaps for the first time. Since Plexiglas is transparent, the child has many opportunities to experience changes in perspective. Two children standing on opposite sides of the Plexiglas can do body tracing—of each other. When they look at their respective tracings, the two children can clearly see the mirror-image reversals. If the Plexiglas is set as in Figure 9-3b, two children can each trace the same object that is sitting on the floor underneath the Plexiglas, one from the top and one from the side, thereby seeing two different perspectives of the same object. In a similar manner they can trace the same object a number of times as the object is moved away from the Plexiglas.

*Variation.* With children who are too young to draw the outline of an object, you can take a familiar asymmetrical object, draw three different perspectives of that object on three sides of a pasteboard box, and cut out the three perspectives. The child then uses the pasteboard box as a "perspective-sorter" puzzle. The important feature of this perspective sorter is that each perspective is a transformation of the same object—the side view, the top view, and the frontal view of the object (see photograph p. 67).

### Representation of Physical Environment

Construct a scale model of the classroom or playground. Make little dolls, and paste on their heads the photographs of all the children in the class. Have the children try to place each doll in the scale model in the same place the real child occupies in the classroom or playground. You can vary the game by having one of the children hide somewhere and placing a doll in the spot that corresponds to the place where the child is hiding. The other children have to run to that spot and find the hiding child. If you make a scale model of the playground, you can use it to give children clues about the places where Easter eggs or other objects are hidden. Ideally the scale model should be placed in a location that permits the children to see the model and the playground simultaneously—for example, in a bay-window area.

*Variation.* With younger children, you can take a photograph of yourself wearing an apron with five or six pockets. Before meeting with the children, you hide several objects in the various pockets. Then you point to one of the pockets in the photograph and ask a child if she can locate that pocket and its contents on your person.

### Seriating Soil

Construct four or five soil sifters with screens of different-size holes or gauges. The frames of the sifters should be at least two inches thick, so that you can stack the sifters one on top of the other. Mix sand, pebbles, and small rocks in the sand table, and have the children pour the composite soil through the sifters. By doing so, the children discover that each sifter traps only soil whose components are larger than a particular size. With further exploration the children discover that, by stacking the sifters according to gauge (the sifter with the smallest holes should be on the table, at the bottom of the stack), the composite-soil mixture can be divided into a number of

Seth places miniature objects in their correct places.

piles ordered according to the size of their particles. As the soil mixture is poured down into the stack of sifters, each sifter catches only those particles too large to pass through the screen. The soil reaching the table is the finest. By rearranging the order of the sifters, the children discover other relationships—for example, what happens when the sifters are stacked so that the sifter with the largest-gauge screen is on the table. This activity should help the children understand that soil, even though it looks like a homogeneous substance, is actually composed of tiny particles of many different sizes.

*Variation.* Give the younger child a set of plastic containers with lids. Each lid has a hole of different size. The child fills each container with the composite soil and covers the containers with the lids. As the child inverts the soil-filled containers, he discovers that different amounts of the composite soil remain in different containers.

## Continuity across Discontinuity

Place a row of dominoes on end, so that pushing one domino causes the whole row to collapse. You and the children can experiment with the amount of space that can be allowed between successive dominoes and with the extent to which the dominoes can be arranged in a curving line for the trick to work. This game increases the child's awareness that what seems like a continuous motion is actually composed of many separate, discontinuous units. Exploring the interval of space needed between dominoes for the trick to work relates to premeasurement skills, such as the reiteration of a standard interval (that is, moving a ruler along a surface).

*Variations.* Hang an I-V (intravenous-feeding) apparatus filled with water from the ceiling over the sand table. As the children move the I-V tube across the sand, the constant rate of drip is marked by spots on the sand. Since the apparatus allows children to control the rate of drip, they can experience the unitizing of motion.

Another way of unitizing motion is by laying sections of rubber tubing at different intervals across the playground slide. As a child rolls a ball down the slide, he

Children write on paper with I-V tubes.

Wedges apart                         Wedges together
Wheels apart                         Wheels together
(a)                                  (b)

*Figure 9-4.*

sees the ball take a quick hop each time it crosses a section of tubing. In this way continuous movement is broken down into intervals (see photograph p. 5).

### Decentering from the Physical

When children are 2 or 3 years old, they are extremely attentive to how wooden objects, like jigsaw pieces and blocks, physically fit. As children progress developmentally, they become more capable of positioning objects on the basis of visual judgment alone. This skill is essential in certain situations. Cut two wedges of wood, and make a groove (about six inches long) in each wedge. Demonstrate to the child how the two wedges can be spaced apart, keeping them parallel, so that a set of wheels on a single axle just fits, one wheel in each grooved edge (Figure 9-4a). The

Using off-sized wheels makes the axle arc.

wheels will roll down the wedges freely only if the two wedges are spaced parallel and at the correct interval. Place a small item at the bottom of the wedges, so that, if the wheels successfully roll down the wedges, the child is rewarded by the fun of seeing the wheels knock down the item. Young children have a tendency to place the two wedges flush together, thereby making it impossible for the wheels to fit one in each grooved wedge. This task requires that the children decenter from the physical flushness of the two wedges and make a visual judgment based on the distance between the two wheels fixed to the axle.

*Variations.* This game can be made more difficult by giving the child a set of wheels that slide on a common axle. This increases the degrees of freedom. The child eventually learns that there are two ways of solving the problem, each the reciprocal of the other. He can either leave the wheels separated and space the wedges to the right parallel arrangement (Figure 9-4a) or he can leave the wedges

Rolling wheels down wedges.

flush together and push the wheels close together on the common axle (see Figure 9-4b).

The young child's orientation to the feel and fit of objects can be seen in the 3-year-old's lack of tolerance for jigsaw pieces that don't fit well (Forman, Laughlin, & Sweeney, 1971). Furthermore, when given an opportunity to create a form either by the physical, touchable outline of an object or by the pattern painted on the surface of a flat piece of wood, 2- and 3-year-olds choose the former. Forman, Kuschner, and Dempsey (1975c) presented children with a task that created conflict between these two means of creating good form. By placing two pieces of wood together, the child could produce either the outline of a square (Figure 9-5a) or the painted pattern of a circle (Figure 9-5b). Teachers can make similar materials using more meaningful objects, like two pieces that join to make either the physical outline of a house or the painted scene of a farmyard. These simple tasks create a conflict that helps the child decenter from exclusive attention to the fit and feel of the physical outline of objects. We are not suggesting that children learn to ignore phys-

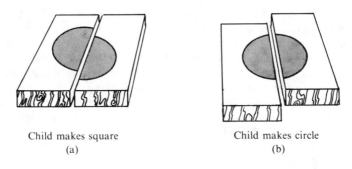

Child makes square          Child makes circle
(a)                                (b)

*Figure 9-5.*

ical outline but that they learn to pay attention to other sources of pattern as well.

We have also used another toy that 2- and 3-year-olds enjoy, a toy that improves their decentration from physical fit and feel of object against object. This toy must be specially made. It consists of a large wooden ring mounted on an aluminum frame. Inside the wooden ring is a small disk that is itself securely glued to an aluminum plate. The aluminum plate can slide within the frame but cannot be removed from the frame. Therefore the small disk can slide within the large ring but cannot be removed. The task for the child is to place another ring in the space that is being created around the small disk when the disk is centered inside the large ring. Young children, around age 2, try to place this second ring into the puzzle by pushing the small disk against the large ring, as illustrated in Figure 9-6a. Once the child begins to use visual judgment rather than physical feedback, he can center the small disk (Figure 9-6b), thereby *making* a space that will accommodate the second ring. This is a good example of a task that requires the child to transform space, which is a better pedagogical procedure than the usual form boards, which require the child only to match shapes (see Chapter Three).

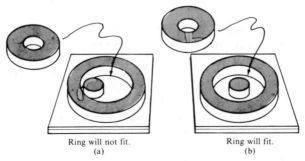

Ring will not fit.          Ring will fit.
(a)                         (b)

*Figure 9-6.*

### Conservation of Discontinuity

Sometimes young children (around 2 years of age) seem to forget that a stack of blocks forever remains a set of discontinuous elements. They try to pick up the whole stack by grasping a center section and lifting, as if it were one, tall object. The following activity gives the child an opportunity to explore the discontinuity of two objects that appear continuous. Cut a large wooden circle and then cut an inner circle within the large one. This will create a disk inside a ring. Paint a picture of a bird on the surface of the wooden disk. When the child grasps the ring and lifts, the disk will remain on the table. Ask the child to place the bird and the nest (the ring) on the hill (a small overturned box), as illustrated in Figure 9-7. Young children have a ten-

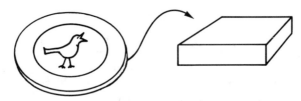

*Figure 9-7.*

dency to grasp the ring very firmly, as if they were trying to prevent the disk from remaining on the table. Even when the child herself places the ring over the disk, she still fails to remember that the two objects are forever discontinuous. With time she will learn to cradle the disk from underneath while lifting the ring with the other hand.

### Recognizing Transformed Shapes

Construct a translucent shadowbox near the kitchen corner. A sheet stretched within a rectangular frame usually works. Place kitchen utensils on hooks hanging on the back of the shadowbox. Turn on a light source behind these utensils. In this way the children can see only the shadows of the utensils. As they play in the kitchen corner, the children will need various objects, like a spoon, a grater, and so on. The shadowbox can be built so that only the teacher has easy access to the utensils. As the child needs a utensil, he points to the shadow that he thinks is cast by the item he desires. The teacher can vary the position of the items so that the child must deal with a variety of perspectives (frontal, top, and side views). Interested children can play these games with each other if they wish.

*Variation.* Younger children can actively manipulate objects behind the screen, noticing how the form of the object changes as the object moves. Hand puppets and the child's own hand are good objects to begin with. Objects that contain open spaces—like toilet-paper tubes or a cup with a handle—produce particularly interesting effects when rotated.

## Anticipating Positions

Certainly the 2-year-old can anticipate where a rolling ball will collide with something. She can even aim the ball toward an object she wishes to knock down. This basic skill can be expanded in the following game, modeled after the pinball machine. Build an inclined plane about four feet by two feet. Construct a retaining wall, about two inches high, around the two long sides and the top narrow side. Insert two-inch pegs at regular intervals both from top to bottom and from right to left on the inclined plane. By using two-inch wide elastic loops, you can create a variety of channels through which a ball can roll down the inclined plane. The child is asked to position a small toy at the foot of the inclined plane, at the point where she believes the ball will exit. You and the child can vary the objective from placing the toy where the ball will exit to placing the elastic loops so that the ball will exit at a designated point.[3]

*Variation.* Younger children can anticipate position by varying the direction of "hot-wheels" tracks. A car is placed in the track and released down an inclined track that the child has positioned so that the car will roll off the track, across the floor, and into a shoe box some feet away.

## Goals with Subgoals

Young children have no difficulty dealing with problems whose solution requires a direct relation between response and goal, such as pushing directly on an object that is stuck. More difficult to solve are problems that contain subproblems —for example, keeping a spring-operated faucet on while trying to wet one's hands. (It should be noted that these kinds of problems are all variations of the detour problem discussed in Chapter Four and illustrated in Figure 4-1.) Here are some problems that contain subproblems: hanging a coat when one has to first insert a peg into a hole in the wall; getting an object out of a desk when one has to first invent

[3]We thank Ada Secrist, Research Coordinator at the Early Childhood Education Project in Buffalo, New York, for this idea.

some way of keeping the spring-operated desk lid or drawer open (such as placing a jam in the opening); pouring juice when one has to first figure how to puncture the juice can; getting an item from a high shelf when one has to first stack two or more stepping blocks to reach the shelf; taking off one's coat when one has to first remove large mittens; swinging in a swing when one has to first tell the teacher to adjust the swing chain to make the seat parallel to the ground; jumping rope with only one other child when one end of the rope must first be secured to an upright post. There are literally hundreds of problems in which the child must keep his main goal in mind while solving a problem that is essential to the goal. As we have said elsewhere, these types of "detour" problems help the child to decenter from a single-path approach to a goal and to increase flexibility of thinking.

*Length versus Distance*

Length is the amount of space an object occupies from end to end. Distance is the amount of space between two points (regardless of whether the space is occupied or not). You can work on this distinction in the sandbox, in the playground, and in the classroom at large. Take some weak elastic strips and attach short sticks to each end of the strips. The elastic strips can be stretched to different lengths to serve as pretend roads in the sandbox. "This road is too short. Can you make it longer so it covers the distance between the car and the garage?" you ask the child. The child stretches the elastic. "Good. Now the length of the road is the same as the distance between the car and the garage." In the playground you can stage a similar problem by stretching a clothesline between two poles. "The length of this one piece of rope is not enough to cover the distance between these two poles. What shall we do?" The children tie another piece of rope to the clothesline. Then you place a large climbing box between the two poles. "Do you think that the distance between the two poles is the same or that it's different now that I put the box there?" The box can be opened at each end, making a tunnel. One child says "If you open the ends, the distance is the same." You continue: "Has the rope between the poles gotten shorter?" By staging problems and asking questions, you can at least make the child think about the distinction between length and distance. "Is the rope shorter now that we are holding it in a circle?" The child will soon discover that changing the shape of the rope does not change its length, for, after all, when it is stretched out again, it will still go from one pole to the other.

*Intervals in Motion*

In our attempts to understand motion, we often break a continuous action into equal intervals. This is what a golf coach does when he shows a pupil a film of his golf swing, first at high speed and then projected on the screen one frame at a time. Many outdoor climbing apparatuses, like ladders and jungle gyms, can be used to break walking, climbing, and even running into equal intervals. What is missing from this outdoor equipment is a means to vary these intervals, so that the child can understand the functional relation between the interval—say, his stride— and the total motion. Take an old ladder and cut out all but the top and bottom rungs. Lay the ladder flat on the ground. Take the nine or ten rungs that you have

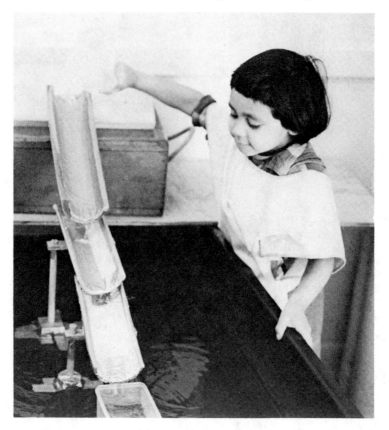

Breaking motion into intervals.

removed and reinsert them inside the ladder in such a way that they can be moved back and forth (for example, by tacking two narrow strips of wood on each side piece of the ladder, thus creating a channel within which the rungs can slide freely). The children can step in the spaces between the rungs as part of an "obstacle course" you have designed. You or the children can vary the intervals between the rungs and then discover how the variation affects the difficulty of the obstacle course. Since running the obstacle course requires the children to step in each space between the rungs, the children will soon discover that equal intervals allow them to establish a rhythm that is impossible with unequal intervals and make the obstacle course easier to negotiate.

# References

Aaron, D., & Winawer, B. P. *Child's play: A creative approach to play spaces for today's children.* New York: Harper & Row, 1965.

Allen, L. E., Henke, L. B., Harris, F. R., Baer, D. M., & Reynolds, N. J. Control of hyperactivity by social reinforcement of attending behavior. *Journal of Educational Psychology,* 1967, *58,* 231–237.

Appel, M. H. Aggressive behavior of nursery-school children and adult procedures in dealing with such behavior. *Journal of Experimental Education,* 1942, *11,* 185–199.

Aronfreed, J. The origin of self-criticism. *Psychological Review,* 1964, *71,* 193–218.

Ausubel, D. P. *Educational psychology: A cognitive view.* New York: Holt, Rinehart & Winston, 1969.

Baldwin, A. A. A is happy—B is not. *Child Development,* 1965, *36,* 583–600.

Barker, R., Dembo, T., & Lewin, K. Frustration and regression: An experiment with young children. *University of Iowa Studies in Child Welfare,* 1941, *18,* No. 1.

Becker, W. S., Madsen, C. H., Arnold, C. R., & Thomas, D. R. The contingent use of teacher attention and praise in reducing classroom behavior problems. *Journal of Special Education,* 1967, *1,* 287–307.

Bee, H. *The developing child.* New York: Harper & Row, 1975.

Beilin, H. Stimulus and cognitive transformation in conservation. In D. Elkind & J. H. Flavell (Eds.), *Studies in cognitive development: Essays in honor of Jean Piaget.* New York: Oxford University Press, 1969.

Beilin, H. *Studies in the cognitive basis of language development.* New York: Academic Press, 1975.

Bell, S. M. The development of the concept of object as related to infant-mother attachment. *Child Development,* 1970, *41,* 291–311.

Blank, M. The wrong response: Is it to be ignored, prevented, or treated? In R. K. Parker (Ed.), *The preschool in action.* Boston: Allyn & Bacon, 1972.

Blank, M. *Teaching learning in the preschool: A dialogue approach.* Columbus, Ohio: Merrill, 1973.

Blank, M., & Solomon, F. How shall the disadvantaged child be taught? *Child Development,* 1969, *40,* 47–61.

Bloom, L., Lightbown, P., & Hood, L. Structure and variation in child language. *Monographs of the Society for Research in Child Development,* 1975, *40* (160, Whole No. 2).

Bower, T. G. R. *Development in infancy.* San Francisco: W. H. Freeman, 1974.

Bowlby, J. *Attachment.* New York: Basic Books, 1969.

Brainerd, C. J., & Allen, T. W. Experimental inductions of the conservation of "First-Order" quantitative invariants. *Psychological Bulletin,* 1971, *75*(2), 128–144.

Bruner, J. S. *On knowing: Essays for the left hand.* New York: Atheneum, 1967.

Bruner, J. S. *Center for Cognitive Studies, Ninth Annual Report.* Cambridge, Mass.: Harvard University Press, 1968. (a)

Bruner, J. S. *Processes of cognitive growth in infancy.* Heinz Werner Lectures, Clark University, Worcester (Vol. 3). Barre, Mass.: Barre, 1968. (b)

Bruner, J. S. *Beyond the information given: Studies in the psychology of knowing.* New York: Norton, 1973.

Bugelski, B. R. *The psychology of learning applied to teaching.* New York: Bobbs-Merrill, 1964.

Cazden, C. B. Suggestions from studies in early language acquisition. In C. B. Cazden (Ed.), *Language in early childhood education.* Washington, D.C.: National Association for the Education of Young Children, 1972.

Charlesworth, W. R. The role of surprise in cognitive development. In D. Elkind & J. H. Flavell (Eds.), *Studies in cognitive development: Essays in honor of Jean Piaget.* New York: Oxford University Press, 1969.

Chomsky, C. Write now, read later. In C. B. Cazden (Ed.), *Language in early childhood education.* Washington, D.C.: National Association for the Education of Young Children, 1972.

Chukovsky, K. *From two to five.* Berkeley: University of California Press, 1974.

Clark, E. What's in a word? On the child's acquisition of semantics in his first language. In T. Moore (Ed.), *Cognitive development and the acquisition of language.* New York: Academic Press, 1973.

Conrad, R. The chronology of the development of covert speech in children. *Developmental Psychology,* 1971, *5,* 398–405.

Decarie, T. G. *Intelligence and affectivity in early childhood.* New York: International Universities Press, 1966.

DeVries, R. Constancy of generic identity in the years three to six. *Monographs of the Society for Research in Child Development,* 1969, *34* (3, Serial No. 127).

Duckworth, E. The having of wonderful ideas. In M. Schwebel & J. Raph (Eds.), *Piaget in the classroom.* New York: Basic Books, 1973.

Duckworth, E. *Piaget in the classroom.* Workshop presented at the School of Education Marathon, Amherst, Mass., Spring 1974.

Elkind, D. Giant in the nursery—Jean Piaget. *The New York Times Magazine,* May 26, 1969, pp. 152–164. (a)

Elkind, D. Conservation and concept formation. In D. Elkind & J. Flavell (Eds.), *Studies in cognitive development: Essays in honor of Jean Piaget.* New York: Oxford University Press, 1969. (b)

Elkind, D. *A sympathetic understanding of the child: Birth to sixteen.* Boston: Allyn & Bacon, 1974.

Erikson, E. *Childhood and society* (2nd ed.). New York: Norton, 1963.

Ervin-Tripp, S. Language development. In L. W. Hoffman & M. L. Hoffman (Eds.), *Review of child development research* (Vol. 2). New York: Russell Sage Foundation, 1966.

Evans, E. D. *Contemporary influences in early childhood education* (2nd ed.). New York: Holt, Rinehart & Winston, 1975.

Fein, G. G., & Clarke-Stewart, A. *Day care in context.* New York: Wiley, 1973.

Ferster, C. B., & Perrott, M. C. *Behavior principles.* New York: Meredith, 1968.

Fiske, D. W., & Maddi, S. R. *Functions of varied experiences.* Homewood, Ill.: Dorsey, 1961.

Flapan, D. *Children's understanding of social interaction.* New York: Teachers College Press, 1968.

Flapan, D., & Neubauer, P. B. *The assessment of early child development.* New York: Aronson, 1975.

Flavell, J. H., Beach, D. H., & Chinsky, J. M. Spontaneous verbal rehearsal in a memory task as a function of age. *Child Development,* 1966, *37,* 283–299.

Flavell, J. H., Botkin, P. T., Fry, C. L., Wright, J. W., & Jarvis, P. E. *The development of role-taking and communication skills in children.* New York: Wiley, 1968.

Forman, G. E. *The role of bilateral symmetry in the early development of logic.* Paper presented at the biennial meeting of the Society for Research in Child Development, Philadelphia, March 1973.

Forman, G. E. On the components of spatial representation. In J. Eliot & N. J. Salkind (Eds.), *Children's spatial development.* Springfield, Ill.: Charles C Thomas, 1975.

Forman, G. E., & Hill, D. F. *The School for Constructive Play.* Workshop presented at the Seventh Annual Symposium of the Jean Piaget Society, Philadelphia, May 1977.

Forman, G. E., Kuschner, D. S., & Dempsey, J. *From action to interval: Early development of spatial relations as seen in the spontaneous block play of young children.* Paper presented at the biennial meeting of the Society for Research in Child Development, Denver, April 1975. (a)

Forman, G. E., Kuschner, D. S., & Dempsey, J. *Transformations in the manipulations and productions performed with geometric objects: An early system of logic in young children.* Final report. Washington, D.C.: National Institute of Education, 1975. (Grant NE-G-00-3-0051) (b)

Forman, G. E., Kuschner, D. S., & Dempsey, J. Visual decentration: From stereometric points to planeometric forms. *Perceptual and Motor Skills,* 1975, *41,* 343–352. (c)

Forman, G. E., Laughlin, F., & Sweeney, M. The development of jigsaw puzzle solving in preschool children: An information-processing approach. *DARCEE Papers and Reports* (Kennedy Center for Research), 1971, *5* (Whole No. 8).

Freud, A. *Normality and pathology in childhood.* New York: International Universities Press, 1965.

Frost, J. L., & Kissinger, J. B. *The young child and the educative process.* New York: Holt, Rinehart & Winston, 1976.

Furth, H. G. *Thinking without language: Psychological implications of deafness.* New York: Free Press, 1966.

Furth, H. G. *Piaget and knowledge: Theoretical foundations.* Englewood Cliffs, N.J.: Prentice-Hall, 1969.

Furth, H. G. Two aspects of experience in ontogeny: Development and learning. In H. W. Reese (Ed.), *Advances in child development and behavior* (Vol. 9). New York: Academic Press, 1974.

Gallup, G. G. Chimpanzees: Self-recognition. *Science,* 1970, *167,* 86–87.

Garvey, C., & Hogan, R. Social speech and social interaction: Egocentrism revisited. *Child Development,* 1973, *44,* 562–568.

Gibson, E. *Principles of perceptual learning and development.* New York: Appleton-Century-Crofts, 1969.

Gibson, J. J. *The senses considered as perceptual systems.* Boston: Houghton Mifflin, 1966.

Ginsburg, H., & Opper, S. *Piaget's theory of intellectual development: An introduction.* Englewood Cliffs, N.J.: Prentice-Hall, 1969.

Gleason, J. B. Do children imitate? *Proceedings of the International Conference on Oral Education of the Deaf,* June 1967, *2,* 1441–1448.

Glucksberg, S., Krauss, R., & Higgins, E. T. The development of referential communication skills. In F. Horowitz (Ed.), *Review of child development research* (Vol. 4). Chicago: University of Chicago Press, 1975.

Gordon, I. J. *Human development: A transactional perspective.* New York: Harper & Row, 1975. (a)

Gordon, I. J. *The infant experience.* Columbus, Ohio: Merrill, 1975. (b)

Grene, M. *The knower and the known.* Berkeley: University of California Press, 1974.

Harlow, H. F. Learning set and error factor theory. In S. Koch (Ed.), *Psychology: A study of a science* (Vol. 2). New York: McGraw-Hill, 1959.

Hawkins, F. P. *The logic of action: Young children at work.* New York: Pantheon, 1974.

Heathers, G. Emotional dependence and independence in nursery school play. *Journal of Genetic Psychology,* 1955, *87,* 37–58.

Hilgard, E. R., & Bower, G. H. *Theories of learning.* New York: Appleton-Century-Crofts, 1966.

Holland, V. M., & Palermo, D. S. On learning "less": Language and cognitive development. *Child Development,* 1975, *46,* 437–443.

Hunt, J. McV. *The challenge of incompetence and poverty.* Urbana: University of Illinois Press, 1969.

Inhelder, B., & Piaget, J. *The early growth of logic in the child: Classification and seriation.* New York: Norton, 1964.

Inhelder, B., Sinclair, H., & Bovet, M. *Learning and the development of cognition.* Cambridge, Mass.: Harvard University Press, 1974.

Isaacs, S. *Intellectual growth in young children, with an appendix on children's "why" questions by Nathan Isaacs.* London: Routledge & Kegan Paul, 1930.

Kamii, C. *One intelligence indivisible.* Paper presented at the annual convention of the National Association for the Education of Young Children, Washington, D.C., 1974.

Kamii, C., & Derman, L. The Engelmann approach to teaching logical thinking: Findings from the administration of some Piagetian tasks. In D. R. Green, M. P. Ford, & G. B. Flamer (Eds.), *Measurement and Piaget.* New York: McGraw-Hill, 1971.

Kamii, C., & DeVries, R. Piaget for early education. In R. K. Parker (Ed.), *The preschool in action* (2nd ed.). Boston: Allyn & Bacon, 1977.

Karplus, R. (Director). *The science curriculum improvement study.* Chicago: Rand McNally, 1972.

Kendler, H. H. *Basic psychology.* New York: Appleton-Century-Crofts, 1963.

Kendler, H. H., & Kendler, T. S. Vertical and horizontal processes in problem solving. *Psychological Review,* 1962, *69,* 1–16.

Knoblock, H., & Pasamanick, B. (Eds.). *Gesell and Amatruda's developmental diagnosis* (3rd ed.). New York: Harper & Row, 1974.

Kritchevsky, S., Prescott, E., & Walling, L. *Planning environments for young children: Physical space.* Washington, D.C.: National Association for the Education of Young Children, 1969.

Kuhn, T. S. *The structure of scientific revolutions* (2nd ed.). Chicago: University of Chicago Press, 1970.

Laurendeau, M., & Pinard, A. *The development of the concept of space in the child.* New York: International Universities Press, 1970.

Lewis, M. Individual differences in the measurement of early cognitive growth. In J. Hellmuth (Ed.), *Exceptional infant. 2: Studies in abnormality.* New York: Brunner/Mazel, 1971.

Luria, A. R., & Yudovich, F. I. *Speech and the development of mental processes in the child.* London: Staples Press, 1959.

Madsen, C. H., Jr., & Madsen, C. K. *Teaching/discipline.* Boston: Allyn & Bacon, 1968.

Mahler, M. S. *On human symbiosis and the vicissitudes of individuation. 1: Infantile psychosis.* New York: International Universities Press, 1968.

Maratsos, M. P. Decrease in the understanding of the word "big" in preschool children. *Child Development,* 1973, *44,* 747–752. (a)

Maratsos, M. P. Nonegocentric communication abilities in preschool children. *Child Development,* 1973, *44,* 697–700. (b)

Martin, W. E., & Stendler, C. B. *Child development: The process of growing up in society.* New York: Harcourt Brace, 1953.

McCarthy, J. J., & Kirk, S. A. *Illinois test of psycho-linguistic abilities: Experimental edition.* Urbana: Institute for Research on Exceptional Children, University of Illinois, 1961.

Meers, D. R., & Marans, A. E. Group care of infants in other countries. In C. A. Chandler (Ed.), *New perspectives in early child care.* New York: Atherton, 1968.

Metz-Hatch, K. *Desociocentering: A theory based on the work of Jean Piaget.* Unpublished dissertation, School of Education, University of Massachusetts, Amherst, 1975.

Miller, G. A. The magical number seven, plus or minus two: Some limits on our capacity for processing information. *Psychological Review,* 1956, *63,* 81–97.

Miller, G. A. *Psychology, the science of mental life.* New York: Harper & Row, 1962.

Miller, L. B., & Estes, B. W. Monetary reward and motivation in discrimination learning. *Journal of Experimental Psychology,* 1961, *61,* 501–504.

Miller, R. S., & Morris, W. N. The effects of being imitated on children's responses in a marble-dropping task. *Child Development,* 1974, *45,* 1103–1107.

Mischel, T. *Cognitive development and epistemology.* New York: Academic Press, 1971.

Montessori, M. *The discovery of the child.* Notre Dame, Ind.: Fides Publishers, 1967.

Murphy, L. B. *The widening world of childhood: Paths toward mastery.* New York: Basic Books, 1962.

Nelson, K. Structure and strategy in learning to talk. *Monographs of the Society for Research in Child Development,* 1973, *38* (1–2, Serial No. 149).

Peed, S., & Forehand, R. Effects of different amounts and types of vicarious consequences upon imitative performance. *Journal of Experimental Child Psychology,* 1973, *16,* 508–520.

Piaget, J. *Play, dreams, and imitation in childhood.* New York: Norton, 1951.

Piaget, J. *The child's conception of number.* London: Routledge & Kegan Paul, 1952.

Piaget, J. *The construction of reality in the child.* New York: Basic Books, 1954.

Piaget, J. *The child's conception of physical causality.* Totowa, N.J.: Littlefield, Adams, 1969.

Piaget, J. Piaget's theory. In P. Mussen (Ed.), *Carmichael's manual of child psychology* (3rd ed., Vol. 1). New York: Wiley, 1970.

Piaget, J. *To understand is to invent: The future of education.* New York: Grossman, 1973.

Piaget, J. *The grasp of consciousness: Action and concept in the young child.* Cambridge, Mass.: Harvard University Press, 1976.

Piaget, J., & Garcia, R. *Understanding causality.* New York: Norton, 1974.

Piaget, J., & Inhelder, B. *The child's conception of space.* New York: Norton, 1967.

Piaget, J., & Inhelder, B. The gaps in empiricism. In A. Koestler & J. R. Smythies (Eds.), *Beyond reductionism.* London: Hutchinson, 1969. (a)

Piaget, J., & Inhelder, B. *The psychology of the child.* New York: Basic Books, 1969. (b)

Piaget, J., & Inhelder, B. *Mental imagery in the child.* New York: Basic Books, 1971.

Poincaré, H. *Foundations of science.* New York: Science Press, 1946.

Pufall, P. B. *Relations between egocentricism and coordinate reference systems.* Paper presented at the biennial meeting of the Society for Research in Child Development, Philadelphia, 1973.

Raths, L. E., Harmin, M., & Simon, S. B. *Values and teaching.* Columbus, Ohio: Merrill, 1966.

Reichenbach, H. *The philosophy of space and time.* New York: Dover, 1958.

Rheingold, H. L., & Eckerman, C. O. The infant separates himself from his mother. *Science,* 1970, *168,* 78–83.

Schaffer, H. R. Some issues for research in the study of attachment behavior. In B. M. Foss (Ed.), *Determinants of infant behavior* (Vol. 2). New York: Barnes & Noble, 1963.

Schwartz, G. E., & Shapiro, D. (Eds.). *Consciousness and self-regulation: Advances in research* (Vol. 1). New York: Plenum, 1976.

Sherif, M., & Sherif, C. W. *Groups in harmony and tension.* New York: Harper & Row, 1953.

Sigel, I. E. Developmental theory and preschool education: Issues, problems, and implications. In I. Gordon (Ed.), *Early childhood education: The 71st yearbook of the National Society for the Study of Education.* Chicago: University of Chicago Press, 1972.

Sigel, I. E., Secrist, A., & Forman, G. E. Psycho-educational intervention beginning at age two: Reflections and outcomes. In J. Stanley (Ed.), *Compensatory education for children, ages 2 to 8.* Baltimore: Johns Hopkins University Press, 1973.

Sigel, I. E., Starr, R., Secrist, A., Jackson, J. P., & Hill, E. Social and emotional development in young children. In E. H. Grotberg (Ed.), *Day care: Resources for decisions.* Washington, D.C.: Office of Economic Opportunity, 1971.

Skinner, B. F. *The technology of teaching.* New York: Appleton-Century-Crofts, 1968.

Smedslund, J. The acquisition of conservation of substance and weight in children. V: Practice in conflict situations without external reinforcement. *Scandinavian Journal of Psychology,* 1961, *2,* 153–155.

Smilansky, S. *The effects of sociodramatic play on disadvantaged preschool children.* New York: Wiley, 1968.

Sommer, R. *Personal space: The behavioral basis of design.* Englewood Cliffs, N.J.: Prentice-Hall, 1969.

Stone, J. L., & Church, J. *Childhood and adolescence: A psychology of the growing person* (3rd ed.). New York: Random House, 1973.

Stone, J. L., Murphy, L. B., & Smith, H. T. *The competent infant: Research and commentary.* New York: Basic Books, 1973.

Strauss, S. Inducing cognitive development and learning: A review of short-term experiments. 1: The organismic developmental approach. *Cognition,* 1972, *1,* 329–357.

Strohner, H., & Nelson, K. E. The young child's development of sentence comprehension: Influence of event probability, non-verbal context, syntactic form, and strategies. *Child Development,* 1974, *45,* 567–576.

Sutton-Smith, B., & Sutton-Smith, S. *How to play with your children (and when not to).* New York: Hawthorn, 1974.

Uzgiris, I. C. Patterns of vocal and gestural imitation in infants. In F. J. Mönks, W. W. Hartup, & J. DeWitt (Eds.), *Determinants of behavioral development.* New York: Academic Press, 1972.

Vurpillot, E. *The visual world of the child.* New York: International Universities Press, 1976.

Walcher, D. N., & Peters, D. L. (Eds.). *The development of self-regulatory mechanisms.* New York: Academic Press, 1971.

Watson, J. S. Smiling, cooing, and "the game." *Merrill-Palmer Quarterly of Behavior and Development,* 1972, *18*(4), 323–339.

Wenar, C. Competence at one. *Merrill-Palmer Quarterly of Behavior and Development,* 1964, *10* (4), 329–342.

Werner, H. *Comparative psychology of mental development.* New York: International Universities Press, 1948.

Werner, H., & Kaplan, E. The acquisition of word meanings: A developmental study. *Monographs of the Society for Research in Child Development,* 1952, *15* (1, Whole No. 51).

Werner, H., & Kaplan, B. *Symbol formation.* New York: Wiley, 1963.

Weyl, H. *Philosophy of mathematics and natural science.* New York: Atheneum, 1963.

White, B. L. *The first three years of life.* Englewood Cliffs, N.J.: Prentice-Hall, 1975.

White, S. H. Changes in learning processes in the late preschool years. In *Early learning.* Symposium presented at the meeting of the American Educational Research Association, Chicago, 1968.

Whitehead, A. N. *The aims of education and other essays.* New York: Free Press, 1967.

Woodcock, L. *Life and ways of the two year old.* New York: Basic Books, 1941.

Zaporozhets, A. V. The development of perception in the preschool child. In W. Kessen & C. Kuhlman (Eds.), *Cognitive development in children.* Chicago: University of Chicago Press, 1970.

Zigler, E. Metatheoretical issues in developmental psychology. In M. Marx (Ed.), *Theories in contemporary psychology.* New York: Macmillan, 1963.

# Index

Aaron, D., 188
Action:
  change of, 133
  consciousness of, 140
  content of, 133
  depersonification of, 9
  direction of, 133
  force of, 133
  form of, 9
  inhibition of, 125
  logic of, 36
  modulation of, 132-133
  product of, 132-133
  reflection on, 126-127, 139-140
  repetition of, 125
  reversibility in, 70-71, 113-114, 137
  significance for learning, 14, 52-53
  target of, 133
Activities:
  exploratory, 160-167
  support, 160-161, 163-164
Adaptation, 25-27
Affect:
  and cognition, 18, 43, 79
  as a diagnostic, 18
Allen, L. E., 99
Arnold, C. R., 99
Aronfreed, J., 90
Associative thinking, 83-86
Assumptions, basic:
  about child development, 169-174
  about knowledge, 4, 36, 47
Ausubel, D. P., 110
Autonomy, 90-91

Baer, D. M., 99

Baldwin, A. A., 79
Barker, R., 18
Batchelder, E., 179*n*
Beach, D. H., 81
Becker, W. S., 99
Bee, H., 82, 86
Behavior modification, 94-107, 114-118
Beilin, H., 84, 110
Bell, S. M., 41
Blank, M., 99, 101, 135*n*, 157, 195
Bloom, L., 14
Body awareness, in infancy, 41
Botkin, P. T., 215
Bovet, M., 88
Bower, T. G. R., 60, 70, 81
Bowlby, J., 90
Bruner, J. S., 18, 40, 81
Bugelski, B. R., 110

Carew, J. V., 142
Causality, and projection of self, 29
Centration, 88-91, 125 (*see also* Decentration)
Chan, I., 142
Change:
  adjustment to, 26
  coordinated with differences, 58
  coordinated with static states, 63
  direction of, 74
  ecological importance, 60
  implications of, 74
  in position of self, 42
  quantity of, 74
  thinking about, 140
  view of, 25-26
Charlesworth, W. R., 112

Chinsky, J. M., 81
Chipman, H. H., 21
Chomsky, C., 60
Chukovsky, K., 14
Chunking, 81
Clark, E., 14
Clarke-Stewart, A., 82
Classification, 57–58
Classroom management, through behavior modification, 114–117
Clustering, 81
Cognitive development, 7, 10–13, 69–93, 106–107
Communication, effective, 211, 213 (*see also* Language)
Compensation, 55, 74
Concrete-operational stage, 69, 76–78
Conflict (*see also* Conflict inducement):
  as a diagnostic, 112–113
  and expectations, 129–131
  as motivation, 10, 11, 12, 113–114
Conflict inducement, 94–95, 107–117 (*see also* Conflict)
  and behavior modification, 94–95
  in learning encounters, 136–137, 198
Conrad, R., 81
Consciousness:
  of actions, 140
  of form, 10
  and knowledge, 36
Conservation:
  of area, 55–56
  and compensation, 55
  of invariant properties, 57
  and language, 84
  of length, 9, 74–76, 85–86
  of number, 52–53
  origins of, 74–76
  precursory experiences, 77
  of quantity, 74
Constructivist theory, 47, 50–52
Continuity:
  in science and mathematics, 58–61
  in teaching, 27
  transfer of learning, 27–28
Conventions, 40
Cooperative behavior, 207–210
Copy theory, 47–49
Correction of performance, 94
Correspondence, and self-knowledge, 43
Creativity, 60
Curriculum materials (*see* Materials)

Decarie, T. C., 86
Decentration, 87–91, 125
Dembo, T., 18
Dempsey, J., 51, 106, 125, 132, 225
Depersonification of action, 9
Derman, L., 99, 110, 118
Detour situations, 9, 70
Development (*see also* Differences, developmental):
  absolute to relative, 86–91
  cognitive, 7, 10–13, 69–93, 106–107
  as continuous process, 7–10
  dimensions of, 10, 79–91, 128
  emotional, 10, 13, 17–18, 79
  empirical to logical, 83–86
  and learning, 106–107, 160
  perceptual, 87–88
  Piagetian theory of, 69–78
  precursory experiences, 9, 11, 74–75, 77
  as qualitative change, 106–107
  reactive to active, 79–81
  social, 7, 10–13, 79, 81–83, 86, 88–91
  stages of, 7–9, 69–78, 204
  views of, 8–9
DeVries, R., 34, 215
Differences:
  and change, 58
  developmental, 12–19
  and similarity, 56–61, 161–163, 166
Discontinuity:
  forms of, 31
  in learning, 39, 62–63
  and representation, 30–31
  and self-knowledge, 29
Discovery learning, 110–111
Discrimination training, 47–49
Displacements, 70–73
Distancing, 17, 136n
Drawing:
  and cognitive development, 84–86
  using inferences, 88
Duckworth, E., 113, 138, 203

Early Childhood Education Project, 12, 15, 18
Eckerman, C. O., 86
Egocentrism, 88–91, 126 (*see also* Decentration)
Elkind, D., viin, 82, 160
Emotional development, 10, 13, 17–18, 79
Empathy, 43, 88

Encounters, learning (*see* Learning encounters)
Environment:
  educational, 187–191
  as factor in learning, 152, 154–155
Equilibration, 160
Erikson, E., 26
Errors, role in learning, 51$n$, 101, 109–110, 128–129
Ervin-Tripp, S., 107
Estes, B. W., 17
Evans, E. D., 21, 47, 118
Exploratory activities, 160–167

Fein, G. G., 82
Fernie, D., 219$n$
Ferster, C. B., 109
Figurative knowledge, 76–77
Fiske, D. W., 17
Flapan, D., 89, 90
Flavell, J. H., 81, 215
Forehand, R., 131
Formal-operational stage, 69, 77–78
Forman, G. E., 12, 15, 29, 51, 105, 106, 125, 132, 217$n$, 225
Free play (*see also* Play):
  as a diagnostic, 123
  importance of, 123–124
  problems of entry, 123–137
Freud, A., 90
Fromanek, R., 93
Frost, J. L., 84
Fry, C. L., 215
Functions:
  precursory experiences, 74–75
  preoperational concept of, 73–74, 78
  and structure, 63, 162–163, 167
Furth, H. G., 37, 50, 160

Gallup, G. G., 205
Garcia, R., 29, 34, 111, 201
Garvey, C., 82
Geometry, transformational, 59
Gibson, J. J., 60$n$
Ginsburg, H., 113
Glucksberg, S., 90, 213
Gordon, I. J., 41, 42
Gravity, 50–51
Group of translations, 70
Gurian, A., 93

Halfar, C., 142

Harlow, H. F., 28
Harris, F. R., 99
Hawkins, D., 168$n$
Hawkins, F. P., 139, 142, 168
Henke, L. B., 99
Hetherington, E. M., 34$n$
Heuristics, use of, 184–187
Higgins, E. T., 90, 213
Hilgard, E. R., 60
Hill, D. F., 217$n$
Hill, E., 82
Hogan, R., 82
Holland, V. M., 84
Hood, L., 14
Hunt, J. McV., 40

Imitation, 19, 73, 131–135
Inferential thinking, 37, 73, 83–86
Inhelder, B., 21, 29, 37, 52, 55, 58, 81, 85, 88, 90, 93, 160, 197
Inhibition of action, 125
Instruction (*see also* Teaching):
  degree of structure, 98–99, 116–117
  individualized, 97–98, 105–106
  one-to-one teaching, 14
Interaction, between child and environment, 185–187
Intrinsic reinforcement, 103–105 (*see also* Motivation; Reinforcement)
Inverse relations, vs. reciprocal relations, 208–209
Isaacs, N., 129
Isaacs, S., 46, 129$n$

Jackson, J. P., 82
Jarvis, P. E., 215

Kamii, C., 7, 28, 34, 99, 110, 118, 209
Kaplan, B., 81
Karplus, R., 29
Kendler, H. H., 62, 106
Kendler, T. S., 62
King, E. W., 192
Kirk, S. A., 57
Kissinger, J. B., 84
Knoblock, H., 81
Knower-known relation, 28–33, 86–91
Knowledge:
  assumptions about, 4–5, 36
  base, 152–153
  categories of, 34–45
  consciousness of, 36

Knowledge (continued)
  construction of, 6
  figurative, 76–77
  logico-mathematical, 151
  operational, 76–77
  physical, 34–35, 150
  rote vs. meaningful, 39
  self-, 29, 34, 41–44, 150, 203–206
  social, 34, 35, 38–40
  sources of, 4, 37
Kohlberg, L., 46, 65
Krauss, R., 90, 213
Kritchevsky, S., 188
Kuhn, T. S., 58, 65
Kuschner, D. S., 51, 106, 125, 132, 225

Language, 10, 13–14, 17–18, 37 (*see also* Communication)
  and conservation performance, 84
  egocentric use of, 90, 126
  and reflection, 126–127
  and representation, 217
  specific, 211–213
  teacher's, 48, 139–140
Laughlin, F., 105, 225
Laurendeau, M., 88, 197
Learning, 10–19
  by actively changing, 50–52, 61–63
  and development, 106–107, 160
  and discontinuity, 39
  as discovery, 110–111
  doing vs. understanding, 100
  episodic vs. disjunctive, 143
  errors, role of, 101, 109–110
  by increased attention, 47–50
  to learn, 99
  level of, 99
  readiness, 112–113
  response chaining, 84
  rote, 60, 100, 107
  self-regulated, 105–106, 114–117, 138
  transfer of, 27–28, 158–160
  transformational approach to, 52–63
Learning encounters:
  *Anticipating Positions,* 227
  *Changing Perspective,* 219–220
  *Cones-through-the-Hole,* 206–210
  and conflict inducement, 198
  *Conservation of Discontinuity,* 226
  *Constructing a Straight Line,* 218
  *Continuity across Discontinuity,* 221–223

Learning encounters (continued)
  *Decentering from the Physical,* 223–225
  encounter-as-presented, 154
  environment-as-prepared, 154
  expansion of, 143–145
  *Funnels,* 198–201
  generalization of, 151–160
  *Goals with Subgoals,* 227–228
  influence on, 152–158
  *Intervals in Motion,* 228–229
  *Invisible Displacement,* 218
  knowledge base, 152–153
  *Length vs. Distance,* 228
  *Mirrors,* 203–206
  motivation, 153
  and negation, 197
  *Negative and Positive Space,* 217–218
  performance, 153
  and prediction, 198
  and reciprocity, 197
  *Recognizing Transformed Shapes,* 226–227
  *Representation of Physical Environment,* 220
  sand-play example, 137–140
  *Seriating Soil,* 220–221
  *Specific Language,* 211–213
  styles of, 12
  summarizing, 146–147
  termination, 147–148
  transfer of learning, 158–160
  *Tunnels,* 201–203
  variations, 197–198
  *Who Am I Now?* 213–217
Lewin, K., 18
Lightbown, P., 14
Logico-mathematical knowledge, 35–38, 77, 151 (*see also* Knowledge)
Luria, A. R., 125

Maddi, D. W., 17
Madsen, C. H., 99, 114
Madsen, C. K., 114
Mahler, M. S., 89
Marans, A. E., 91
Maratsos, M. P., 88, 90
Martin, W. E., 90
Materials:
  choosing, 189–191
  discrete, 196
  fluid, 196
  moldable, 196

Materials (continued)
types of, 196
Mayer, R., 46
McCarthy, J. J., 57
Meers, D. R., 91
Memory, 70, 81
Metz-Hatch, K., 43
Miller, G. A., 41, 81
Miller, L. B., 17
Miller, R. S., 131
Mischel, T., 55
Montessori, M., 48, 116, 139, 190
Morris, W. N., 131
Motivation (*see also* Reinforcement):
by cognitive conflict, 10, 11, 12
by external rewards, 10
intrinsic, 17, 19, 139
and learning encounters, 153
paradox vs. surprise, 111–112
using conflict, 113–114
Murphy, L. B., 11, 89, 90

Negation, 70, 197, 204
Negativism, stage of, 89
Nelson, K. E., 86
Neubauer, P. B., 89

Objectives, sources of, 143
Object permanence, 41, 70, 87
Observation, importance of, 128–131
Operational knowledge, 76–77 (*see also* Knowledge)
Opper, S., 113
Opposition, 62
Ordered relations, 201–203

Palermo, D. S., 84
Pasamanick, B., 81
Peed, S., 131
Perception, seeing vs. understanding, 50–52
Perceptual development, 87–88
Performance:
correction of, 94
vs. knowing, 153–154
as process, 100
as product, 100
Perrot, M. C., 109
Perspective (*see* Decentration)
Peters, D. L., 95
Physical knowledge, 34–35, 81, 84–86, 87–88, 150

Piaget, J., 7, 9, 15, 17, 28, 29, 34, 37, 46, 52, 53, 54, 55, 58, 60, 65, 70, 81, 84, 90, 93, 102, 111, 113, 126, 131, 140, 160, 164, 197, 201, 202
Piagetian theory of development, 7–10, 69–78
Pinard, A., 88, 197
Play (*see also* Free play):
expansions on, 134–135
self-regulation of, 138
teacher's entry into, 131–139
and transformations, 137–139
Poincaré, H., 52
Precursory experiences, 9, 11, 74–75, 77
Preoperational stage, 73–76, 78
Prescott, E., 188
Pretense:
and distancing, 136$n$
with objects, 81, 164
with others, 82
Pufall, P. B., 203

Questioning, use and strategies of, 61–63, 110–111, 136, 140

Raph, J., 21, 192
Reciprocity:
vs. inverse relations, 208–209
in learning encounters, 197
vs. negation, 204
in sensorimotor stage, 70, 204
Reinforcement:
extrinsic, 94–98
intrinsic, 103–106
Relations, inverse vs. reciprocal, 208–209
Repetition, 125
Representation:
importance of, 167
and the knower-known relation, 29–31
and language, 217
literal drawings, 84–86
in sensorimotor stage, 73
and spanning discontinuity, 30–31
Reversibility:
in action, 70–71, 113, 114, 137
implications of, 78
Reynolds, N. J., 99
Rheingold, H. L., 86
Roles, social, 216–217
Role taking, 213–217
Rowen, B., 142, 192

School for Constructive Play, ix, 217n
Schwartz, G. E., 95
Schwebel, M., 21, 192
Secrist, A., 12, 15, 82, 227n
Self-knowledge, 29, 34, 40–45, 150, 203–206
Self-regulated learning, 105–106, 114–117, 138
Sensorimotor stage, 69–73, 78, 204
Shantz, C., 34n
Shapiro, D., 95
Sherif, C. W., 210
Sherif, M., 210
Sigel, I. E., 12, 15, 17, 82, 123n, 136n
Similarity, 56–61, 161–163, 166
Sinclair, H., 88, 119
Skinner, B. F., 110
Smedslund, J., 107
Smilansky, S., 82, 214
Smith, H. T., 11
Social development, 7, 10–13, 79, 81–83, 86, 88–91 (*see also* Social knowledge)
    autonomy, 90–91
    cooperative behavior, 207–210
    empathy, 88
Social knowledge, 34–35, 38–40, 81–83, 86, 88–91 (*see also* Social development)
Social roles, 216–217
Solomon, F., 99
Sommer, R., 188
Spatial relations, 77, 87, 88, 199–201
Sponseller, D., 168
Staff development:
    assumptions about children's development, 169–174
    openness to change, 174–177
    use of videotapes, 177–183
Stages of development:
    concrete-operational, 69, 76–78
    formal-operational, 69, 77–78
    preoperational, 73–76, 78
    sensorimotor, 69–73, 78, 204
Starr, R., 82
Static states, 63
Stendler, C. B., 90
Stevens, J. H., Jr., 192
Stone, J. L., 11
Strauss, S., 88
Strohner, H., 86
Structure and function, 63, 162–163, 167
Support activities, 160–161, 163–164
Sutton-Smith, B., 82

Sutton-Smith, S., 82
Sweeney, M., 105, 225

Teaching, 12–19, 123–140 (*see also* Staff development)
    approaches to, 12–19
    closed view vs. open view, 25
    continuity in, 27
    entry into play, 131–136, 137–139
    expansions on play, 134–135
    and exploration, 160–166
    imitation, use of, 19, 73, 131–135
    improvement of, 169–191
    influence of basic assumptions on, 47, 169–174
    and knowledge of developmental theory, 107, 113–114
    monitoring of, 183–187
    process, of, 27–28
    questioning, use and strategies of, 61–63, 110–111, 136, 140
    reflecting on activity, 149–151
    stating objectives, 103
    taking child's perspective, 146–147
    teacher as troublemaker, 114
Temporal relations, 199–201
Theory:
    importance of theoretical base, 124–128
    and practice, 3, 11, 124–127
Thinking:
    associative, 83–86
    about change, 140
    inferential, 83–86
    and knowledge base, 152–153
Thomas, D. R., 99
Transfer of learning, 27–28, 158–160
Transformations:
    continuous vs. discontinuous, 196, 202
    and creativity, 60
    and curriculum materials, 190–191
    and educational environment, 188–189
    and geometry, 59
    implicit in paradox, 111–112
    and knower-known relation, 204
    and play, 137–139
    and self-knowledge, 43
    and static states, 52
    use in preschool education, 61–63
    use in thought, 54–58
    using both directions, 63
    views of evolution, 59
    views of mental health, 59

Transitive relation, 73
Transivity, 84, 201
Translations:
  and conservation of length, 74–76
  group of, 70

Uzgiris, I. C., 133, 197

Videotaping, use and techniques of, 177–183
Vurpillot, E., 81

Walcher, D. N., 95
Walling, L., 188
Watson, J. S., 84

Wenar, C., 90
Werner, H., 17, 81, 205
Weyl, H., 59
White, B. L., 82, 93
White, S. H., 14
Whitehead, A. N., 25
Winawer, B. P., 188
Woodcock, L., 55
Wright, J. W., 215

*Young Learners Puzzles,* 190
Yudovich, F. I., 125

Zaporozhets, A. V., 163
Zigler, E., 106

# Information about NAEYC

## NAEYC is . . .

. . . a membership-supported organization of people committed to fostering the growth and development of children from birth through age 8. Membership is open to all who share a desire to serve and act on behalf of the needs and rights of young children.

## NAEYC provides . . .

. . . educational services and resources to adults who work with and for children, including

• *Young Children, the* journal for early childhood educators

• **Books, posters, brochures,** and **videos** to expand your knowledge and commitment to young children, with topics including infants, curriculum, research, discipline, teacher education, and parent involvement

• An **Annual Conference** that brings people from all over the country to share their expertise and advocate on behalf of children and families

• **Week of the Young Child** celebrations sponsored by NAEYC Affiliate Groups across the nation to call public attention to the needs and rights of children and families

• **Insurance plans** for individuals and programs

• **Public affairs** information and access to information available through NAEYC resources and communication systems for knowledgeable advocacy efforts at all levels of government and through the media

• The **National Academy of Early Childhood Programs,** a voluntary accreditation system for high-quality programs for children

• The **National Institute for Early Childhood Professional Development,** providing resources and services to improve professional preparation and development of early childhood educators

• **Young Children International** to promote international communication and information exchanges

For free information about membership, publications, or other NAEYC services, visit the **NAEYC Website** at **http://www.naeyc.org**

**National Association for the Education of Young Children**
**1509 16th Street, NW**
**Washington, DC 20036–1426**
**202–232–8777 or 800–424–2460**